W9-DIM-531

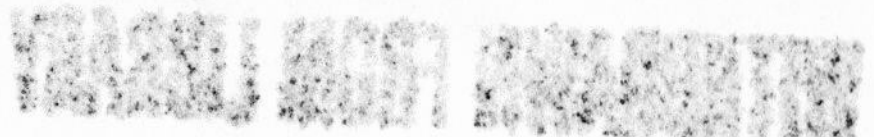

STRATEGIES AGAINST POVERTY IN AMERICA

STRATEGIES AGAINST POVERTY IN AMERICA

JOHN B. WILLIAMSON

Jerry F. Boren, Frank J. Mifflen,
Nancy A. Cooney, Linda Evans,
Michael F. Foley, Richard Steiman,
Jody Garber, Nancy Theberge,
Donna J. B. Turek

SCHENKMAN PUBLISHING COMPANY

HALSTED PRESS DIVISION

JOHN WILEY & SONS

New York—London—Sydney—Toronto

Schenkman Publishing Company, Inc.
Cambridge, Massachusetts 02138

Distributed solely by Halsted Press, a Division
of John Wiley & Sons, Inc. New York.

Library of Congress Cataloging in Publication Data

Strategies against poverty in America.

Includes bibliographical references and index.
1. Economic assistance, Domestic—United States.
i. Income maintenance programs—United States.
3. Public welfare—United States
I. Williamson, John B.
HC110.P63S73 338.973 74-19464
ISBN 0-470-94883-3
ISBN 0-470-94884-1 pbk.

CONTENTS

LIST OF TABLES

Foreword

LEE RAINWATER

Understanding the welfare state, its evolution and contemporary dynamics, is one of the central intellectual challenges to the social sciences in the 1970s. The welfare state program has proved a compelling solution to the conflicting imperatives of productivity and social justice in modern societies, both capitalist and socialist. Now that a large part of the program of the original advocates of welfare state policies has been adopted in most Western capitalist countries we are begining to understand something of the limits of these policies.

The debacle of the War on Poverty can teach us a great deal. In this book, Williamson and his co-workers have advanced our knowledge of what can and cannot be expected from the armamentarium of anti-poverty strategies. The War on Poverty has involved extremely varied actual and proposed policies. On the one hand anti-poverty policy has simply extended approaches first put forward in New Deal days; on the other hand, a wide range of relatively new policy proposals have been put forward. These, in turn, are diverse in their intellectual origins and in the diagnosis of poverty on which they are based. Some are highly psychological in conception such as the child development strategies of Head Start. Others are based on a direct economic view of poverty, for example, the guaranteed income strategy.

A simply intellectual solution to the variety of diagnoses of the causes of poverty and policies for its amelioration or eradication has been to say that we need a multi-faceted attack on the problem, no one policy can do the job.

This view has proved a convenient rationale for the great proliferation of Federal government programs on behalf of the poor that began in the 1960s and continued even under a Republican administration into the 1970s. The political dynamics of bureaucracy and of powerful constituencies has been such that all sorts of interests have put forward their claims to a role in solving the problem of poverty by participation in the anti-poverty business.

How then is one to sort out issues of cost and effectiveness of different approaches to fighting poverty? Ideally, one would seek empirical research which tests under rigorous experimental conditions the effects of anti-poverty programs, separately and in combination, on the prevalence of the problem. Such empirical research would have to be carried out on a scale far beyond the present imagination of social scientists, let alone research funders. Many anti-poverty strategies are directed toward effects in the distant future rather than immediate effects and therefore rigorous experimental research could take decades or longer.

But if fighting poverty is to be other than a political slogan, we cannot wait. Ways must be found to assess the effectiveness of anti-poverty strategies on the basis of the best information that is available. This is what Williamson and his co-workers have done. In this book, they report the results of an effort to assess such information as is available concerning the gamut of anti-poverty strategies and to evaluate these policies against each other and against the absolute criterion of the degree to which they might reasonably be expected to contribute to a reduction in poverty. They have devoloped a standard schema for evaluating anti-poverty strategies and assessed each of the significant actual or proposed anti-poverty policies against this standard set of criteria. The book clearly reflects their insistence on care and detachment in assessing each policy regardless of their own predilections. The results of the study are impressive. For the first time they give us a systematic comparison of competing anti-poverty policies in such a way that we are able to have a much more realistic understanding of what particular policies can and cannot be expected to accomplish. The results of their work will prove of great use both to readers whose primary interests are those of policy planning and action and to those whose interests are more those of the scholarly understanding of how the American welfare state operates.

In 1966, I argued in testimony before Senator Ribicoff's subcommittee holding hearings on the urban crisis that it was useful to think of anti-poverty programs as reflecting one of two kinds of strategies, a *services strategy* or an *income strategy*. I argued that the services strategy had almost totally monopolized our approach to problems of poverty and disadvantage, and that such programs were doomed to failure if one took as the goal of the War on Poverty the eradication of poverty. Reading this book, I see that such a dichotomy is overly simple and that it would perhaps be most useful to think of four major kinds of anti-poverty strategy, each type being the combination of a choice about whether to attack poverty *directly* or *indirectly* and whether to do so by the provision of *income* or *services*. Indirect attacks on poverty emphasize approaches that in one way or another increase the "human capital" of the poor. The goal is to allow them thereby to earn more money, to better use the resources available to them, to exercise their power as citizens more effectively, and so on. Policies emphasizing a direct approach focus more on directly changing the consumption of the poor. The goal is to increase the goods and services used by poor families either through providing the income with which to acquire those goods and services or by directly providing the services (as with public housing, surplus food, free medical clinics, etc.). The anti-poverty strategies analyzed here fall rather neatly into these four types:

Income Strategies

Direct (oriented to consumption): Public assistance, social insurance, family allowances, negative income tax.

Indirect (oriented to increasing human capital): Unionization, "black capitalism," community corporations.

Services Strategies

Direct: Housing, food, medical care, day care, family planning, neighborhood legal services.

Indirect: Education, manpower, casework social services, community organization.

Of course, in any particular program these orientations may overlap, producing a kind of hybrid. The proposed housing allowance is perhaps one of the best examples of a hybrid strategy. Cash is used to confer the benefit, but this addition to income is tied to a particular good, housing. The direct services strategy argues that some goods are more important than others and therefore anti-poverty strategies will be more effective if they require the poor to spend money in ways that are known to be particularly beneficial—as for example, on housing or food. Other kinds of hybrids have been suggested, for example, for the use of education/training vouchers which confer a cash benefit on individuals or families but require that benefit to be used in a particular way, that is, for education or job training.

More interesting are the situations in which these different orientations to the goals of a particular program can have important effects on the way a program is carried out. For example, day care can be seen as reflecting either a direct or indirect anti-poverty strategy. Clearly it is a service (although again some proposals argue for day care vouchers, there introducing an element of income strategy). But what is the main purpose of the service? Is it the personal and educational development of the children—that is directed toward a "human capital" goal? Or is it a direct service to provide child care so that the mother is able to work? (This has been somewhat pejoratively termed the "custodial orientation" to day care.) An alternative direct service orientation would emphasize not so much freeing the mothers to work but rather providing free to poor children, a good ("nursery school") which a great many less poor parents purchase for their children. These different orientations within the same program have important effects in terms of program design, the kind of work force that is employed by the program, and its cost.

One of the most depressing findings from many evaluations of so-called anti-poverty programs is how much they contribute to the well-being of the non-poor who find jobs in the programs and how little they pay off for the poor themselves. Particularly dramatic examples have been the new housing programs instituted in the late 1960s, and the special education programs designed to remedy educational disadvantage. Given the great increase in educated manpower in this country and the popular expectation of the desirability of earning a living in the "human services" profession, it seems likely that it will probably prove extraordinarily difficult in the future, as it has proved impossible in the past, to prevent anti-poverty strategies from simply serving to guarantee a market for the labor services of that portion of educated manpower which cannot be absorbed by the rest of the economy.

It is against the background of considerations such as these that this book argues that the most effective anti-poverty strategy will be a "national income insurance plan" designed to achieve a progressive shift of the income distribution from the bottom toward the middle. The case made here for such a guaranteed income approach is all the more persuasive because it is based on a detached and fair-minded evaluation of competing services and human capital approaches to the poverty problem.

Whether the constructive programs which this book argues for become a reality is an issue of political will and creativity. But work such as this makes it clear that the intellectual problems of designing anti-poverty problems that would be effective can be solved. It may well be that other effective policies will be invented (recent work on the idea of wage subsidy suggests the possibility of a valuable companion to income insurance), but the challenge now is clearly a political one. Part of effective policies, however, will involve using the knowlege developed in books like this to prevent the wastage of national initiative that we can now see occurred because from its inception the War on Poverty adhered so closely to services and human capital strategies.

Acknowledgements

A book such as this is not possible without the combined efforts of many people. We want to express our appreciation to the Institute of Human Sciences of Boston College and its Director Marc Fried for the research funds that made this study possible. Lee Rainwater, Michael Useem, Mildred Rein, and Barbara Wishnov have all read portions of preliminary drafts of the manuscript; their comments have been most useful. Nancy Williamson and Andre Daniere have also made a number of very useful suggestions. Janet Caruso and Ellen Delaney have provided very competent editorial assistance. Jerry Blake made a number of valuable contributions to our preliminary evaluation of the manpower strategies. And most of all we want to thank Roz Beck for her outstanding contribution as a typist and editor through numerous preliminary drafts of the manuscript. John Williamson had the primary responsibility for the Introduction, Chapters 1, 2, 3, and 6. Jerry Boren, Donna Turek, and Jody Garber had primary responsibility for the material in Chapter 4. Linda Evans, Nancy Theberge, Frank Mifflen, Michael Foley, Richard Seiman, and Nancy Cooney had primary responsibility for the material in Chapter 5. For a more detailed presentation of the material in Chapters 5 and 6 see our preliminary report, *Reducing Inequality: Comparisons among Alternative Anti-poverty, Programs and Proposals.*

To Alex Inkeles

Introduction

In the early 1960s the poverty problem was rediscovered. Poverty was explicitly mentioned in the 1960 Democratic platform. During the Kennedy Administration a number of pilot studies such as Mobilization for Youth (in New York City) were initiated. In his 1964 State of the Union message President Johnson called for an "unconditional war on poverty." In a message to Congress on poverty a few months later, he went on to specify that the objective was total victory. The elimination or at least a marked reduction in the extent of poverty was to be a major national priority. In response to this national concern, a host of anti-poverty proposals were made and many were eventually introduced as federally funded programs. But with escalation in Vietnam anti-poverty efforts began to sag.

During the first years of the Nixon Administration the funding for many of these programs was cut back: by his second term it was clear that the goal was to dismantle many of these programs altogether. In little more than ten years the focus on poverty in America had come full circle. Poverty had been rediscovered, had become defined as a high priority national social problem, and then had quietly been all but forgotten.

Why? An answer we frequently hear today is that the liberal reforms of the 1960s had not worked. Not only had they not succeeded in eliminating poverty or markedly reducing the extent of poverty, it was not even clear that they could be expected to achieve such results in the long run. The extravagant promises with which these programs had been introduced were taking their toll: the programs were uniformly falling short of their stated objectives. Poverty and economic inequality were turning out to be integrated into the social and economic structure of our society in a much more fundamental way than many liberals had anticipated.

In view of the apparent failure of the liberal reforms of the 1960s and in view of the present hiatus in efforts to reduce the extent of social inequality, this is an appropriate time to reflect on what went wrong. Hopefully we can learn from the experience of the 1960s and put what we have learned to use in the formulation of strategies for that time in the future when today's more conservative approach is itself discredited.

In this book we focus on the major anti-poverty strategies of the 1960s. In addition to programs introduced during the 1960s we also consider some strategies that had been introduced as far back as the 1930s, some that would most accurately be described as pilot studies, and some that were merely proposals. Many of the strategies we consider have been the subject of previous evaluations, some of numerous evaluations. But these evaluations have often considered only one program and never more than a few. There has to date been no effort to be comprehensive. The present study has been undertaken to fill this gap.

The strategies considered can be grouped into the following six general anti-poverty approaches: (1) income-in-kind, (2) income, (3) manpower, (4) education, (5) economic development, and (6) organization. The relationships between these approaches are summarized in the diagram below.

The income-in-kind strategies include programs and proposals which would deliver to the poor goods and services which others purchase on the open market. An assumption of this approach is that the income that is or could be made available to the poor would not be sufficient to assure their being able to purchase these needed goods and services on the open market.

The income strategies include those programs and proposals which provide the poor with money. The assumption is that the poor will use this money to buy goods and services that they would not otherwise have been able to afford.

The manpower strategies consist of those programs and proposals which would provide more or better jobs to the poor. These are based on the assumption that with better jobs the poor would be able to earn a higher income and with it purchase needed goods and services.

Among the manpower programs to be considered are those which would create more jobs for the poor, train the poor for better jobs, help the poor locate existing jobs, and reduce job discrimination against the poor.

The education strategies refer to those programs and proposals which would provide the poor with a better education than is presently available to them. The objective is to provide the educational background that is necessary for better jobs. Better jobs would in turn increase the income of the poor. Included among the education programs and proposals to be considered are those which would provide compensatory education, those which would provide an opportunity for persons currently out of school to return, and those which would reorganize the school system.

The economic development strategy includes programs and proposals which would create jobs for the poor in response to local or national economic development. The object is to stimulate economic growth.

RELATIONSHIPS BETWEEN THE PROPOSED GENERAL CATEGORIES OF ANTI-POVERTY STRATEGIES

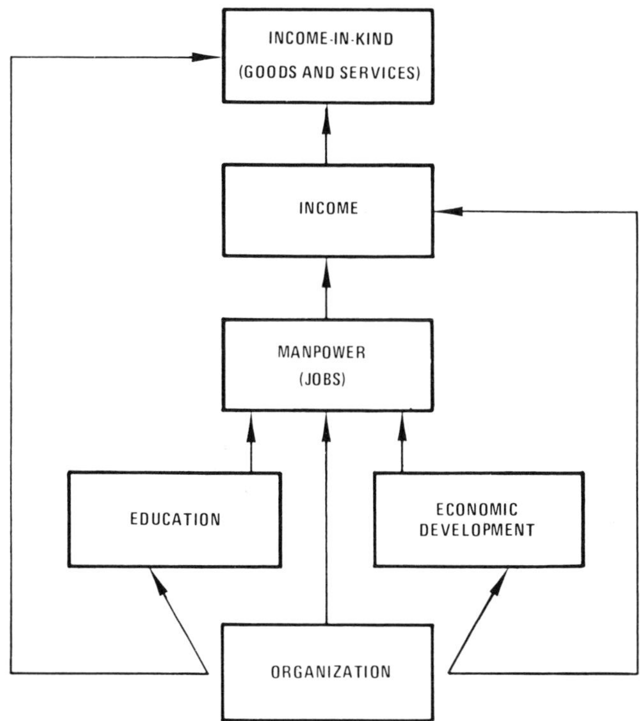

This creates more jobs which in turn increase the income of the poor.

The organization strategy includes those efforts which would encourage the poor to act together and in cooperation with others so as to increase their political influence. Many such strategies are appropriate for use within the existing social structure. Such efforts can be directed toward increasing benefits from income-in-kind programs, income programs, manpower programs, education programs, and economic development programs. There are other organization strategies which call for social structural changes as a first step towards improving the conditions for the poor.

The reader will note that we have devoted approximately the same amount of space to the income strategies as to all other strategies combined. This is not indicative of the emphasis in the actual evaluation effort carried out in each of the six general areas; each was given roughly the same emphasis. But we have found that some focus was necessary to keep an already long book to a reasonable length. The income strategies are given disproportionate emphasis here because several of the most highly rated strategies turned out to be included in this approach.

Our analysis is designed to meet the following three objectives. The first is to *evaluate* the major anti-poverty strategies within each of the six general approaches being considered. As part of this effort we also evaluate each of the six general approaches themselves. The second objective is to *compare* the strategies *within* each of the six general approaches.

The third objective is to *compare* programs and proposals *across* the six general approaches. As part of this effort we consider how well a given approach tends to compare with the other general approaches. Although most policy decisions involve choices among alternative strategies within the same general approach, such as choices among alternative educational strategies, there is a very real need for more explicit criteria for use in making comparisons across general approaches.

For each of these three objectives we have used a set of twenty-six dimensions described in the Appendix. Included are such dimensions as proportion of the poor who benefit, impact on the distribution of income, and the extent to which recipients are stigmatized. We have selected a subset of eighteen out of the twenty-six dimensions for most of our conclusions as to the overall ratings of the strategies, but the reader is free to make his or her own selection. Readers exercising this option may come to some quite different conclusions, but the source of the discrepancies will be evident.

Our evaluations are heavily dependent upon this set of twenty-six dimensions. It should come as no surprise to our readers that the quality of the information used in making these ratings was better for some dimensions than for others; this is reflected in the description of the dimensions and in the rating procedure used. With some dimensions we have been able to provide specific quantitative ratings and with others the ratings are clearly more qualitative and impressionistic. An effort was made to keep the dimensions sufficiently open and general so that they could be used across the entire range of strategies being considered.

We expect that our evaluations and particularly our ratings will stimulate a debate. We see them as a point of departure and in no sense do we view ourselves as passing final judgement. It is our hope that by taking a stand we will stimulate a discussion which will lead to further clarification and eventually to modifications in the present ratings.

Much of what has been presented in recent years as evaluation research would be more accurately described as public relations. This is particularly true when the evaluation is conducted by administrators of the program being evaluated. Funding has generally been precarious and program administrators have been all too willing to accept the flimsiest of evidence when it is favorable and to reject adverse findings of more competent evaluation research as premature or irrelevant.

Much of the literature available on a program has been prepared by those who are apologists for that approach. In the unusual event that comparisons are made between the chosen strategy and alternatives, it is often to compare the weaknesses of the alternatives to the advantages of the chosen strategy.

Our study has a very different orientation. We consider both the strengths and the weaknesses of those strategies we favor as well as those we look upon with less favor. We make it a point to include even those arguments we disagree with when there is evidence that others find merit in them. This is not to say that our analysis is free of bias. But we have not used the inevitability of bias as a rationale for not attempting to present a balanced discussion.

We have selected 1969 as the base year for much of our statistical analysis. Statistics are often presented for 1969 or as close to 1969 as possible. On the grounds that the most recent statistics are the most relevant statistics a case could be made for 1973 as the base year, but such a choice would have the disadvantage that the liberal reform anti-poverty efforts of the 1960s were by then very much on the decline. A case could also be made for an earlier year such as 1966 on the grounds that the decline had already clearly begun by the end of the decade. Our choice of 1969 is a compromise with some of the advantages and limitations of each of these alternatives.

We now turn to a brief sketch of the contents of the chapters that follow. The first chapter is a general introduction to the poverty literature. It includes: a discussion of which segments of the population run the greatest risk of poverty, a discussion of the relative merits of the numerous alternative ways of measuring poverty, and a review of the most frequently cited causes of poverty and consequences of being poor.

The second chapter is a discussion of the major existing income strategies. The most familiar of these are Aid to Families with Dependent Children (AFDC), Social Security, Unemployment Insurance, and Workmen's Compensation. The third chapter considers several family allowance and negative income tax proposals. The United States has never had a family allowance, but many other countries have and there is much to be learned from their experience. The negative income tax is an American conception which has never been tried except on a small scale pilot study basis.[1] The negative income tax strategy is often referred to as a guaranteed income because a guaranteed income is a major component of any negative income tax plan. The Family Assistance Plan (FAP) proposal of the Nixon Administration is the closest this country has ever come to the enactment of a negative income tax.[2] One of the most ambitious negative tax proposals to date is that proposed by Senator McGovern early in his 1972 presidential campaign.

In the fourth chapter various income-in-kind strategies are considered. Included are such housing strategies as public housing, leased housing, rent supplements, and the national housing allowance proposal which is currently being tested in pilot studies.[3] The food strategies considered include food stamps, school lunches, and the commodity distribution program. Neighborhood health centers, the national health insurance approach, medicare, and medicaid are the medical care strategies considered. The social service strategies examined include casework social services, neighborhood legal services, day care, and family planning.

In the fifth chapter we consider manpower, education, economic development and organization strategies. Among the manpower strategies presented are the JOBS program, New Careers and the Neighborhood Youth Corps. The education strategies considered include Head Start, open enrollment, school integration, and school vouchers, a proposal that is currently being tested in several pilot studies. Among the economic development strategies considered are black capitalism, the community development corporation, and economic growth. Some of the organization strategies evaluated are the Community Action Program, rent strikes, NWRO, and the unionization of farm workers.

In the sixth chapter we present a detailed comparison among the five most highly rated strategies presented in the preceding chapters. We also present an outline of a national income insurance plan which attempts to combine the strengths of a number of the most highly rated income strategies. Most of the strategies examined in this book can be characterized as falling within the liberal reform tradition. The national income insurance plan is also consistent with this tradition.

We argue that Congress will in all probability pass a national program similar to what we refer to as a national income insurance plan at some point in the not too distant future. There are many strong arguments both liberal and conservative for preferring such a program to the existing welfare system. We go on to argue that once such a program is introduced it will lead to a gradual unification of the poor and then to a unification of the poor with the working class. The process once started will be very difficult to stop and may lead to a major shift in the distribution of power, income, and wealth. Such a program could well contribute to shifts in such basic values as acceptance of the work ethic and contribute to significant changes in the social and economic structure of our society.

Notes

1. For a recent discussion of the status of the negative income tax experiments see Joseph Heffernan, "Negative Income Tax Studies: Some Preliminary Results of the Graduated-Work-Incentive Experiment," *Social Service Review* 46, 1(1972): 1–12.
2. For a thorough discussion of the fate of the FAP plan see Daniel P. Moynihan, *The Politics of a Guaranteed Income* (New York: Random House, 1973).
3. For a discussion of the status of the housing allowance experiments see Anthony Phipps, "Locational Choices of Direct Housing Allowance Recipients," mimeograph prepared for Midwest Council for Model Cities, December, 1972.

1

The Nature Of Poverty

People without the economic resources to live at an adequate standard of living are poor, but adequacy is a matter of degree and for this reason there is no clear dividing line between the poor and the rest of society. The conditions often associated with poverty such as substandard housing, poor schools, malnutrition, drug addiction, and family instability, to name only a few, become less prevalent as income increases. Some conditions associated with poverty, such as malnutrition, are primarily found at the very bottom of the income distribution; others, such as poor schools, affect a much wider income range. Some of those who would never be classified as poor and who would never consider themselves poor experience in a milder form many of the adverse conditions commonly associated with poverty. A number of the consequences of poverty are a function of income deprivation relative to the rest of society rather than absolute income deprivation. It is likely that these conditions will persist as long as the distribution of income, wealth, and associated opportunities remains as unfavorable to the poor as it is today.

A PROFILE OF THE POOR

The most commonly used measure of the extent of poverty in the United States is the Social Security Administration's poverty line index. The index is based on family income; it is adjusted to take into consideration differences in family size and whether or not the person lives on a farm. In 1969, the poverty line for a nonfarm family of four was $3,720 per year. In that year 24.3 million Americans were classified as poor including 4.9 million families and 4.8 million unrelated individuals.[1] For each year between 1959 and 1969 there was a decline in the number of poor and their proportion of the total population. In 1959, there were 39.5 million poor and they made up 22.4 percent of the population. In 1969, there were 24.3 million poor and they made up 12.2 percent of the total population.[2] Between 1969 and 1970, for the first time since the Social Security Administration's statistics were reported, there was an increase in the number of Americans living in poverty. In 1970, 25.5 million persons or 12.6 percent of the population had incomes below the poverty line.[3] This reversal is likely to be temporary: the general downward trend in the proportion of the population who are poor will in all probability continue.

Each year, the Social Security Administration's poverty line index is adjusted for increases in the cost of living. Between 1959 and 1970 the poverty line increased from $2,973 to $3,968 for a nonfarm family of four.[4]

It would have taken $10 billion to raise the aggregate income of all poor families and single individuals to the poverty line in 1969.[5] That is, if each family and single individual had been given exactly the amount of money needed to reach the poverty line, the amount of money distributed would have been $10 billion. This represents a minimum cost for any income approach to the elimination of poverty but any real program would cost much more due to the expenses involved in getting the right amount to the right people. There would also be leakage to those who are not poor with any of the methods of distribution which have been proposed to date.

Contrary to popular belief, more of the poor are white than are non-white. In 1969, whites accounted for 69 percent of the poor and non-whites accounted for only 31 percent (over 90 percent of non-whites are blacks). In the same year 10 percent of whites as opposed to 31 percent of non-whites were poor. The discrepancy between these alternative ways of presenting the statistics is due to whites making up a much larger segment of the total population. The high percentage of non-whites who are poor helps to clarify why so many people view programs to help the poor as programs to help non-whites, particularly blacks.

Families in which the head is unemployed are often poor. In 1969, 10 percent of all families were poor. In the same year 31 percent of families in which the head did not work at all were poor; 20 percent of families in which the head worked part-time for the full year were poor; 16 percent of families in which the head worked, but for less than a full year were poor; only 3 percent of families in which the head worked full-time all year were poor. The preceding illustrates the extent to which unemployment and underemployment contribute to poverty.

The poor work more than they are generally given credit for. In 1969, 26 percent of the heads of poor families worked all year and an additional 28 percent worked part of the year.[6] When interpreting these statistics it is useful to keep in mind that many of the poor hold jobs that are seasonal and due to low seniority they are often the first to be laid-off. Of the male heads of the poor families who did not work at all, 90 percent were either ill or disabled.

A commonly held misconception is that the heads of poor black families work less than the heads of poor white families. If anything, the trend is in the opposite direction. Considering poor male headed families in 1969, the head of household was employed in 71 percent of black families and in 59 percent of white families. Looking at poor female headed families in the same year, the head of household was employed in 49 percent of black families and in 39 percent of white families.

Female headed families are more often poor that male headed families. In 1969, 32 percent of female headed families in contrast to 7 percent of male headed families were poor. Women who are household heads are often from a lower-class backround and as a result have been deprived of the education and training necessary for high wage jobs. Other factors which serve to depress their wages are the generally low wages paid in many of the occupations characterized as women's jobs, the tendency for women to be paid less than men for the same work, the tendency for an absence of unions in many of the occupations women work in, and the tendency for women who do work to be employed only part-time. In 1969, 95 percent of male family heads were employed in contrast to only 71 percent of female family heads. Considering only persons who did work, 36 percent of the female heads worked part-time in contrast to 15 percent for male heads. For women with small children who cannot work, in many cases the only alternative source of support is the AFDC program. AFDC, however, provides an income that is substantially below the poverty line in most states.

Children make up a sizable fraction of the poor. In 1969, 40 percent of the poor were under the age of 18. In the same year 14 percent of persons under the age of 18 were poor. Children in large families are particularly likely to be poor. In 1969, 8 percent of one child families were poor, 11 percent of three children families were poor, and 30 percent of families with six or more children were poor (recall that 10 percent of all families were poor).

The aged are another substantial segment of the poor. In 1969, 30 percent of the poor were aged 65 or over, while 25 percent of persons aged 65 and over were poor. The aged poor tend to differ from other categories of the poor in several ways. One is that many lived at levels substantially above the poverty line prior to retirement. Another difference is that the aged are often living on savings or income from savings and as a result their income is likely to be more steady than is the case for younger families at the same income level.

The risk of poverty is greater for persons living in central cities than for those living in suburban areas, but the risk of poverty is greater for those living outside of metropolitan areas than it is for persons in central cities. In 1969, 17 percent of persons living outside metropolitan areas were poor, 13 percent of those living in central cities were poor, and 6 percent of those living in suburban areas were poor (recall that 12 percent of all persons in the U.S. were poor that year). The movement of the rural poor into central cities and the movement of the middle class from the central cities to the suburbs both contribute to the high rate of poverty in central cities.

The risk of poverty decreases as level of education increases. In 1969, 25 percent of families in which the head had less than an eighth grade education were poor; 11 percent of families in which the head had completed between 9 and 11 years of education were poor; and only 5 percent of families in which the head had completed high school but not attended college were poor.

In the discussion so far, the poor have generally been classified by one characteristic at a time. When several factors are considered simultaneously, it is possible to classify many people into categories which show a higher risk of poverty than is indicated when the same factors are considered one at a time.[7] For this reason any description of the poor which considers only one factor at a time tends to understate the risk of poverty faced by many categories of the population. For example, some 10 percent of all families are poor, 22 percent of families with seven or more members are poor, 28 percent of black families are poor, and 32 percent of female headed families are poor. Taking two characteristics at a time, we find that 53 percent of black female headed families are poor and that 66 percent of female headed families with seven or more members are poor. Considering all three characteristics together, we find that 73 percent of black female headed families with seven or more members are poor.

MEASUREMENT OF POVERTY

The Social Security Administration's poverty index is based on family income as are many other measures of poverty. Much attention has been given to the problem of selecting a specific income level which can be used to separate the poor from the rest of the population. There is general agreement that a uniform, even if somewhat arbitrary, criterion does have advantages. One advantage is that it facilitates efforts to describe long-term trends in the proportion of the population living in poverty. Another advantage is that it increases comparability between studies of the poor. When there is disagreement between two studies, each of which uses a different indicator of poverty, it is sometimes difficult to determine whether the disagreement is substantive or merely the result of differences in the way poverty is measured.

Now that the Social Security Administration's poverty index has become widely used, this in itself is a major factor contributing to its further use. The following are some of the characteristics which have led to its becoming so widely accepted in the first place: (1) it provides alternative poverty lines depending on the size of the family, (2) it provides a different income line for farm families, which often produce much of the food they consume, than for nonfarm families, (3) it is updated yearly for increases in the cost of living, (4) it defines poverty at a sufficiently low level to be acceptable to many of those who want to restrict government poverty programs to as few people as possible, (5) the Social Security Administration is viewed by many as a less partisan source than the various organizations and individuals outside of the federal government who have suggested other alternatives, and (6) it is based on the adequacy of the diet available to persons at the specified income level. This last reason is used to argue that the index avoids the subjectivity and arbitrariness of other poverty lines. However, as we shall see, the case is not as clear cut as some would have us believe.

One of the most salient characteristics of the poor in many underdeveloped countries is that they are malnourished. There is often a sharp increase in the death rate when there are food shortages in such countries. To the casual observer this might suggest that an income line (or more appropriately the equivalent in food) can be established below which starvation will occur and above which starvation will not occur. Such a poverty line, could it be found, would avoid the subjectivity of other poverty lines. But the need to take into consideration differences in food requirements due to variation in body weight, variation in extent of physical activity, and variation in metaboblism would require many alternative poverty lines and constant monitoring of the needs of each individual in the population of interest. Since the risk of disease increases as the adequacy of diet decreases, it would also be necessary to consider the increase in susceptibility to disease. In recent years medical services have been introduced into areas that did not formerly have them, and as a result many of those who would have in the past died of diseases contracted while malnourished are now kept alive. But in many cases the actual diet continues to be as inadequate as it was in the past. In short, food shortages contribute to increases in the death rate; but the extent of the impact is mediated by other factors making it difficult, if not impossible, to specify how much of the actual increase is due to undernourishment and malnourishment. While the goal of constructing an absolute poverty line based on the minimum amount of food necessary for subsistence may be attractive to those wishing to avoid the subjectivity of other poverty lines, this goal is for all practical purposes unachievable. Even a poverty line based on the adequacy of the diet provided is necessarily somewhat arbitrary.

For many years the U.S. Department of Agriculture has prepared a series of alternative food plans to be used by families at different income levels. Each of these food plans if followed exactly would assure an adequate diet, but the lower cost plans allow less variety and call for more skill in food preparation. The lowest cost plan, the low income food plan, was commonly used by welfare departments in making up food budgets for their recipients. In 1964, a lower cost food plan referred to as the economy food plan was created. This plan had a cost approximately 80 percent that of the low income food plan. Of families spending an amount equal to the cost of the economy food plan, approximately 75 percent met at least two-thirds of the National Research Council's recommendations for each of eight nutrients. The higher the food budget, the greater the proportion of families that meet these recommendations; but even with a large food budget, there are some families who because of unusual eating habits do not.[8] The selection of a 75 percent cut-off point was arbitrary, but it would not have been possible to specify an income level at which all families would have met the National Research Council's recommendations.

The Social Security Administration's poverty index was based on the cost of the economy food plan. Data from a 1955 survey by the U.S. Department of Agriculture indicates that families with a food budget at the level of the economy food plan spent approximately one-third of their income on food. Based on this, the poverty line was set equal to three times the cost of the economy food plan.[9] Prior to 1969, the poverty index was adjusted yearly for increases in the cost of the economy food plan; since then, the Consumer Price Index has been used. In 1970, the poverty line was $3,968 for a nonfarm family of four.

It is clear then that the number of people classified as poor is a function of the income level used as the poverty line. When comparing poverty lines for different years, it is necessary to take into consideration changes in the cost of living. However, even when we do take into consideration such changes, there has been a trend to raise the level of the poverty line. Consequently, many of those who are considered poor today would not have been classified as poor at the turn of the century. In 1904, a poverty line of $460 was suggested ($1,787 in 1968 dollars); in 1950, a poverty line of $3,000 was suggested (or $2,893 in 1968 dollars); and in 1968, the Social Security Administration's poverty line was $3,553.[10] The widespread acceptance of the Social Security Administration's measure has temporarily put an end to the trend. It is increased yearly, but the increase only takes into consideration increases in the cost of living.

When a fixed income is used as an indicator of poverty, the trend since the Depression has been, with only minor fluctuations, for the proportion of the population classified as poor to decrease. This generalization holds even after inflation is taken into consideration. Using the Social Security Administration's poverty index, between 1959 and 1970 the number of persons classified as poor decreased from 39.5 million to 25.5 million; this represents a decrease from 22.4 to 12.6 percent of the total population.

Comparisons can be made between the person living at the poverty line in America and the middle class in an underdeveloped country which suggest that the poor in America are very well off. However, the poor in America do not compare themselves with people living in other countries. The cost of living they face in America is quite different than it would be in India or Egypt. Through television and other mass media the poor in America are constantly exposed to the standard of living of the "typical" American family. This "typical" American family lives at a standard that is substantially above that experienced by many of the poor; in fact, it is even above that of the median income American family. The standard of living for the poor in America compares quite favorably to that of most Indian peasants, but it does not compare favorably to that of middle-class Americans.

Because social comparison is unavoidable for the poor, the suggestion has been made that relative measures be taken into consideration in the assessment of the extent of poverty. One of the most commonly suggested indicators of relative poverty is an income equal to half the median income. In 1947, 19 percent of the population lived in families below half the median income; in 1965, 20 percent were below half the median income.[11] By this indicator not only was there a slight increase in the percentage of the total population that was poor; but far more importantly, the absolute number of persons in poverty increased from 28 million to 39 million. This represents a 38 percent increase in the number of poor persons. Critics of this indicator argue that a measure which shows no decrease in the extent of poverty when the actual income level for the poorest segment of the population increases is measuring something other than what most people mean by poverty. Rather than choosing a relative or an absolute measure of poverty, an alternative is to retain both and to keep in mind the discrepancy between them. A family may experience an improvement in standard of living but experience no improvement relative to other families.

So far we have only considered current income as an indicator of the extent of poverty. Another important dimension of income to take into consideration is stability. The income of the poor tends to be quite unstable. Of those who were poor in 1965, 36 percent were not poor in 1966. Similarly, of the poor in 1966, 34 percent had not been poor in 1965.[12] By taking a family's present income as the indicator, we assume that their situation is better than that of another family when, in fact, their respective positions might have been the reverse during the previous year and might reverse again next year. Present income may give a less accurate picture of a family's true situation than a measure that averages income over a period of years. But even an average income figure would fail to differentiate between families that have had a steady income and those which have had a highly fluctuating income. Large fluctuations in income are not conducive to long-term planning.

Another dimension for analysis of the extent to which a family experiences poverty is the earning potential of family members. A family which is poor because the head of household is temporarily out of work due to a slowdown in the economy is in quite a different situation than the family which does not have a head who is capable of earning an income at a level above the poverty threshold.

Another relevant dimension is wealth and other available family resources. The earning potential of members of the family is one such resource. The availability of relatives who in an emergency will provide cash or in-kind support is another resource. Personal wealth including equity in a house, land, savings, and insurance is another important resource. A family's income may temporarily drop below the poverty line, but the availability of resources may make the experience much less harsh than it would otherwise be.

As was mentioned earlier, the extent to which the poor in America own consumer items is sometimes used to argue that they are well off in comparison to even the middle class in less developed countries. A family can be poor in America and own a car, a television set, a refrigerator, and a washing machine.[13] In many less developed countries only the upper class could boast of such an array of consumer goods. But the comparison does not take into consideration the cost of such goods relative to the cost of food needed for subsistence or relative to the pay for a day's labor. A run-down second hand car can be purchased for two weeks in wages at even a poverty income level in America, but the same car would cost several years wages for the typical peasant in many developing countries. Similarly, that car would be worth a lot more food in the developing country than it is in America. Such comparisons also fail to take into consideration the consequences of not having some of these consumer items in a society that is organized on the assumption that people do have them.

The emphasis so far has been on defining poverty in terms of income and wealth. The suggestion has been made that such a focus is too narrow. A proposed alternative is to consider poverty in terms of a number of indicators of social welfare.[14] The emphasis would not be on how much money the poor have relative to the rest of society, but rather on the quality of the goods and services that they obtain with their money. Considering health, for instance, some indicators that could be considered are infant mortality, per capita visits to doctors and dentists, and per capita cost of medical services received. In education some of the indicators that could be used are school drop-out rates, rates of college attendance, per pupil school expenditure, and performance on standardized achievement tests. Possible welfare indicators include adequacy of diet, family living space, housing quality, and family stability. Other possible social indicators are rate of victimization by assault, armed robbery, or burglary, rates of drug addiction, quality of neighborhood services, and differential treatment by police and other social agencies. It is clear that any attempt to delineate poverty in terms of such social indicators would call for rather arbitrary decisions as to where the line should be drawn. But then again, there is also much subjectivity in the income criterion that is generally used at present.

Another alternative is to ask a representative sample of the population to indicate where they would draw the income line separating the poor from the rest of society. Based on interviews in 1972 with 300 residents of the Boston Area, we have found that the poverty line tends to be drawn between $7,000 and $8,000 per year for a family of four. This is considerably above the $4,000 figure used by the federal government. We also found that the poverty line so indicated did not vary much with the income of the respondents. The poverty line tended to be drawn closer to $8,000 by respondents living in high income suburbs and closer to $7,000 by respondents living in low income central city areas.

One of the most important implications of the preceding analysis is that the selection of a poverty line is much more a political decision than is generally realized. For example, if the Social Security Administration had not come up with a "reasonable" poverty line, its index would not have gained wide acceptance. The poverty line had to be reasonable in the context of measures of poverty that were currently being used by other federal agencies and advisory groups. Once a poverty line is selected it is then justified in terms of some standard such as the adequacy of the diet provided. But there are always many other criteria that might as legitimately have been selected, but they were not, such as the adequacy of the income for assuring that the children in the family can afford to attend college or adequacy for assuring that the family can afford to live in a safe neighborhood. If those with low incomes were more influential than they are, it is likely that the federal poverty line would be higher than it is.

CAUSES OF POVERTY

A few years ago the following question was included in a Gallup Poll of a representative national sample, "In your opinion, which is more to blame if a person is poor—lack of effort on his part, or circumstances beyond his control?" Approximately one-third of the sample felt that the lack of effort was the most important reason. About the same percentage felt that circumstances beyond his control were most important. The rest of the sample gave responses indicating that both factors were equally important.[15]

Stated in more general terms, the distinction the respondents were asked to make was between individualistic and situational causes of poverty. The controversy between these perspectives exists and will continue to exist for many of the same reasons that the free will versus determinism question has remained a source of controversy for so long. Those taking a situational perspective emphasize circumstances beyond individual control such as characteristics of the social and economic system a person lives in. Those taking an individualistic perspective emphasize personal decisions and other personal factors for which the poor are held individually responsible. Those who tend to take a liberal or radical perspective on welfare issues emphasize situational causes in their explanation; those who take a more conservative perspective tend to emphasize individualistic causes.[16]

Both individualistic and situational factors contribute to poverty. One reason that it is difficult to determine how much to attribute to each is that they are so interdependent. Situational factors influence personal decisions, but personal decisions shape which situational factors operate at a later time. There are frequently alternative arguments based on the situational and the individualistic perspectives. The discrepancy is often the result of a difference in choice about how far back to trace the causal chain. For example, those taking an individualistic perspective might trace a poor man's failure to achieve upward mobility to his lack of personal motivation; while those taking a situational perspective might choose to go back another step in the causal chain to look at the environmental factors which influenced his level of personal motivation.

In the discussion which follows we consider a number of the factors commonly mentioned as causes of poverty. Some would be mentioned by those who take a situational perspective, others by those who take an individualistic perspective. Many of the causes mentioned are not mutually exclusive; consequently, there is a certain amount of overlap among them.

Depending on the perspective taken, it is often possible to argue that the purported effect of one factor is due in large part to other causally prior factors. For this reason the extent to which each contributes to poverty is a matter of debate. Among those who agree on an ideological perspective, it is possible to reach some consensus as to the relative importance of various factors, even though the data are not adequate for precise estimates. But in the absence of unambigous data, the perceived importance of various factors is hotly contested by those who do not share the same basic ideological perspective.

Causes most frequently presented by those who take a situational perspective are considered first:

The experience of being socialized in a lower-class social environment contributes to poverty.[17] Growing up in a poor family is one factor. Unsuccessful parental role models, family conflict, family instability, parental values, attitudes, aspirations, beliefs, and the behavior of parents are all relevant aspects of the lower class family social environment. The experience of growing up with lower class peers is another factor. Peer group associations have an effect on educational aspirations and school behavior, occupational aspirations and choice of occupation, sexual behavior (with the chance of teenage pregnancy), use and experimentation with drugs and alcohol, and on many other decisions which have implications for an individual's long-term economic success. The experience of attending a low quality school is another aspect of being socialized in a lower-class social environment. Poor schools increase the probability that students will drop out, which in turn has implications for future earning capacity.

A related argument from an individualistic perspective is that it is a waste of time, money, and effort to attempt to provide more opportunities for the poor until they learn to live more like the rest of society. A reply is that the lower-class life style is more a response to, than a cause of being poor. A related argument from a situational perspective is that it is unjust for those children who have had the bad luck to be born into poor families to be required to pay a penalty for their fate.

A central theme of the Moynihan Report is that the disorganized family environment in which lower-class blacks are socialized is a major reason for subsequent failure to compete successfully with whites in adult life. The report emphasizes instability, extent of illegitimacy, and the tendency to have a female head of the household as symptoms of the weakness of the black family. Evidence is presented suggesting that the situation has been getting worse, not better in recent years. The report calls for efforts to strengthen the black family, but it does not make suggestions as to how this might be done. The conclusions drawn by readers of the report have been quite diverse and often heavily influenced by their prior ideology.[18]

The following are some of the interpretations of the findings from those taking individualistic perspectives. One has been that the poor are immoral and consequently unworthy of the money that is already being spent to say nothing of spending more on them. Another interpretation has been that it is a waste of good money to educate, train, and find jobs for blacks before something is done about the family situation. Others conclude that blacks need marriage counseling and other forms of psychotherapy designed to help the black family function more effectively in today's world.

From a situational perspective the structure of the black family is viewed as largely a response to the dismal economic outlook faced by blacks, particularly black males. The focus suggested is changing opportunities available to blacks rather than changing family patterns. The proposed emphasis is on policies which improve the wages, job security, and opportunities for advancement for those who are presently at the bottom of the occupational structure.

The opportunity structure faced by those from a lower class background contributes to poverty.[19] The educational and occupational opportunities that exist are limited. For those who have completed high school, college is often too expensive. For those who have not, many of the available jobs are dead-end, low paying, or insecure.

From an individualistic perspective a related argument is that not all persons socialized in a lower class milieu end up in poverty. Many are at least moderately successful and some become very successful. The evidence that some manage to escape poverty is interpreted as an indication that others could too if they were willing to make the required effort.

One reply to the preceding argument is based on the assumption that there is a small and relatively fixed number of good jobs open to persons from lower-class backgrounds. Some of the poor can obtain good jobs, but the demand for such jobs far exceeds the supply. As the good jobs are filled, it becomes increasingly difficult for others to find them. Consequently, hard work will result in more upward mobility when a relatively small segment of the lower-class population makes the necessary effort. If all of the poor were to make an effort to obtain these jobs, the majority would fail because the supply is limited.

From a situational perspective the conclusion is drawn that the economic failure of persons from a lower-class background is often due to lack of those opportunities which lead to long run economic success. Furthermore, the adverse effects are cumulative. Those who are excluded from certain opportunities early in life are at a disadvantage for the rest of their lives. In many cases they will not be able to compete successfully later in life if they are given an equal chance at that time. A parallel argument can be made for the cumulative effect of inequality of opportunity between generations.

Low wages contribute to poverty.[20] In 1969, 22 percent of the heads of poor families were employed all year, but the wages earned were not sufficient to keep the family out of poverty. Many of these workers had jobs in low-wage industries. This includes many service jobs as domestic, laundry, hospital, and restaurant workers as well as many farm labor jobs. It also encompasses some factory jobs particularly in non-unionized industries. Worker productivity is low in many low-wage industries due in part to the low capital investment. In many cases, the industry has a highly competitive produce market. In some instances, the corporation could not provide decent pay and at the same time maintain competitive prices. Many of the low-wage industries are not unionized. This is in part due to lack of effort by the unions. There is often less interest in organizing the smaller and more isolated units. It is also in part due to resistance from the employers who realize that they would have difficulty staying in business and paying decent wages. Many of those in low-wage industries are not covered by minimum wage legislation. In many cases the low wages can be linked to discrimination on the basis of race or sex.

In recent years there has been frequent mention of a dual economy in the United States. The primary sector has been expanding; it provides adequate wages and decent working conditions. The secondary or irregular sector includes many of the low-wage jobs. This sector is characterized by poor working conditions and low wages. Although the skill level of the work involved in the secondary sector is often equal to that for at least some of the jobs in the primary sector, those who enter the secondary sector often find few opportunities to shift to the primary sector.

From an individualistic perspective a related argument is that if a man does not like the wages offered by these low-wage industries, he can obtain the education and training necessary for the better jobs or migrate to an area in which there are higher paying jobs for those with his skill level. A response from a situational perspective would be that often people are unaware that there are better opportunities for persons with their skills in other locations. Also, in many cases they do not have the opportunities to obtain the additional training needed for the better jobs.

Another argument from the individualistic perspective is that many low-wage earners are not worth more than what they are being paid. If wages are "artificially" forced up, many of these workers will be out of jobs and consequently worse off than they are with low wages. One reply is to question whether workers can be assumed to be worth what they are being paid. For example, two workers doing identical work may receive very different salaries if one works in a unionized industry and the other a non-unionized industry. Another reply is that studies of industries recently covered by minimum wage legislation do not show substantial increases in unemployment rates.

Unemployment contributes to poverty. In 1969, 46 percent of the heads of poor families were unemployed for the entire year and an additional 28 percent were unemployed part of the year. Unemployment is a fundamental component of a capitalistic economic system. In many industries it is standard practice that employees be laid-off during slack periods. In some seasonal industries such as farming it is assumed that a high proportion of the workers will be unemployed for a substantial part of each year. Unemployment is particularly high for blacks and youths. The standard published unemployment figures tend to understate the full extent of unemployment because many of those who have been unemployed for an extended period are classified as being out of the labor force rather than unemployed.

A related argument from an individualistic perspective is that unemployment is a necessary aspect of our economic system and it is with this economic system that we have been able to achieve the highest standard of living of any country in the world. While unemployment is a source of discomfort to some, this disadvantage is more than compensated for by the long-run benefits to the poor as well as to the rich. Another argument is that a successful corporation can employ many people and keep them out of poverty most of the time. But if it does not lay-off workers during slack periods, it runs a risk of failing. In such an event the workers would be worse off than if they had been temporarily unemployed. A reply to these arguments is that there are some countries, such as Sweden, which manage to keep unemployment levels substantially below those of the United States. While profit margins may be lower and government intervention may be necessary, this is not an unreasonable price to pay for the improvement in general welfare for the workers involved.

Work related injuries and health problems contribute to poverty.[21] Many of the industries in which the poor are most likely to be found working have a relatively high risk of injury or illness. In industries such as coal mining, the owners sometimes choose not to make certain safety improvements because of the cost involved. They find it more economical to plan to pay pensions to a limited number of injured workers than to spend an even greater sum of money on safety measures. While many of those who are injured receive pensions, these pensions are often not adequate to keep the recipient's family out of poverty. Others are disqualified from receiving any pension at all due to some technicality (e.g., the company doctor will not certify them as totally disabled). In addition to those who are injured on the job, there are many more workers who gradually develop work-related health problems. Sometimes the problem develops over a period of time during which the worker has held a series of jobs. The worker in a coal mine, saw mill, or other environment in which there are particles in the air is particularly prone to develop diseases related to the gradual deterioration of his lungs. In many such cases workers are forced into early retirement due to poor health and often they are not eligible for compensation.

From the individualistic perspective an argument is that the worker himself must often take a certain amount of the responsibility for the disability. The worker in many cases had the choice between a low paying job with little chance of a job related injury and a higher paying job with a greater chance. The higher pay is in part his compensation for taking this risk.

From the situational perspective a reply is that lower class youth often have a limited number of job options. The alternatives to a high risk occupation may pay very low wages and have very low status among peers. Even if a high risk occupation is selected, the risk may be sufficiently low that it would be economically rational to select the higher risk job. In many high risk occupations it would be possible for the employer to reduce the risk of injury, but on economic grounds the decision is not to make the changes. This raises the question of why the worker should be held responsible for an injury that was in part due to his employer's efforts to maximize profits.

The emphasis in a capitalist economy on efficiency and profit maximization contribute to poverty. Efficient production calls for keeping the labor costs to a minimum. The emphasis on efficiency leads to efforts to employ the most productive persons in the available labor pool. This increases the risk of unemployment for the aged, the partially disabled, the mentally retarded, the poorly educated, and other low productivity workers.

In some instances, the goal of efficient production and profit maximization lead to policies which have adverse effects in localized areas. In the effort to reduce labor costs some industries move from one section of the country to another. Many of the least skilled are left behind without jobs. In some industries technological advances reduce the number of workers needed; in areas that have become dependent on one industry this often means extended unemployment for many workers. Industries which cannot compete successfully must leave the market; the consequences of the failure of an industry are again particularly severe in areas which have become dependent on that one industry. While these factors contribute to poverty in isolated areas, the overall impact is not necessarily adverse. Some workers in one area fall into poverty when an industry fails; at the same time workers in another area may be rising out of poverty due to the jobs created by the competing industry. In other words, when an industry relocates, it may increase poverty in one area and decrease poverty in another. However, it is not always the case that the gain will match the loss; there may be fewer jobs created than are lost. In addition, jobs created may go to those who would not otherwise have been poor.

Many of the adverse consequences of the emphasis on profit maximization can be modified with appropriate legislation and labor union organization. Over the years working conditions have been improving. But the slow rate of change is not accidental. Our economic system is organized with a higher priority on the maximization of profit than on employee welfare.

One reply to the preceding calls for making a distinction between efficiency from the perspective of an individual corporation and efficiency in terms of general social welfare. While an individual corporation may run very efficiently, what it produces may not contribute in an important way to general social welfare. Competition between producers often results in extensive duplication which is not efficient in terms of the goal of maximizing general social welfare. For example, the production and maintenance of cars would be much more efficient if there were fewer models to choose from. The defense industry is a major sector of our economy. Even if the individual contractors were to operate efficiently, the massive defense spending may not be efficient when measured in terms of its contribution to general social welfare. As a final example, many industries pollute the environment, but the extent of the pollution is not taken into consideration in the assessment of the efficiency of production except in those few cases in which there are fines for pollution above a specified level. These examples illustrate that our capitalistic economic system may be efficient in certain respects, but quite inefficient if looked at in terms of contribution to general social welfare.

Discrimination contributes to poverty.[22] One source of discrimination is the tendency to exclude women and minority group members from certain higher paying occupations. Another is to pay them less for the same work. Many women work part-time and are paid at a lower rate for doing so. Many blacks hold jobs in the irregular labor market and are not covered by minimum wage legislation. In the South prejudice against blacks has inhibited the organization of labor unions among low-income blacks and whites with unfortunate economic consequences for both groups. The lower wages for women have on occasion been defended on the grounds that women can generally rely on their husband's wage for their primary support. But many women in the work force are single.

While race and sex discrimination are two of the most obvious categories, others exist. Often a person who would be competent to handle a job is turned away because of his age. There is often a reluctance to hire a person with a disability of some type even when the disability does not interfere with his capacity to do the required work.

A related argument from an individualistic perspective is that in many cases an employer is accused of discrimination when he is just attempting to hire the most qualified applicants. The individual employer cannot be held responsible if his white male applicants are more qualified than the black and female applicants. A reply to this argument is that excessive emphasis on present qualifications often serves to perpetuate the effects of past discrimination.

The preceding causes of poverty would be most likely to be mentioned by those who view poverty primarily from a situational perspective. The causes that follow are more likely to be mentioned by those who take an individualistic perspective. There is necessarily a certain amount of overlap because many of the causes to be mentioned attempt to explain some of the same phenomena that the preceding causes purport to account for.

Many personal decisions made early in life contribute to subsequent poverty. Among the decisions being referred to are (1) dropping out of school; (2) taking a dead-end job in a dying industry, a job with a high risk of disease or disability, or a job with little opportunity for social mobility; (3) experimentation with hard drugs; (4) taking the chance of pregnancy at an early age, early marriage, having several children early in marriage; (5) participation in various delinquent activities that can lead to jail sentences; (6) and other such decisions which decrease the opportunities for economic success in adult life.

From the individualistic perspective the argument is that the youths consciously make such decisions and have the option of making other decisions. Further, if people are not held responsible for such decisions there is the danger that there will be an increase in the number of people making similar decisions. An alternative explanation from the situational perspective is that there is substantial pressure for a youth growing up in a lower-class social environment to make many decisions which reduce the chance of long-run economic success. In part, these decisions are a reaction to the perceived lack of opportunities to actually long-term economic success. Many of the lower-class youth's peers who do try the more legitimate paths to economic success are frustrated in their attempts. One response to this failure is the development of norms in support of other categories of success such as being tough, being successful in sexual exploits, being successful in various delinquent activities, and in other ways which tend to reduce the chances of long-run economic success.

Lower-class values, attitudes, aspirations, and beliefs contribute to poverty.[23] The poor often have lower achievement motivation, lower educational aspirations, lower occupational aspirations, less self-esteem, a weaker sense of personal efficacy (fate control), and show less belief in the value of planning for the future. There is some evidence that they are more present-oriented, and show less faith in the efficacy of hard work.

An argument based on the individualistic perspective is that the poor cannot avoid exposure to the emphasis in American culture on the value and efficacy of hard work, upward social mobility, future orientation, and other attitudes which contribute in the long run to economic success. If a person chooses to reject these values and attitudes, that is his choice; but he should be held responsible for having done so. If his alternative attitudes prolong poverty, he and not society is responsible.

Upholders of the situational perspective would counter that the differences in values and attitudes between the poor and others may in large part be the result rather than the cause of the social class differences. This interpretation assumes that attitudes and values are strongly influenced by social structural factors and represent an adaptation to them. The acceptance of modified or different values and attitudes by the poor is viewed as an attempt to cope with the situation of being unable to live up to dominant culture's values.

Old age contributes to poverty.[24] Many people are capable of keeping themselves out of poverty as long as they can participate full-time in the labor force. But with advancing age many are forced into partial or full retirement or at least into lower paying occupations. The result is that many who were never poor previously slip into poverty.

With reference to the individualistic perspective, it can be argued that everyone knows he must eventually retire and has the responsibility to plan accordingly. Those who choose a higher standard of living prior to retirement do so knowing that this advantage is achieved at a cost of a lower standard of living and possibly poverty after retirement.

From the situational perspective a reply to the preceding argument is that often a person is forced into retirement many years prior to original expectations. Not only are several earning years lost, but several years of high medical expenses may be added. Furthermore, many of those who are not able to save an adequate income for retirement have been living quite modestly prior to retirement. They might have reduced spending to an even more modest level, but it would have meant raising their children in a lower-class neighborhood, not being able to send their children to college, or not being able to adequately meet certain health needs.

Genetic and prenatal factors contribute to poverty.[25] There has been considerable debate over the relative importance of heredity and environment as determinants of intelligence. The debate will not be reviewed here. For our purposes it is sufficient to point out that there is general agreement that genetic factors are important as determinants of intelligence. Mental retardation can often be linked to genetic factors. While there is much debate over the extent to which mental illness can be accounted for in terms of genetic factors, there is evidence that in at least some cases of schizophrenia this is true. There are a number of hereditary diseases and other physical defects which reduce adult productivity. Physique and physical attractiveness have genetic components; they too have implications for adult success. There are also physical and mental defects due to complications during pregnancy or birth. A poorly nourished mother is more likely to have a premature baby, and prematurity is associated with a number of complications. If the mother contracts certain diseases, such as German measles, or uses certain drugs , the child is more likely to have certain physical defects.

Upholders of the individualistic perspective would argue that the physically deformed and mentally retarded are less productive and should be willing to accept a lower standard of living because they contribute less to society. From the situational perspective the argument is that a person does not pick his parents and has little influence over his prenatal environment; consequently, he should not be penalized for the limitations that are passed on to him.

Lack of work effort (laziness) contributes to poverty.[26] Some of those who are poor would not be poor if they were willing to make more of an effort to find a job, were more willing to accept the kinds of jobs that are available, or were willing to spend a higher percentage of their time at work.

It is argued from the individualistic perspective that people who could work and could support themselves if they did work should be held personally responsible for their poverty and should not be supported with public money. A response to this argument from a situational perspective is that it is often difficult in practice to differentiate people who are willing to work, but unable to find an employer from those who are unwilling to work. The stated goal of excluding persons who are able but unwilling to work often results in the exclusion of persons who are able to work but unable to find a job.

An argument based on the situational perspective would assert that many of those who appear to be able-bodied unemployed have problems such as low skill, mental retardation, alcoholism, drug addiction, personality problems, relatively advanced age, or some other disability. Such persons may have spent substantial effort in the past attempting to locate a job only to be turned down or laid-off soon after being employed.

Lack of ability contributes to poverty. To some extent ability is a function of intelligence and other physical characteristics with important genetic components. Ability is also influenced by prior experience and training.

From the individualistic perspective the argument is made that those with the most ability must be rewarded for their ability as an incentive to maximize the contributions of the most able to society. The legitimacy of basing rewards on differences, however, can be questioned as they could be due to training and genetic endowment. A person does not, for instance, pick his parents. Many kinds of training are more accessible to persons from higher social class background. We can also question whether the discrepancy in the magnitude of rewards that presently exists between the less able and the more able is needed.

Low productivity contributes to poverty. This cause is closely related to the preceding cause. Worker productivity can be viewed as in part due to ability and in part due to motivation.

Upholders of the individualistic perspective would argue that the productive workers must be rewarded so as to assure that society will reap the full benefits of their potential capacity. A necessary corollary is that the less productive workers are often worth very little. In some instances they may not even be able to find an employer who feels they are worth a living wage. A counter argument is that in many cases it would be possible to reduce the economic incentive for the most productive workers somewhat without substantially reducing their productivity; the resources could be used to provide a more adequate standard of living for the less productive. The assumption, that the added productivity of the potentially most productive is worth the human cost of the poverty experienced by the least productive, can also be called into question. The few studies that have been conducted suggest that rates of taxation on the upper income groups could be increased without a substantial drop in productivity.[27]

The counter culture contributes to poverty. Many of those referred to as hippies, street people, and so on, live in what might be called voluntary poverty. The reference here is primarily to those persons from a middle-class background who have accepted the poverty associated with dropping-out over the option of obtaining and holding a job that would pay an above poverty wage. Now that such a social movement is in full swing, it itself becomes a source attracting others to this type of poverty. It would be a mistake to conclude that all or even most of those who have chosen this style of life prefer poverty to affluence. Many may be willing to accept the poverty as the price for the opportunity to drop-out, but many would undoubtedly prefer not to be poor if it were possible within the framework of their preferred life style.

From the individualistic perspective it is argued that these poeple have chosen poverty and should be willing to take the consequences. They certainly do not have any legitimate claim for support from those who hold regular jobs within the main culture. As a response from the situational perspective it can be pointed out that the decision that some make to drop out is in reaction to the options that are available within the regular job market. In many cases with less emphasis on the maximization of profits, jobs could be made more personally satisfying.

While some people do voluntarily choose to live in poverty, this group makes up a small minority of those who are poor. It is a common mistake for higher income groups to assume that many of the poor are where they are because they really do not want to get ahead in life.

CONSEQUENCES OF POVERTY

Many of the causes of poverty which were discussed earlier will again be mentioned here, but this time as consequences rather than causes of poverty. The reason for this is that many of the consequences of being born into a poor family and of being raised in a lower class social milieu contribute to poverty in adulthood. In other words, many of the consequences of poverty become transformed into causes of the persistence of poverty. Thus the circular relationship between the causes and consequences form a vicious cycle of poverty.

If it were not for the many situational factors that generally accompany low income, the consequences would be substantially less adverse. This is illustrated by certain immigrant groups, such as the Jews, which have experienced extremes of poverty, but have nonetheless avoided some of the consequences that are often associated with being poor. If the family and the community can provide values and patterns of behavior that are consistent with upward mobility, many of the consequences that often accompany poverty can be avoided. It is less likely that a family will succeed in providing the necessary values and behavior patterns when that family lives in an area in which most other families have adopted lower-class values and behavior patterns.

Because low income is generally accompanied by a number of other conditions, it is difficult to specify precisely how much the fate of the poor family should be attributed to income alone and how much the fate of the poor family should be attributed to the other accompanying factors. A few of the most important consequences of poverty are considered here. Some of the consequences are of most direct relevance to the poor themselves, others are of relevance to those who are not poor. Those of particular relevance to the poor are considered first.

The poor have access to fewer educational and economic opportunities. The poor are less likely to attend college for a number of reasons that are related to being poor and to being socialized in a lower-class milieu. Among the reasons are the expense involved, poor performance in secondary school, poor quality secondary education, and lack of support for the decision to attend college by parents or peers. A number of the same factors increase the chance that a person growing up in poverty will become a high school drop-out. In addition, the desire to earn more money than is possible while attending school full-time and the irrelevance of the school curriculum to anticipated future activities also contribute to the decision to become a drop-out.

The educational disadvantage with which the poor begin is one factor limiting occupational choice. Another is lack of information about where to obtain good jobs and what must be done to qualify for them. In addition there is substantial discrimination against the poor, particularly against those who are members of minority groups. The jobs that are most easily accessible to the poor pay low wages, offer poor working conditions, few opportunities for advancement, and little job security. Many of the jobs are tedious, undignified, or menial. Some are physically dirty, others involve considerable physical labor, and many involve both. A disproportionate number involve a risk to good health and personal safety.

The poor acquire values, attitudes, aspirations, and beliefs that hinder long-run economic success. The lower-class values and attitudes of those who are socialized by lower-class parents and peers are better suited for coping with the frustrations of being poor than they are for escaping poverty. Some argue that the values and attitudes of the poor would persist even if they were given ample opportunities to become upwardly mobile. Others argue that the attitudes and values of the poor are for the most part a response to the opportunity structure that they face; that is, if the opportunities were to change, there would be a rapid shift in attitudes, values, and related behavior. In a short time the previously poor would be indistinguishable from those who had always been in these higher income and occupational categories. The most reasonable position lies somewhere between these two extremes. If there were a substantial improvement in the opportunities for the poor, there would be marked shifts in relevant attitudes, values, and related behavior; but for many there would continue to be some adjustment problems related to their prior lower-class socialization.[28]

There is some disagreement as to whether the poor accept the major cultural values of American society such as the importance of economic success and planning for the future. One argument is that the poor reject many of the values of the dominant society and substitute their own values. An alternative is that the poor maintain the values on such matters as economic success and planning for the future, but they have fewer sanctions for those who fail to live up to them. Related to this is the greater acceptance of the decision to live by alternative values when special circumstances make it difficult to live up to the values of the dominant culture. In place of economic success, other forms of success such as toughness or sexual conquest are accepted as substitutes. An orientation primarily in terms of the present rather than the future is less stigmatized when there is reason to believe that the future is very uncertain due to job instability, marital instability, and other similar sources of uncertainty in the lives of the poor. Such modifications of the values of the dominant culture often lead to decisions which reduce the likelihood of long-term economic success.[29]

The poor often receive low quality health care.[30] The poor cannot afford the cost of high quality medical and dental services. In some rural areas medical and dental services for the poor are nonexistent. In cities such services are available in public clinics, but the care available is generally of much lower quality than that available to private patients. In some instances medical decisions that could prolong life at a high cost are not made for the poor patient who does not have the insurance to cover the cost. An example would be the decision of whether or not to make use of an artificial kidney machine.

The poor are often malnourished.[31] The poor are more likely to be malnourished than other segments of society. This is due to the limited funds available for food, food preferences learned from the more affluent, and the desire for other goods and services. It is impossible to provide an adequate diet on the available income of the poorest families. For the others who are a bit better off it is possible to purchase an adequate diet with the available family resources, but in many cases the diet still remains inadequate. One contributing factor is the decision to spend the available money in such a way that the funds for food are insufficient to provide an adequate diet. In some cases the family is not fully aware of the implications of the allocation being made; in others, a conscious decision is made to economize on food in the effort to pay for a television set, a washing machine, or some other such high priority purchase. In many poor families, the actual funds spent on food are sufficient to provide an adequate diet, but the diet is inadequate because the money is not spent in such a way to maximize the nutritional value per dollar. The food preferences of the poor are substantially influenced by the eating habits in the dominant culture. Such preferences emphasize meat, although meat is not the most economical source of protein. Since most food buyers are willing to pay for convenience foods, the foods that are most readily available in the corner store are those that sell best and not necessarily those that provide the most nutrition for the money spent. In short, the buyer who seeks to obtain the maximum nutritional value per food dollar is going to have a diet that would be unfamiliar and unappealing to most Americans.

The poor are more likely to be victims of crimes against the person.[32] This includes such crimes as armed robbery, assault, and murder. The poor are also more likely to be victimized by property crimes such as burglary. A related consequence of poverty is that the poor are often given harsher treatment by the law enforcement officials: a poor youth is more likely than a middle-class youth to have his offense recorded officially rather than handled unofficially.[33]

The poor are more vulnerable to marital instability.[34] The poor have more marital conflict, less marital satisfaction, and less marital stability than the general population. One factor that contributes to this instability is the husband's inability to provide a steady income to the family. Another is the present AFDC program which provides benefits to a woman if her husband has left the family. This makes it economically advantageous to the family if the husband leaves the household.

The poor have less political influence.[35] The poor are a minority, they cannot contribute much to campaign funds, they do not tend to run candidates, and they usually have a low voter turnout. All these factors contribute to not having their interests well represented by elected politicians. In many areas their already weak political position is often further undercut by job and welfare discrimination against those who vote, by the gerrymandering of election districts, and by the emphasis on electing local officials at large rather than from specific districts, and other similar forms of discrimination.

The poor have less influence on the job and within the community itself. In addition to having little influence in electoral politics, the poor are less likely to be in a position of authority over others at work or to be able to obtain improvements in working conditions. They are also less likely to be influential in church and other community voluntary organization, or within the school system. Also their influence with the police and other community service agencies tends to be limited. One form this lack of influence takes is that the poor are given less prompt and less considerate attention.

Although the consequences of poverty unquestionably fall heaviest on the poor themselves, there are also consequences for the rest of society. A few of the most important of these are considered here.

The existence of a substantial poor segment of the population contributes to the decay of central cities. The rural poor contribute to the decay of central cities by their migration to these areas; the urban poor contribute to the worsening situation by their generally higher rates of social pathology and their inability to pay high taxes to improve the quality of police protection, schools, transportation and other public services. A response to this situation by many of the more affluent members of society is to move to the suburbs. This migration further reduces the tax base and the proportion of city population that is middle class. This in turn makes conditions worse and increases the incentives for the remaining middle-class residents to make the move to the suburbs.

Many of the poor are dependent on public support. In most states welfare makes up a substantial percentage of the state budget. In addition to the direct costs of welfare benefits there are other indirect costs associated with the poor such as increased spending on law enforcement and upkeep on school buildings. Much of the direct and indirect cost of supporting the poor is borne by other segments of society.

Poverty has contributed to civil strife in recent years. Civil strife has divided our country. It has undermined the confidence of many in the leadership of our country. For some this has led to a questioning of the viability of our economic and political system. Many Americans feel that it would be desirable for the nations in the world to adopt political and economic systems similar to ours. However, the existence of the poor and the evidence of their discontent suggest that even though our social system is effective for creating great wealth, it is not successful in eliminating poverty.

Poverty in America is increasingly becoming a source of guilt for the rest of society. While in the past it has not been possible to eliminate poverty, today many feel that it is. This situation is a source of guilt for many Americans, as evidenced particularly among college students. It has led some to question the capacity of our ecconomic and political system to provide a fair distribution of resources, power, and opportunities. This lack of confidence in the government is reflected in a reluctance to plan a career in government service or to participate in such programs as VISTA.

In our discussion, we have focused on the disadvantages to society if a substantial segment of the population is poverty stricken. In a poor country poverty is an unavoidable necessity. In a rich country such as the United States, poverty could be eliminated. When attempting to explain why our society permits poverty to exist, it is useful to consider some of the needs of the more affluent that are met by allowing poverty to continue to exist. Gans has outlined thirteen functions which poverty serves for the affluent.[36] The following discussion is in large part based on some of the functions which he mentions.

The poor provide the labor pool for many low-wage industries. In some of these industries it would be economically feasible to pay higher wages, but profits would fall off. But many others are so highly competitive that they could not continue to compete unless their competitors also increased wage levels. In some cases, the main competition is from an alternative product in a more highly mechanized industry; in other cases foreign competition is the main threat. Many such industries could not weather any uniform increase in wages and would go out of business if forced to pay higher wages. Many low income women work as domestics. If their wages were increased, some of the upper income families which can presently afford this service would no longer be able to do so. Even those who could afford to pay higher wages have a vested interest in maintaining low wages for domestic workers.

The poor provide the labor pool for society's menial and undignified jobs. They also provide the labor pool for many of the jobs that involve minimal job security, no opportunity for advancement, and serious health hazards. These are the jobs that would not get done unless there were workers with no other alternatives. Many of the jobs in low-wage industries would be included here. This argument has been included to emphasize that there are many undesirable characteristics of such jobs in addition to their low wages.

The poor provide a source of status to many in the working class. Our society places a high value on success. There is a tendency to use an individual's economic status relative to some reference group in evaluating success. Many of those who are working class get a certain amount of satisfaction in knowing that there are others who are much less successful. For such persons efforts to improve the position of the poor are a threat to their own status. In many areas the poor are predominantly black and the working class is predominantly white. In such cases the race difference is confounded with the difference in economic status. Many working-class whites get satisfaction from being able to point to poor blacks as their economic and social inferiors.

The poor provide a source of upward mobility for many of those who provide goods and services to them. These businesses often involve illegal or dishonest activities. Some such activities are providing the poor with housing, drugs, and stolen goods. Also included are prostitution, gambling, and loan sharking. These businesses are generally of low prestige and many of those who are successful in taking this route to upward mobility subsequently shift to more legitimate types of business activity.

ALTERNATIVES FOR DEALING WITH POVERTY

This book deals with a wide range of strategies for reducing the extent of poverty. Most of the programs considered are supported by public, primarily federal, funds. Similarly, most of the proposals considered call for programs which would be paid for out of public funds. Before turning to an evaluation of the relative merits of the alternative strategies, it is appropriate to examine the assumption common to all of these strategies that substantial public funds should be spent in the effort to reduce the extent of poverty. There are several different perspectives from which the decision to support or oppose public spending on anti-poverty programs can be made. In figure 1.1 the eight alternatives to be considered here are summarized.

To put these alternative perspectives in context, we begin by distinguishing between those persons who emphasize situational factors and those who emphasize individualistic factors in their accounts of why poverty exists in the United States. For those who emphasize individualistic factors, the distinction can be made between those who feel that it is not possible to substantially reduce the extent of poverty by means of various anti-poverty programs and those who feel that it is possible to do so. The reference here and throughout this discussion is to politically feasible, publically funded programs. Those who feel that a substantial reduction would be possible (perspective 1) would generally support at least certain categories of anti-poverty programs. Those who do not feel that it would be possible to make a substantial reduction (perspective 2) would tend to oppose most anti-poverty spending.

Considering those who tend to emphasize situational factors, the distinction can again be made between those who feel that it is possible to have a substantial impact on the extent of poverty through public-

ALTERNATIVE PERSPECTIVES FROM WHICH TO SUPPORT OR OPPOSE PUBLICALLY FUNDED ANTI-POVERTY EFFORTS

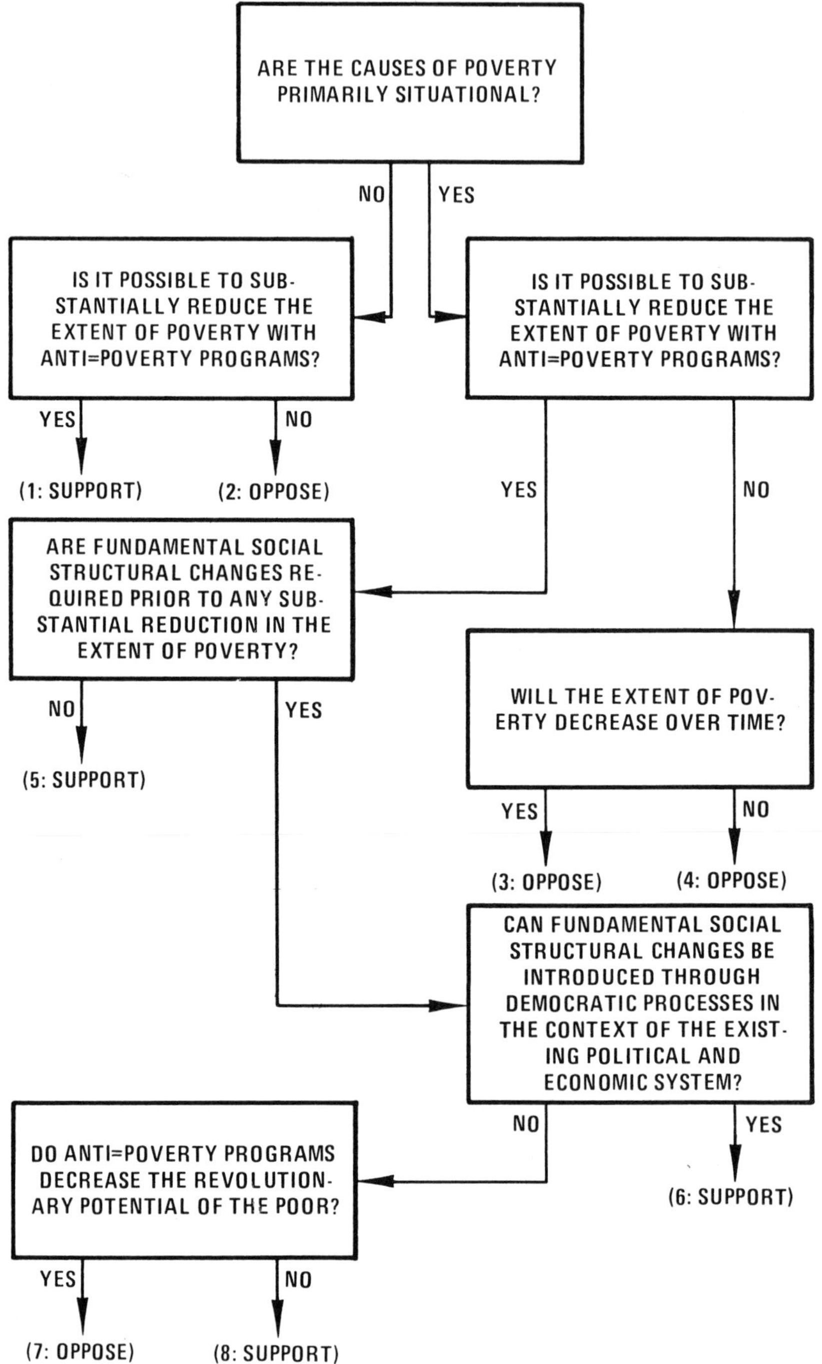

ly supported anti-poverty efforts and those who feel that it is not. For the latter, the distinction can be made between those who feel that there will be a reduction in the extent of poverty independent of specific anti-poverty efforts (perspective 3) and those who feel that the situation of the poor is going to remain pretty much as it is today at least for the foreseeable future (perspective 4). From both of these perspectives, there is likely to be opposition to anti-poverty spending.

In considering those who feel that it would be possible to substantially reduce the extent of poverty, the distinction can be made between those who do and those who do not feel that fundamental social structural changes would be required. The social structural changes being referred to would involve a shift from a predominantly capitalistic economy to a more socialistic economy. This would involve government ownership or control of all or most major industries. Those who feel that such fundamental social structural changes would not be necessary (perspective 5) would tend to support anti-poverty spending.

For those who feel that fundamental social structural changes would be necessary, the distinction can be make between those who feel that such changes could be brought about through democratic processes and those who feel that other, possibly more violent, means would be required. Those who feel that such changes can be brought about by democratic processes within the framework of the present economic and political system (perspective 6) would tend to support anti-poverty spending. They would tend to view the enactment of major public anti-poverty programs as one aspect of the shift to a more socialistic economy.

Those who assert that the fundamental social structural changes cannot be introduced by democratic processes within the framework of the present political and economic system, can be divided between those who feel that anti-poverty programs would increase revolutionary potential and those who feel that such programs would decrease revolutionary potential. Those who feel that anti-poverty programs would decrease revolutionary potential (perspective 7) would oppose them. Those who feel that such programs would increase or at least not decrease revolutionary potential (perspective 8) would support them.

The eight perspectives which have been outlined do not exhaust all possibilities. Many of the distinctions are based on dichotomies when it would have been quite reasonable to include a third or even a fourth alternative. We now turn to a more detailed consideration of each of these eight perspectives.

Perspective 1 is upheld by many of those who believe that poverty is primarily due to characteristics of the poor themselves. It is argued that with anti-poverty programs it would be possible to compensate, at least in part, for these personal limitations. The result would be a substantial reduction in the extent of poverty. Anti-poverty programs and spending would be supported from this perspective.

Perspective 2 is the standard conservative viewpoint. It is based on the view shared with upholders of perspective 1, that poverty is primarily due to characteristics of the poor themselves. The major difference is the rejection of the argument that anti-poverty programs could substantially reduce the extent of poverty. A common argument from this perspective is that human nature cannot be changed and consequently there will always be some people who will not be willing to make the effort that is necessary to avoid living in poverty. Most anti-poverty programs and spending would be opposed from this perspective.

Perspective 3 is shared by those who think that poverty is largely due to situational factors over which the poor and the makers of public policy have little control. The poor are raised in a lower-class social milieu with consequent disadvantages. It would not be possible to substantially reduce the extent of poverty by any anti-poverty programs that are at present politically feasible. The extent of poverty will in any case tend to decrease due to general expansion of the economy, increases in per capita productivity, and other such trends. Anti-poverty programs and spending would generally be opposed from this perspective.

Perspective 4 is basically the same as the preceding one. The major difference is the lack of optimism that the extent of poverty is likely to decrease in the long run. The condition of the poor relative to the rest of society is more likely to be emphasized than the absolute condition of the poor which has undeniably been improving in recent years. Those who share this perspective are likely to oppose anti-poverty efforts.

Perspective 5 is the standard liberal view shared by many who support anti-poverty efforts. Liberals believe that it is possible to reduce the extent of poverty in the United States. Furthermore, they feel this is possible without fundamental social structural changes; they can be made through reform efforts within the context of the present political and economic system.

Perspective 6 takes the view that it would be possible to substantially reduce the extent of poverty in the United States, but extensive social structural change would be required. It is further argued that the necessary social structural change can and should be brought about through democratic means within the context of the existing political and economic system. This approach would involve efforts to elect politicians with ideologies consistent with the social democratic tradition.[37] Many anti-poverty efforts would be supported because they would form part of the social democratic legislative program.

Perspective 7 is the basis of the argument that the social structural changes which would be necessary to cause a substantial impact on the extent of poverty could not be introduced through democratic processes; some form of social revolution would be necessary. From this perspective anti-poverty efforts within the context of the existing political and economic system only serve to divert attention from the structural aspects of the system which contribute to the continued existence of poverty. Anti-poverty efforts would be opposed because they would tend to reduce the discontent and revolutionary potential of the poor. Anti-poverty programs would bring some minor improvements, but at a cost of reducing the chance of the much more fundamental changes that would be necessary to have a truly substantial impact on the extent of poverty.

Perspective 8 is similar to perspective 7; the major difference being that at least some anti-poverty programs are seen as increasing or at least not decreasing the revolutionary potential of the poor. The evidence that the most repressed segment of the population is less likely to express dissatisfaction is used to argue that anti-poverty programs might contribute to an increase in revolutionary potential. In this context anti-poverty programs are viewed as bringing a small improvement in living conditions to many people and in the course of doing so they increase expectations and decrease acceptance of the existing social order. This perspective is also justified on grounds that efforts should be made to improve the lot of the poor until the time for social revolution is ripe. From this perspective anti-poverty programs and spending would be supported.

On the basis of the preceding analysis the following observations can be made. It is possible to support anti-poverty efforts while holding a basically individualistic perspective in the causes of poverty (perspective 1). Some of those who view poverty from a basically situational perspective will oppose anti-poverty efforts (perspective 3, 4, and 7). Some of those with the most radical views about poverty (perspective 7) will join some welfare conservatives (perspective 2, 3, and 4) in opposing anti-poverty efforts.

Any effort to evaluate the relative merits of the alternative perspectives is beyond the scope of the present analysis. The preceding discussion illustrates that support for public programs designed to reduce the extent and impact of poverty derives from a wide range of perspectives. For those who agree that some form of public anti-poverty effort is in order, the next question to ask is which strategies should be used? The major objective of the present study is to compare the relative merits of a wide range of alternatives.

Notes

1. U.S. Bureau of the Census, *Current Population Reports,* Series P–60, No.76, "24 Million Americans—Poverty in the United States: 1969," (Washington, D.C.: U.S. Government Printing Office, 1970). The data base for this report is the March 1970 Current Population Survey of approximately 50,000 households. All 1969 statistics in this section are either drawn directly from this report or based on simple calculations using the data presented therein.
2. U.S. Bureau of the Census, "24 Million Americans."
3. U.S. Bureau of the Census, *Current Population Reports,* Series P–60, No. 77, "Poverty Increases by 1.2 Million in 1970," (Washington, D.C.: U.S. Government Printing Office, 1970).
4. U.S. Bureau of the Census, "Poverty Increases by 1.2 Million in 1970."
5. U.S. Bureau of the Census, "24 Million Americans."
6. This statistic is frequently reported in a misleading way. The reader is told that in 1969, 54 percent of the heads of poor families worked. Many would interpret this statement as indicating that all or most of those referred to worked the full year, but this was true for only 26 percent. Many of the others worked for much shorter periods. Another way in which statistics on work are often misleading is that the distinction is not made between part and full-time work. For example, we report that 26 percent of the heads of poor families worked all year. Many readers would assume that the reference is to full-time work. Of the 26 percent, 22 percent is due to full time-work and 4 percent to part-time work.
7. While some of the resulting categories include persons with a greater risk of poverty, others include persons with less risk. Overall the increase in risk to certain catetories must be balanced by a decrease in risk to other categories.
8. Rose Friedman, *Poverty Definition and Perspective* (Washington, D.C.: American Enterprise Institute, 1965). In 1955 for families spending $187 per person on food, 50 percent met their requirements for adequate nutrition. For families spending $262 per person, 75 percent met their requirements. For families spending $325 per person, 90 percent met their requirements.
9. Mollie Orshansky, "Counting the Poor: Another Look at the Poverty Profile," *Social Security Bulletin* 28, 1(1965): 3-29. The poverty line was published in 1965, but it was based on 1963 data so it was actually the 1963 poverty line. The necessary data was available back to 1959 and poverty lines have since been calculated for each year back to 1959.
10. The $460 figure was suggested by Hunter. See Robert Hunter, *Poverty* (New York: Macmillan, 1904), p. 52. For the 1950 and 1968 poverty lines see Anthony Downs, *Who Are The Urban Poor?* (New York: Committee for Economic Development, 1970), p. 10.

11. See Victor R. Fuchs, "Redefining Poverty and Redistributing Income," *The Public Interest* 8 (Summer 1967): 89-94. Also see *Report of the President's Commission on Income Maintenance Programs, Poverty Amid Plenty,* Ben W. Heineman, Chairman. (Washington, D.C.: U.S. Government Printing Office, 1969), p. 40. Another relative indicator is the Gini index which measures the extent of inequality in the overall income distribution.
12. Heineman, *Poverty Amid Plenty,* p. 31.
13. U.S. Bureau of the Census, *Statistical Abstract of the United States: 1970* (91st. ed.; Washington, D.C.: U.S. Government Printing Office, 1970), p. 327. In 1969 of households in America with income under $3,000 per year, 45 percent had a car, 77 percent had a television, 75 percent had a refrigerator, and 50 percent had a washing machine.
14. S.M. Miller et al., "Poverty, Inequality and Conflict," *The Annals of the American Academy of Political and Social Science* 373 (1967): 18-52. Also, see S.M. Miller and Pamela A. Roby, *The Future of Inequality* (New York: Basic Books, 1970), Chapter 5.
15. The question was asked in an American Institute of Public Opinion (AIPO) poll December 5, 1964. In the total sample 30 percent responded "lack of effort", 31 percent responded "circumstances", and 34 percent responded "both". The lack of effort response was given by 42 percent of respondents with an income of $7,000 or over and by 18 percent of respondents with an income under $3,000. Reported in Amitai Etzioni and Carolyn O. Atkinson, *Social Implications of Alternative Income Transfer Systems* (Washington, D.C.: Bureau of Social Science Research, 1969), Table IX-1.
16. Most social scientists emphasize situational factors in accounting for poverty. Representative of this view are Gans, Rainwater, and Lumer. Among social scientists individualistic factors are emphasized by those who feel that many of the poor live in a separate subculture and those who emphasize psychological factors; Banfield, Lewis, and Walter Miller are representative of this emphasis. See Herbert J. Gans, "Culture and Class in the Study of Poverty: An Approach to Anti-Poverty Research," and Lee Rainwater, "The Problem of Lower-Class Culture and Poverty-War Strategy," both in *On Understanding Poverty,* ed. Daniel P. Moynihan (New York: Basic Books, 1969); Hyman Lumer, *Poverty: Its Roots and Its Future* (New York: International Publishers, 1965); Lee Rainwater, *Behind Ghetto Walls* (Chicago: Aldine, 1970). Also see Walter B. Miller, "Focal Concerns of Lower Class Culture," in *Poverty in America,* ed. Louis A. Ferman, Joyce L. Kornbluh, and Alan Haber (Ann Arbor: University of Michigan Press, 1965); Edward C. Banfield, *The Unheavenly City* (Boston: Little, Brown and Company, 1970); Oscar Lewis, *La Vida* (New York: Random House, 1966).
17. See Lewis, *La Vida.* He gives a theoretical discussion of the culture of poverty concept in the introduction. For evidence of the inverse relationship between family income and marital stability see William J. Goode, "Economic Factors and Marital Stability," *American Sociological Review* 16, 1(1951): 802-812. For evidence for a positive relationship between parental aspirations and social class see Herbert H. Hyman, "The Value Systems of Different Classes: A Social Psychological Contribution to the Analysis of Stratification," in *Class, Status, and Power,* eds. Reinhardt Bendix and Seymour M. Lipset (New York: Free Press, 1966).

18. The Moynihan Report is the popular name for a U.S. Department of Labor report "The Negro Family: The Case for National Action," which is reprinted in Lee Rainwater and William L. Yancey, *The Moynihan Report and The Politics of Controversy*, (Cambridge Mass: M.I.T. Press, 1967). The present discussion draws on the following articles presented in the same volume: Christopher Jencks, "The Moynihan Report," Herbert J. Gans, "The Negro Family: Reflections on the Moynihan Report," William Ryan, "Savage Discovery: The Moynihan Report," Also see Warren D. TenHouten, "The Black Family: Myth and Reality," *Psychiatry* 33, 2(1970): 145-155.
19. For a more technical treatment of this cause see Lester C. Thurow, *Poverty and Discrimination* (Washington, D.C.: The Brookings Institution, 1969).
20. Barry Bluestone, "The Poor Who Have Jobs," *Dissent* 15, 1 (1968): 410-419. Hyman Lumer, "Why People are Poor," in *American Society, Inc.*, ed. Maurice Zeitlin (Chicago, Ill: Markham, 1970).
21. President's Commission on Income Maintenance Programs. *Background Papers* (Washington, D.C.: U.S. Government Printing Office, 1969), pp. 139-142.
22. Paul M. Siegel, "On the Cost of Being a Negro," *Sociological Inquiry* 35, (1965): 41-58; Herbert Hill, "Racial Inequality in Employment: The Patterns of Discrimination," *The Annals of the American Academy of Political and Social Science 357,* (1965): 30-47; Thurow, *Poverty and Discrimination*; For more on job discrimination against women see Marijean Suelzle, "Women in Labor," *Trans-action* 8, 1 and 2 (1970): 50-58; Joan Jordan, "Working Women and the Equal Rights Amendment," *Trans-action* 8, 1 and 2 (1970): 16-22.
23. Oscar Lewis, *La Vida.* For information on achievement motivation differences see James N. Morgan et al., *Income and Welfare in the United States* (New York: McGraw-Hill, 1962). For information on educational aspirations see John A. Michael, "High School Climates and Plans for Entering College," *Public Opinion Quarterly* 25, 1(1961): 585-595. For self-esteem see Morris Rosenberg, *Society and the Adolescent Self-image* (Princeton, N.J.: Princeton University Press, 1965). For personal efficacy see Zahava D. Blum and Peter H. Rossi, "Social Class Research and Images of the Poor: A Bibliographic Review," in *On Understanding Poverty,* ed. by Daniel P. Moynihan (New York: Basic Books, 1969). For present orientation see Edward C. Banfield, *The Unheavenly City,* Chapter 10. For information on ability to defer immediate gratification see Louis Schneider and Sverre Lysgaard, "The Deferred Gratification Pattern: A Preliminary Study," *American Sociological Review* 18, 2(1953): 142-149. Also see the criticism of this work by S.M. Miller, Frank Riessman, and Arthur A. Seagull, "Poverty and Self-indulgence: A Critique of the Non-deferred Gratification Pattern," in *Poverty in America,* eds. Ferman et al. (Ann Arbor: University of Michigan Press, 1965).
24. For a review of information on the economic consequences of being old, see Joseph A. Pechman, Henry J. Aaron, and Michael K. Taussig, *Social Security* (Washington, D.C.: Brookings Institution, 1968), Chapter 2. Also see *Background Papers,* pp. 135-138,
25. For a review of the evidence pointing to the importance of the genetic component of intelligence see Arthur R. Jensen, "How Much Can We Boost

IQ and Scholastic Achievement," *Harvard Educational Review* 39, 1(1969): 1-23. Evidence of the relationship between IQ and social class is reviewed by Blum and Rossi, "Social Class Research and Images of the Poor". For a discussion of genetic factors and mental health see Bruce P. Dohrenwend and Barbara S. Dohrenwend, *Social Status and Psychological Disorder,* (New York: Wiley, 1969). Also see Christopher Jencks et al., *Inequality* (New York: Basic Books, 1972).

26. This argument is discussed in Robert E. Lane, *Political Ideology: Why The American Common Man Believes What He Does* (Glencoe, Ill.: Free Press, 1962).
27. George F. Break, "The Effects of Taxation on Work Incentives," in *Private Wants and Public Needs,* ed. Edmund S. Phelps (New York: Norton, 1962).
28. For a more detailed treatment of this issue see Gans, "Culture and Class in the Study of Poverty: An Approach to Anti-Poverty Research."
29. For further discussion of this issue see Rainwater, "The Problem of Lower-Class Culture and Poverty-War Strategy."
30. Evidence exists of a negative relationship between mortality rates and socio-economic status; see John M. Ellis, "Socio-economic Differentials in Mortality from Chronic Diseases," in *Patients, Physicians, and Illness,* ed. E. Gartly Jaco (Glencoe, Ill.: Free Press, 1958). There is also evidence of an inverse relationship between infant mortality and social class. See Odin W. Anderson, "Infant Mortality and Social and Cultural Factors," in Jaco, *Patients, Physicans and Illness.* There is evidence of less frequent visits to physicians and dentists by lower-class persons. Similarly the lower-class patients were less likely to be seeking preventive services. See John A. Ross, "Social Class and Medical Care," *Journal of Health and Human Behavior* 3, 1(1962): 35-40; Louis Kriesberg and Beatrice R. Treiman, "Socio-economic Status and the Utilization of Dentists' Services," *Journal of The American College of Dentists* 27, 3(1960): 147-165.
31. See Citizen's Board of Inquiry, *Hunger U.S.A.* (Boston: Beacon Press, 1968).
32. Philip H. Ennis, *Criminal Victimization in The United States: A Report of a National Survey* (Washington, D.C.: U.S. Government Printing Office, 1967).
33. Martin Gold, "Undetected Delinquent Behavior," *Journal of Research in Crime and Delinquency* 3, 1(1966): 27-46.
34. Goode, "Economic Factors and Marital Stability."
35. For data on the political participation of the poor see Angus Campbell et al., *The American Voter* (New York: John Wiley and Sons, 1960).
36. Herbert J. Gans, "The Uses of Poverty: The Poor Pay All," *Social Policy* 2, 2(1971): 20-24; Herbert J. Gans, "Income Grants and 'Dirty Work'," *Public Interest* 6(Winter, 1967): 110-113. Also see Herbert J. Gans, "The Positive Functions of Poverty," *American Journal of Sociology* 78, 1(1972): 275-289.
37. The term "social democrat" is used when referring to the noncommunist socialist parties in several Western European countries. The social democrats call for a mixed economy including both public and private ownership and control of the means of production. The social democrats argue in favor

of gradual transformation of society through democratic methods. While some social democrats hold public control of all industry as an ultimate goal, most are quite willing to accept the mixed economy as their goal. Social democrats tend to push for social welfare measures.

2

Public Assistance And Social Insurance

Public Assistance and social insurance are the two major income maintenance strategies currently used in the United States. In some respects these strategies have been quite successful, but there have also been some serious problems. Dissatisfaction with existing Public Assistance and social insurance programs has led to proposed alternatives including the negative income tax and the family allowance, discussed in the next chapter. One of the most important conclusions of the present chapter is that many, if not most, of the criticisms that have been made of Public Assistance and social insurance programs could be remedied within the framework of the same general strategies without shifting to alternatives such as the negative income tax or the family allowance.

We first consider the Public Assistance programs; included are Old Age Assistance, Aid to the Permanently and Totally Disabled, Aid to the Blind, Aid to Families with Dependent Children (AFDC), and General Assistance. The AFDC program is by far the most controversial of the Public Assistance programs and is given particular emphasis for this reason. Later in the chapter, Unemployment Insurance and Workmen's Compensation are considered. The emphasis is on the Social Security program which delivers more benefits to the poor than all the other income maintenance programs combined.

PUBLIC ASSISTANCE

The goal of this strategy is to confine income maintenance benefits to certain categories of people who are for the most part universally considered deserving public support. This is not to say that all persons in the specified categories are more deserving than those who are not. But restrictions of the benefits to persons in this category gives assurance that at least a very substantial proportion of the recipients will be deserving. The Public Assistance programs are an outgrowth of prior state and local relief programs.

Public Assistance includes four categorical assistance programs. In the Social Security Act of 1935, three categorical assistance programs were established: Aid to the Blind, Old Age Assistance, and Aid to Dependent Children. In 1951, Aid to the Permanently and Totally Disabled was added. These programs are all financed jointly by federal and state governments. Public Assistance also includes state and local General Assistance programs which do not receive any federal funding. General Assistance programs are not categorical and they would substantially alter the character of the Public Assistance approach if they did not represent such a small share of total Public Assistance benefits.

Aid To Families With Dependent Children (AFDC) Prior to 1962, this program was referred to as Aid to Dependent Children (ADC). The goal of the program is to provide economic assistance to needy families with dependent children when the children are deprived of the support of at least one parent (usually the father), due to absence, disability, or death. After 1961, each state had the option of adding an AFDC-UP program which would extend AFDC eligibility to families in which there was an unemployed father. By 1969, only twenty-five states had elected to participate in the AFDC-UP program. The reluctance of some states to participate is no doubt due in part to the increase in costs to the state that would be involved. Participation in AFDC-UP has always been low even in those states which have elected it. This is partly due to the requirement of a recent attachment to the labor force. Most of those who can meet the stringent assets test do not have a recent attachment to the labor force.[1]

In addition to the federal eligibility requirements for AFDC, there are a number of economic and noneconomic state and local eligibility requirements.[2] These requirements vary considerably from state to state and are sometimes used to restrict eligibility in the effort to keep down welfare expenditures. Some states have had residency requirements of up to five years, although this practice has been overturned by the Supreme Court. Nonetheless, the decision of the Court did not rule out the use of such requirements in emergency situations. New York State has already taken advantage of this loophole and used it as grounds for introducing a residency requirement; other states may do the same. Some states have required that a mother maintain a "suitable home"; this criterion was used to exclude women on the basis of their sexual morals; it too has been overturned by the courts. However, state and local authorities still have control over a variety of eligibility criteria. One of the most important is the decision as to the maximum assets a family can have and still be eligible for assistance.

As the program was originally designed, a recipient who chose to take on an outside job was required to deduct all earnings from the welfare payment; that is, there was effectively a 100 percent tax on outside earnings. This often meant a net loss to a recipient of AFDC who decided to take a job because no deduction was allowed for clothing, transportation, and other costs related to being employed. In 1962, the rules were modified so that a part of earned income could be kept to cover some of the costs of being employed, but the effective tax rate was still close to 100 percent. In 1967, the program was again modified so that AFDC recipients could keep the first $30 per month and certain costs associated with being employed, but any additional income was taxed at a rate of 67 percent.[3] At the same time a manpower program, the Work Incentive Program (WIN), was created for AFDC and AFDC-UP recipients. An aspect of the 1967 amendments that was unpopular with recipients was that many were required to register for training and eventual job placement as part of the WIN program.

In 1969, there were 7.3 million AFDC recipients who received a total of $3.6 billion in cash benefits. The average benefit level varied among states from $12 to $70 per month per recipient. Between 1960 and 1969, the number of recipients increased by 138 percent and the total value of money payments increased by 260 percent.

In 1969, the median number of children in AFDC families was three. Approximately 88 percent of AFDC families had only one adult recipient. About 75 percent of AFDC families had fathers who were absent due to divorce, separation, illegitimacy, or desertion. The mother was absent in 8 percent of families. Only 6 percent of families were headed by widows. In 1969, 36 percent of AFDC families included an employable mother; but the mother was actually working in only 13 percent of AFDC families. She was working full time in only 8 percent of these families. In addition to the 36 percent of families with an employable mother, there was another 36 percent with mothers who were needed as homemakers; it is quite possible that many of these women would take work if attractive jobs and adequate day care facilities were available. In another 21 percent of AFDC families, there was a mother who was considered unemployable. In addition to incapacitated women, this category also included those who were unemployable due to lack of an employable skill or the lack of an available job. These latter two alternatives are determined to some extent by labor market conditions. It is possible that some of these women would be employed in a period of high employment.[4]

The AFDC program has become the most controversial of the Public Assistance programs. In the discussion that follows, a number of the criticisms that have been made of the program are reviewed. Characteristics of the AFDC program which are considered weaknesses by those who view welfare issues from a conservative perspective are often considered strengths by those who view welfare issues from a liberal perspective and vice versa.

The cost of the AFDC program has increased rapidly in recent years. The cost of the AFDC payments has increased by 260 percent from 1960 to 1969; this rate of increase was greater than for any other Public Assistance program. In 1960, 30 percent of all Public Assistance payments went to AFDC recipients; in 1969, the percentage had increased to 53 percent. The only Public Assistance program that approaches the AFDC program in rate of growth is Aid to the Permanently and Totally Disabled, but in 1969 this program still constituted less than 12 percent of Public Assistance payments.

A reply to the preceding criticism is that an increase in cost alone is not sufficient grounds for criticizing the program. If evidence could be found indicating that a substantial proportion of the increase was due to increases in administrative cost, graft, or other misuse of funds, the criticism would be well taken. But the increase was primarily due to the increases in the number of recipients and the level of benefits.[5] Even in 1969, the payment levels remained considerably below the poverty line in most states; this fact substantially weakens any criticism of the increase in benefit levels.

The number of AFDC recipients has increased rapidly in recent years. The number of AFDC recipients has increased by 138 percent between 1960 and 1969. A number of factors have contributed to the increase in the number of AFDC recipients. Some factors can be used to argue against the program, others cannot. One source has undoubtedly been the increase in the number of female-headed families. This source could be used to argue that the existence of the program makes it economically advantageous to some families, for the father to leave so that other members of the family will be eligible for AFDC benefits. But the increase in the number of female-headed families has been too small to account for more than a small fraction of the total AFDC increase.[6] Another possible source of the increase in the AFDC caseload would be an increase in the size of AFDC families. But the size of the AFDC family did not increase between 1960 and 1969.[7]

It is possible to point to a number of factors that have contributed to the increase in the size of the AFDC population in recent years, but the available data are not adequate for making quantitative assessments of their respective contributions. One contributing factor is the increase in the number of people eligible to apply for benefits. This is partly due to modifications in the AFDC program which have extended coverage. The AFDC-UP modification has extended eligibility to many families with an unemployed male head of household. Coverage has also been extended to include a second adult member of the household and older children who remain in school. The elimination of residency requirements in 1969 was still another factor contributing to the increase in the number of eligible families.

The recent increase in the AFDC population is also due to the fact that many people are now applying for benefits who were eligible to apply in the past, but who did not do so for a number of reasons. The social stigma associated with being on welfare had kept many from applying. The efforts by various welfare rights groups to convince people that it was their right to receive benefits have somewhat reduced the stigma associated with becoming an AFDC recipient. The increase in the benefit levels for AFDC families is another factor that has contributed to the increase in enrollment.[8]

Also contributing to the increase is that many applicants who would have been rejected in the past are now being accepted. The Supreme Court's rejection of residency requirements, as well as the "suitable home" and "man in the house" rules have all contributed to reducing the number of applicants who are disqualified. There has also been a general liberalization of many other local eligibility criteria.[9]

Opinions about the recent increase in the size of the AFDC population are likely to be strongly influenced by basic beliefs about the proportion of the poor who are deserving of public support. Those who feel that very few of the poor are deserving of public support generally believe that such support should be kept to a minimum. They are likely to disapprove of the increase in the AFDC population and to oppose many of the changes that have contributed to the increase, including the liberalization of the eligibility criteria. On the other hand, those who feel that a high percentage of the poor are deserving of public support also tend to favor an increase in public support for the poor. They are likely to have a positive evaluation of many of the changes in eligibility criteria and of the resulting increase in the number of AFDC recipients.

The administrative cost of the AFDC program is high. One estimate is that the administrative cost of the AFDC programs is roughly 18.5 percent of benefits paid. This can be contrasted with the administrative cost of Social Security which runs about 3 percent.[10] It has been estimated that from 50 to 70 percent of the administrative cost of AFDC is related to eligibility determination.[11] While the administrative cost of AFDC is high, it does not account for the marked increase in the total cost of the program in recent years.

The means test procedure that is presently used for eligibility determination and redetermination requires several home visits yearly by a social worker. If a self-administered income test were substituted, the administrative cost of AFDC could be reduced. It is likely that there would be some cheating, but this could be reduced by having spot checks on a specified percentage of recipients in the same way the Internal Revenue Service rigorously checks about 10 percent of self-administered income tax returns.

Most of the time of AFDC staff members goes into eligibility determination; very little goes into counseling and other social services. In some states as much as 75 percent of a social worker's time goes into eligibility determination. This criticism is more likely to be made by persons who favor liberalization of the AFDC eligibility requirements; it is not likely that this criticism would be made by those who feel that AFDC money is going to many people who do not deserve it. It would be possible to increase the amount of the social worker's time that goes into the delivery of social services, but this would require a simplification of the eligibility determination procedure.

Social stigma is attached to being an AFDC recipient. In part this is due to the low regard with which the general public holds those persons who are dependent on public support. The criticism is stronger for AFDC recipients than for any of the other categorical Public Assistance programs. This was not true when the program was introduced in 1935 because at that time more than 30 percent of the recipients' families were headed by widows. But since then the composition has changed substantially. Today less than 6 percent of AFDC family heads are widows; in the vast majority of families the father is absent from the home due to desertion, divorce, separation, or illegitimacy.[12] Widows are much more likely to be viewed as deserving poor, than women who have become heads of household for these other reasons.

The means test is another source of social stigma. The means test is a procedure for the determination of eligibility for Public Assistance which takes into consideration all resources at the disposal of the applicant or recipient. There is a certain amount of embarrassment associated with the low level of assets that are allowable, that is, to qualify a person must demonstrate that she is destitute. Another factor that makes the means test unpleasant is the use of the periodic personal visit by a social worker for redetermination of eligibility. Such visits are made much more frequently for AFDC recipients than for recipients of other Public Assistance programs. In 1971, the personal home visits were discontinued for all Public Assistance programs except for AFDC. This difference in eligibility redetermination procedures reflects an attitude of greater distrust toward AFDC recipients than toward other Public Assistance recipients. The personal visits may make it necessary to determine where the funds for some new household item came from. Such visits can prove embarrassing when the item was purchased with unreported income received as a gift or obtained in some other way that would not meet with the approval of the social worker.

While there are a number of possible sources for any social stigma that AFDC recipients may feel, there is some recent evidence suggesting that the means tests may not be as unpleasant to the AFDC recipients as was once believed.[13] It is likely that the efforts of the National Welfare Rights Organization and other welfare rights' groups are reducing the stigma associated with being an AFDC recipient.

The AFDC program contributes to family instability. In many states a family with an able-bodied male is not eligible for the program. If the earnings of the male head of household fall substantially below the benefits provided by AFDC program, there is an economic incentive for him to leave the family. Sometimes a husband finds it economically advantageous to establish a separate residence with full intention of frequent "visits" to the original household. Even if the desire to increase his family's income does not influence the husband's decision, the existence of the AFDC program may increase the probability that he will leave for other reasons. For example, one reason is that he may know there would be a source of support in his absence. If the AFDC program provides an income as great or greater than that which a husband could himself provide, this would reduce the extent of his family's economic dependence on him. If they would be taken care of, there would be less incentive for him to remain at home in the face of family conflict.

After a woman has become an AFDC recipient, the rule that there be no able bodied husband in the household may reduce her interest in remarriage. If she restricts herself to casual short-term relationships, she can maintain the independence and security of the AFDC income. In most states the decision to get married would mean that she would lose AFDC benefits. While a husband may be able to provide an income that is higher than the AFDC income, it is likely to be less secure. If either the marriage or her husband's job were to fail, she would be worse off than if she had remained on AFDC.

The introduction of the AFDC-UP program, which allows families with an unemployed father to receive benefits, is a step toward decreasing the extent to which AFDC contributes to father absence. But this program has only been adopted in twenty-five states; even in these states the eligibility requirements are sufficiently strict to keep participation very low.

The AFDC program contributes to father absence, but the evidence that is available is not adequate to allow any quantitative estimate of the impact. The AFDC program contributes to father absence in families with an unemployed or poorly employed father, but it is likely that it contributes to family stability in those families in which the father is blind or disabled. The program may also increase the stability of the matriarchal family. The program makes it possible for many women to keep and raise all their children; without the program it would be necessary in many cases to institutionalize some of the children or offer them for adoption.

The AFDC program discourages employment among recipients. Originally the payment to an AFDC recipient was reduced $1 for every $1 earned. In 1962, the rules were liberalized so that some of the costs associated with taking a job could be deducted from earnings, but for many women the costs involved still exceeded the allowed deductions. In 1967 the rules were futher liberalized with the introduction of the Work Incentive Program (WIN). Recipients were allowed to keep the first $30 per month and 33 percent of any income above that level. This reduced the effective tax rate to roughly 67 percent of earnings. This is high but is nonetheless an improvement over the 100 percent tax rate prior to WIN. Before the introduction of the WIN program, two experimental studies were conducted in which AFDC recipients were allowed to keep a fraction of their earnings. The results of these studies were quite inconclusive.[14] By comparing the percentage of AFDC women working in 1961 to that in 1969, it is possible to get some idea of the impact the reduction in the effective tax rate has had on extent of employment. In 1961, 12.9 percent of AFDC women were employed part or full time. By 1969 there had been an increase to 13.3 percent.[15] This suggests that a reduction in marginal tax from 100 to 67 percent has not proven to be much of a work incentive.

In the analysis of the impact of AFDC on work incentives, it is important to keep in mind the number of women who are potentially employable. This determination is complicated by the existence of a large number of women who give as a reason for not working, the need for their presence in the family. If we assume that the unemployable category includes only those women who are incapacitated or do not have the level of skill required for the available jobs, this category has remained constant from 1961 to 1969 at approximately 21 percent. In 1969, only 13 percent of AFDC families were headed by women who were in job training, awaiting training, or seeking work.[16]

Some AFDC families have higher incomes than many working families not on AFDC. This criticism is similar to that made of relief in the 19th century. One aspect of the English poor law "reform of 1834" was that relief support was to be kept below the income of the poorest category of employed workers.[17] Sometimes an AFDC family with no employed member ends up with an income that is greater than that of a similar size non-AFDC family with an employed member. No estimates are available of the frequency with which this occurs, but in 1969, 22 percent of poor families were headed by persons who worked full time for 50 to 52 weeks per year. Since there will always be some people who choose to work at very low wages rather than seek public support, the effort to keep AFDC support below that of the lowest paid workers not on AFDC would result in very inadequate benefit levels. It would be more appropriate to criticize the AFDC program for its lack of support to the working poor than to criticize it for providing an income that exceeds that of some of the working poor.

AFDC encourages long-term dependency on public support. Since some families vacillate between welfare and non-welfare status, it is difficult to accurately estimate the cumulative amount of time families have spent as AFDC recipients. Considering only the length of the present stay on AFDC, the median duration is approximately two years. But this is an understatement of the cumulative duration of AFDC status over the lifetime of those who at some point become recipients. In 1969, 41 percent of AFDC recipients had been enrolled in the program at some point prior to their present enrollment; that is, they had been on AFDC, gotten off, and eventually returned to enroll again.[18]

In addition to the preceding criticisms of the AFDC program, there are a number of arguments in support of the program. Many of the supporting arguments have been mentioned in the responses to and discussion of the preceding criticisms; they will not be reviewed here.

Other Public Assistance Programs Aid to the Blind provides economic assistance to poor persons who are blind or nearly blind. In 1969, there were 80,000 recipients who received a total of $92 million in cash benefits. The average benefit level varied among states from $54 to $154 per month per recipient. Between 1960 and 1969 the number of recipients decreased by 25 percent, but the total value of money payments increased by 7 percent.

Old Age Assistance provides economic assistance to poor persons who are sixty-five years or older. In 1969, there were two million recipients who received a total of $1.7 billion in cash benefits. The average benefit level varied among states from $45 to $119 per month per recipient. Between 1960 and 1969 the number of recipients decreased by 12 percent, but the total value of money payments increased by 7 percent.

Aid to the Permanently and Totally Disabled provides economic assistance to poor persons over eighteen years old who cannot support themselves because of some physical or mental disability. In 1969, there were 803,000 recipients who received a total of $788 million in cash benefits. The average benefit level varied among states ranging from $50 to $136 per month per recipient. Between 1960 and 1969, the number of recipients increased by 234 percent, and the total value of the money payments increased by 138 percent.

The General Assistance program provides economic assistance to poor persons who are not covered by the other categorical Public Assistance programs. In 1969, there were 857,000 recipients who received a total of $470 million in cash benefits. The average benefit level varied among states ranging from $4 to $81 per month per recipient. Between 1960 and 1969 the number of recipients decreased by 31 percent, but the total value of money payments increased by 47 percent.

Evaluation Of The Public Assistance Strategy A number of arguments for and against the AFDC program have already been considered earlier in the chapter. In this section arguments that apply to the other Public Assistance programs as well as to the AFDC program are considered. We first consider arguments in support of the Public Assistance strategy:

A high proportion of the spending on Public Assistance programs reaches the poor in the form of cash benefits. With a number of other income maintenance strategies, such as social insurance or Unemployment Compensation, much of the cash assistance goes to those who are not poor. In 1961, 93 percent of Public Assistance benefits went to those who would have been poor without those benefits. In the same year 63 percent of Social Security benefits and 36 percent of Unemployment Compensation benefits went to those who would have been poor without the benefits.[19] While a higher proportion of Public Assistance benefits than Social Security benefits go to the poor, the discrepancy is somewhat reduced due to the difference in administrative costs between the programs. For Public Assistance the administrative cost runs about 16 percent of benefits paid; for the Social Security program the administrative cost runs 2 to 3 percent. In both cases these costs represent funds that do not reach the recipient.

Most Public Assistance benefits go to the deserving poor. The categorical Public Assistance programs provide benefits to persons who welfare conservatives would generally consider more deserving than the recipients of the General Assistance program. In 1969, 7 percent of Public Assistance benefits were paid to General Assistance recipients; the other 93 percent went to persons who were eligible for the various categorical programs. While the welfare liberal would probably be in favor of Public Assistance going to the poor rather than to those who are not poor, he would not necessarily feel that it is an advantage that the benefits go primarily to the categories of the poor designated as deserving poor by welfare conservatives. He is likely to believe that there are some people who are equally as deserving, if not more deserving, who are being excluded.

Although the benefits of the categorical Public Assistance programs generally go to those who welfare conservatives consider deserving poor, this is not always the case. Some welfare conservatives feel that many, if not most, women on AFDC could adequately provide for their family through their own employment if they chose to do so. One estimate is that 36 percent of AFDC women would be able to support themselves at the AFDC level or above if they left welfare and went to work.[20] If the cost of child care and periods of involuntary unemployment are taken into consideration, the number who could be self-sufficient would be substantially less than 36 percent. In 1969, approximately 21 percent of AFDC mothers would not have been employable under any circumstances. Another 36 percent felt their role as homemakers precluded the possibility of employment. It is likely that a substantial proportion of these women could have been employed if there had been adequate day care facilities and attractive job possibilities. Another 8 percent of AFDC mothers were absent from the home. This leaves roughly 35 percent of AFDC mothers who were employable. Of these, 13 percent worked part or full time and another 12 percent were seeking employment, already in job training, or awaiting job training.

The cost of the Public Assistance program is substantially less than the cost of an income maintenance program that would provide the same level of support to all poor persons. In 1969, somewhat less than 46 percent of all poor persons were Public Assistance recipients; needless to say, the total cost of the program would have been substantially increased had all of the poor been recipients.[21] This is an argument in favor of Public Assistance from the point of view of a welfare conservative. A welfare liberal would not view the lower cost of Public Assistance as an advantage because it is kept lower by excluding many of those who he considers deserving of public support. The following are some of the criticisms that have been made of Public Assistance:

Many poor people are excluded from the Public Assistance programs on a categorical basis. Over one-half of the non-aged poor are excluded from the Public Assistance programs on a categorical basis. In 1966, 11.7 million out of 19.8 million of those persons who were classified as non-aged poor lived in families with a male head who worked part or full time. Such families were generally excluded from Public Assistance benefits on categorical grounds. This is a criticism made by welfare liberals; welfare conservatives are likely to feel that most of those excluded have no right to receive public support.

Many poor people who fall into one of the broad categories specified by the Public Assistance programs are not receiving benefits. One factor that contributes to this is the existence of numerous local eligibility requirements that are often used to exclude recipients. This is particularly true of the AFDC population. This criticism is made by welfare liberals. The welfare conservative is likely to feel that local eligibility requirements are necessary because not all persons within the general categories are deserving of public support. Another factor is the requirement that an individual must apply for the status of a welfare recipient. Some people are in isolated rural areas and are not aware of the benefits for which they would be eligible. Others do not enroll because of the social stigma that is associated with being on welfare. In 1969, some 18 percent of poor female-headed families with dependent children were not receiving AFDC benefits.

Public Assistance benefit levels are not adequate to provide a decent standard of living. In 1961, 69 percent of recipients of Public Assistance were poor even after receiving their benefits. In 1969, the mean monthly payment per recipient nationally was $45 for AFDC, $50 for General Assistance, $74 for Old Age Assistance, $90 for Aid to the Permanently and Totally Disabled, and $99 for Aid to the Blind. The AFDC family always includes a mother and one or more children. But there is often only one recipient in the family eligible for benefits from the other categorical programs. In 1969, the poverty line for a person living alone was $160 per month; for a person in a family of four it was $78 per month. The difference is due to the economies of scale for a family. Caution must be exercised when interpreting the figures on payment per recipient. Persons receiving the same payment levels may have quite different standards of living because of variations in the number of persons living off the benefit, variations in the availability of in-kind support from relatives, and variations in the extent to which economies of scale can be achieved. A recipient who receives a special price on a room or an apartment from a relative is in a better position than a recipient who must pay the current price. An elderly couple, both of whom receive Old Age Assistance, is in a better position than one elderly person receiving Old Age Assistance due to the economies of scale that can be achieved by two people living together. Some families receive benefits from more than one Public Assistance program. For example, the husband may receive benefits from the Aid to the Permanently and Totally Disabled program while the wife and children receive AFDC benefits.

Those who receive Public Assistance get higher or lower benefits depending on which categorical program they are eligible for. In some states, a family of four on AFDC gets about the same payment as a single elderly person receiving Old Age Assistance. While this is an extreme case, discrepancies do exist to some extent in all states. If the differences in payment levels accurately reflected differences in economic need, there would be little criticism; but this has not been demonstrated.

There is inequity in the Public Assistance program due to the extent of variation among states in the level of Public Assistance benefits. The discrepancy among states in the level of AFDC payments is the most often mentioned, but the discrepancies for the other Public Assistance programs are also substantial. Small variations among states could be defended on the basis of differences in the cost of living, but the differences in benefit levels far exceed the cost of living differences.

Social stigma is associated with being a Public Assistance recipient. This point has been discussed in connection with the AFDC program because the stigma is greatest for that program, but the stigma also exists for recipients of the other Public Assistance programs. The welfare liberal sees the social stigma as an undesirable characteristic of Public Assistance. The welfare conservative is likely to feel that the social stigma is at worst a necessary evil; that is, it is necessary as an encouragement to those who can be self-supporting to avoid dependence on public support.

The Public Assistance programs reinforce the distinction between the deserving and the underserving poor. To the welfare conservative who feels that it is important to make such a distinction, this is an argument in favor of Public Assistance. To the welfare liberal who feels that such a distinction leads to the exclusion of many who should receive public support, this is an argument against it.

In some areas Public Assistance benefits have been used to restrict voter turnout. Salamon reports that in Mississippi and presumably much of the rural South, the welfare administrators are white. The economic dependence of the blacks on Public Assistance benefits is one of the ways in which the voter participation of blacks is restricted. Salamon makes the argument that a program such as the Nixon's Family Assistance Plan, which would be administered at a federal as opposed to a local level, would have the advantage that it could not be used to restrict the political participation of blacks. While it is common for blacks in the rural South to report that economic dependence on whites is a major reason for not voting, dependence on welfare is only one of many forms that this economic dependence assumes.[22]

Public Assistance is one of the many possible approaches to income maintenance that would be consistent with the general strategy of providing cash benefits to specific categories of the poor based on the extent of need. Most of the arguments both pro and con which have been made with reference to Public Assistance would not necessarily hold for all programs consistent with the general strategy. Since any alternative to the present Public Assistance programs would be achieved by modifying these programs in some way, many of the advantages and disadvantages of the existing programs would be likely to characterize the resulting alternatives, at least to some degree.

One aspect of the general strategy is to provide cash benefits on the basis of economic need. This assures that a high proportion of the assistance benefits go to the most needy. Unfortunately, there are some disadvantages associated with the procedure that is necessary to achieve this goal. The use of a means test, which takes into consideration not only income, but also all assets and other possible sources of income, assures that Public Assistance benefits go to the most needy. One disadvantage of the means test procedure is that the administrative cost is too high. It can be argued that it would be preferable to allow some leakage of assistance to those on the borderlines of poverty, rather than having the same money spent on the administration of a more thorough means test procedure which involves personal visits to the home several times a year. The procedures used for eligibility determination for AFDC recipients are considerably more exhaustive than for any other major income maintenance program. The implication is that the AFDC recipient is more likely to cheat and is more deserving of public distrust. This distrust contributes to the social stigma associated with being an AFDC recipient.

Another aspect of the general strategy is to provide cash benefits to specific categories of the poor. An advantage of this procedure is that the assistance benefits will generally go to people who are quite deserving of public support. A program that provides assistance to those whom welfare conservatives consider deserving of public support is likely to receive more political support than a program which provides benefits to many of those whom the welfare conservatives consider the undeserving poor. Even the welfare liberal will agree that some people are more deserving of public support than others. He is likely to agree that those who are capable of supporting themselves are less deserving of public support than those who are incapable of so doing. If the categorical approach yielded programs that called for support to all who were incapable of adequately providing for themselves and excluded only those who were capable of adequately providing for themselves, it is likely that the approach would receive much more support from welfare liberals. But in practice, the categorical approach is often used to exclude many of the poor who the welfare liberal feels are not capable of adequately providing for themselves.

Public Assistance has undergone substantial modification through the years. A number of additional modifications could be made that would yield programs that were still consistent with the general strategy of providing cash benefits to specific categories of the poor based on the extent of need. In the discussion that follows, a number of possible modifications are considered. In many instances these modifications would have implications for the validity of the arguments that have been made both for and against Public Assistance in its present form.

Increase the number of categories of the poor covered. A step in this direction was recently taken with the introduction of the AFDC-UP program which extended coverage to some families with an unemployed father. Coverage could, in theory, be extended to cover as great a proportion of the poor as desired it. But as the proportion of the poor covered increases, the rationale for the categorical approach is weakened. Beyond a certain point it would be administratively simpler and less costly to shift to a universalistic income maintenance program such as a negative income tax. To the welfare conservative a disadvantage of this modification is that it tends to increase the number of recipients who are not deserving of public support. Related to this would be the loss of the political support of welfare conservatives. This might in turn have consequences for the benefit levels that would be politically feasible.

Extend benefits to a greater proportion of those in categories presently covered by existing programs. This could be achieved by reducing the number of local eligibility criteria that are presently used to exclude some applicants in the covered categories. Efforts to reduce the social stigma associated with being a recipient of Public Assistance and efforts to recruit persons who are potentially eligible, but not currently receiving benefits, would also help. A consequence of this modification is that many more of those whom conservatives consider undeserving poor and whom welfare liberals consider deserving poor, would receive assistance benefits. This would increase the political support of the program among welfare liberals and reduce it among welfare conservatives.

Increase the size of assistance payments. The payments have increased substantially during the past several years, but they are still so low that most Public Assistance recipients are left below the poverty line. A possible consequence of higher benefit levels is that Public Assistance would become more attractive as an alternative to employment. It is possible there would be an increase in the number of those who are capable of supporting themselves, but instead choose to remain on Public Assistance. Welfare conservatives might use evidence of such behavior to argue for reduced benefit levels and restrictions on the number of persons eligible for benefits. On the other hand, the higher benefit levels would improve the quality of life in recipient homes. It would probably increase the frequency of participation in training programs, continued education, and other such future-oriented activities that could reduce long-term dependence on public support.

Reduce the effective tax rate on earned income. The present 67 percent tax rate for AFDC recipients may be acting as a work disincentive. If such a modification were made, it would become necessary to allow payments to families with substantial earned incomes. This would result in a higher proportion of benefits going to those who are not poor. It would also increase the frequency with which recipients had incomes higher than comparable families not enrolled with the program.

Substitute a self-administered eligibility test for the present means test. Such a shift would reduce the social stigma associated with being a Public Assistance recipient; it would also reduce the cost of administering the program. On the other hand it would increase leakage to those who are not poor. This leakage might be used by welfare conservatives to argue for low benefit levels and restrictions on the number of persons eligible for benefits. The problem of leakage would be particularly likely if the self-administered eligibility test involved only a report of recent earnings and did not require information about available assets and payments in kind. In 1971, a shift to mailed self-report forms was made for eligibility redetermination for all components of Public Assistance except AFDC.

Take steps to reduce the social stigma associated with being a Public Assistance recipient. In part this could be achieved by making the eligibility determination procedures less humiliating. The payments could be made automatic to persons meeting certain economic criteria so as not to require application for special status as a welfare recipient. Efforts by the National Welfare Rights Organization to convince the poor to look at welfare as a right rather than as a privilege are likely to contribute to a reduction in the stigma. As the stigma associated with being a welfare recipient is reduced, it is likely that there will be an increase in the proportion of recipients who choose to remain on Public Assistance even though they are capable of becoming self-sufficient.

Require that the benefit levels for recipients in different categories be comparable. Any differences in payments would be based on differences in living costs for persons in the various categories. This would eliminate the arbitrary differences in payment level that characterize the present Public Assistance programs.

Require that benefit levels for the various programs be the same from state to state. This could be achieved by having the federal government take on the full responsibility for financing and administering Public Assistance. This would eliminate the arbitrary differences in benefit levels among states that now exist.

Standardize the eligibility criteria from city to city and state to state. At present, local Public Assistance administrators are allowed a certain amount of discretion in eligibility determination. The result is that people who would be accepted as recipients in one city or state are rejected in another. Standardization is called for in both economic and non-economic eligibility criteria.

The preceding discussion suggests a number of ways in which the present Public Assistance program could be modified and still remain consistent with the general strategy of providing cash benefits to specific categories of the poor based on economic need. Such changes would answer many of the criticisms that have been made of Public Assistance. But some of the criticisms would be difficult to deal with adequately using a program consistent with the general strategy.

One of the criticisms of Public Assistance is that it tends to encourage family instability. This is due in large part to the categorical exclusion of families with an employed father with low earnings and the excluson of many families with unemployed fathers (some do receive benefits under the AFDC-UP program). If the AFDC eligibility criteria were broadened so that poor families with employable fathers were generally eligible for benefits, there would be less father absence; but such a change is unlikely as long as the categorical approach is maintained. One of the reasons for establishing a categorical program was to exclude families with employable fathers from public support. Thus, it is likely that an incentive for father absence will remain as long as a categorical approach is maintained.

Another criticism is that some recipient families end up with higher incomes than do some non-recipient poor working families of comparable size. As long as the categorical approach is maintained it is likely that the working poor will be excluded from benefits. As AFDC benefit levels increase and as an increased proportion of recipients take on part or full-time jobs, the number of AFDC families with incomes greater than some of the working poor will increase. If efforts are made to reduce the work disincentive of a high tax rate on the earnings of AFDC recipients, it will be necessary to allow benefits to AFDC families with higher family incomes. This will mean even more AFDC families will have incomes above some of the working poor.

SOCIAL INSURANCE

The goal of this strategy is to provide income maintenance when a worker leaves the labor force as a result of unemployment, disability, retirement or death. In the present discussion the three social insurance programs considered are Social Security, Unemployment Insurance, and Workmen's Compensation. These are the major programs, but several others do exist which will not be considered here.[23]

Employment related social insurance was first introduced in 1884 in Germany. Great Britain introduced a Workmen's Compensation program in 1897 and an Unemployment Insurance program in 1911.[24] In the United States, Workmen's Compensation programs existed in most states by 1920. The first Unemployment Insurance program was introduced in 1932 and Social Security was introduced in 1935.

Social Security Old age insurance was enacted as part of the Social Security Act of 1935. The program originally provided retirement benefits for aged workers. Within a few years the program was expanded to cover survivors of deceased workers. In 1956, the program was further expanded to provide coverage to disabled workers and their dependents, and in 1969 a health insurance component was added. Today the Social Security system is made up of old age and survivors insurance, disability insurance, and health insurance; the set of programs is sometimes referred to collectively as OASDHI.

Social Security benefits are only available to workers who have attained insured status. There are several categories of insured status; each requires a specified number of calendar quarters of "covered employment;" that is, earnings subjected to the payroll tax. To receive maximum retirement benefits, a worker must have at least 40 quarters of covered employment.[25]

When a worker becomes eligible to receive Social Security benefits, the size of his benefits is a function of his earnings during the period of covered employment and, consequently, of his contribution to the program in payroll taxes. The formula used to compute the size of benefits replaces a higher percentage of the earnings for a low income worker, but in spite of this adjustment, the low income worker ends up with a smaller benefit than the higher income worker. If a worker under age 72 continues to work after becoming eligible for Social Security, the size of his benefit is reduced. The earned income at which the Social Security benefit is reduced to zero depends on the size of the original benefit, but it is never reduced to zero for an earned income under $2,900 per year, and it is always reduced to zero for an earned income over $7,500 per year.[26]

The insured worker has the option of starting Social Security retirement benefits at age 62 rather than age 65; but if this option is taken the payments are lower and as a consequence, the expected lifetime benefits are reduced by 20 percent. This option is frequently taken by workers who are forced into early retirement by unemployment or poor health. The same factors that have led to early retirement have often kept earnings low prior to retirement. Since the benefits are based on prior earnings, those who must retire early have their generally low benefits further reduced.

Depending on prior earnings in 1969, the Social Security retirement benefits at age 65 ranged from $55 to $218 per month for an individual alone and from $82 to $434 per month for an individual with dependents. In 1969, the mean Social Security benefit was $113 per month for a disabled worker, $100 for a retired worker, and $87 for the widow of a deceased worker.

In 1965, of the total households receiving Social Security benefits, 59 percent would have had incomes below the poverty line had they not received their benefits. With their benefits, only 32 percent were poor. These data illustrate that the program was a major factor in reducing poverty among recipient families. But it also shows that many families who receive the benefits are left below the poverty line.

Due to the dependence of Social Security benefits on past employment experience, many people age 65 and over are ineligible for benefits. In 1960 approximately 62 percent of persons age 65 and over were recipients; and although by 1969 the percentage had increased to 85 percent, many were still excluded in spite of the fact that all persons age 72 and over were at least minimally covered. Between 1960 and 1969 Social Security payments increased by 138 percent to a total of $26 billion in 1969. These payments were made to 25 million recipients in 1969. In that year an estimated 8 million of the poor and another 7 million who would have been poor received approximately 16 billion dollars in benefits from the program.

A problem with the Social Security as a strategy against poverty is that a substantial portion of any increase in benefit levels would go to the non-poor. One study estimates that if an increase in Social Security benefits in the 10 to 50 percent range were made, less than 20 percent of the increase in benefits would go to the poor.

Despite the substantial sum of money that is transferred to the poor by Social Security, there are some aspects of the program that are quite inconsistent with a welfare orientation. One such aspect is the regressive impact of the system used to finance the program. There is a payroll tax of 9.6 percent (one-half of which is paid by the employee) on the first $7,800 per year of salary. Because only the first $7,800 per year is taxed, the effective tax rate is lower for all people with incomes above this level. Another aspect of the program that is inconsistent with a welfare orientation is the tendency for the greatest benefits to go to those who least need them. Those who have had high earnings prior to retirement are more likely to have other sources of income and wealth to live on than those who have had low earnings; but the benefits are a function of prior income, not current need. There is an income test for recipients under age 72, but only earned income is taken into consideration. Unearned income such as return on investments in securities is not taken into consideration and neither is personal wealth.

Unemployment Insurance Each state has its own Unemployment Insurance program. The objective of these programs is to provide economic assistance to workers who are temporarily out of work. The procedures used to determine eligibility vary from state to state. In many states the worker must have been employed for a specified length of time; for example, in several states the requirement is that the applicant has been employed for the first four out of the preceding five calendar quarters. In each state a maximum is set for the number of weeks that unemployment compensation (Unemployment Insurance benefits) can be received; in most states this is at least 26 weeks. The actual duration of benefits depends on the recipient's earning prior to unemployment. In 1968, the average duration of benefits for those who did not find jobs before exhausting their benefits was 21 weeks. Depending on the overall unemployment rate, the proportion of persons who exhaust their benefits while still unemployed ranges from 20 to 33 percent.

The size of the weekly benefit is a specified fraction of the recipient's earnings prior to unemployment up to a specified maximum benefit limit. The maximum benefits vary quite substantially from one state to another. In 1969, the range was from $34 to $72 per week. There is also marked variation among the states in the proportion of workers covered; in 1967, the states ranged from 59 to 100 percent of all non agricultural wage and salary workers. Because certain employers and the self-employed are exempted from participation, nearly one-third of the labor force is not covered.

Unemployment Insurance is financed by a payroll tax that is paid entirely by the employer in all but three states. There is a federal unemployment tax, but the employer can claim a tax credit for most of the tax if he participates in an approved state Unemployment Insurance program. In 1969, there were 4 million Unemployed Insurance recipients. The average benefit was $46 per week nationally, with a range of from $32 to $56 among states. In some states there is an increment in the size of the benefit for dependents up to a specified limit. The average duration of benefits was 11 weeks. In 1971, approximately 67 percent of those who were unemployed and seeking full-time work were receiving Unemployment Insurance benefits. In 1960, approximately 25 percent of Unemployment Insurance recipients were poor. In 1969, there were an estimated 8 million persons living in families that received Unemployment Insurance benefits and an estimated 2 million of these were poor.

Workman's Compensation The goal of this program is to provide cash benefits and medical care to the victims of work-related injuries. There is much between-state variation in the magnitude of the benefits and in the procedures used to finance the program. The amount paid for a specified type of injury and the duration of payment varies from state to state. Some states pay benefits for life in the case of a permanent and total disability; others pay for a specified number of weeks or up to a specified money limitation. In 1965, the maximum permissible weekly benefit ranged from $35 to $152; the national average was $54.

The majority of compensation cases involve temporary total disability; the benefits for this component are generally based on a percentage (e.g., 60–66 percent) of the worker's average wage during a specified period. But due to other provisions such as upper limits on allowable payments, in 40 percent of states the benefits replace less than 50 percent of the average prior salary. In 1967, Workmen's Compensation programs covered 80 percent of the labor force. Since there were approximately 2 million workers injured that year, a reasonable estimate is that there were approximately 4 million persons in recipient families of whom approximately 1 million were poor. In 1969, the cash payments from the Workmen's Compensation program were $1.7 billion of which an estimated $700 million went to the poor. In addition to cash benefits, $900 million was paid in medical benefits.

The states differ in the procedures used to finance the program. A common practice is for a small employer to purchase a Workmen's Compensation insurance policy with a private insurance corporation and for a large employer to be self-insured. In many states, participation by employers is optional, but those who choose not to participate give up certain legal defenses in damage suits. Certain categories of workers such as casual laborers and agricultural workers frequently are not covered. In many states the program does not cover disability due to occupational diseases.

Evaluation Of Social Insurance Programs Social Security, Unemployment Insurance, and Workmen's Compensation are all classified as social insurance programs; understanding the differences among them is useful in the analysis of what a social insurance program is. One similarity of all three programs is that they replace at least part of earnings that are lost due to death, disability, unemployment, or retirement. Income replacement is one of the functions of private insurance and to this extent there is an analogy between these programs and private insurance. In private insurance the more a person pays in premiums, the greater the potential yield of his policy. This aspect of private insurance is reflected in the Social Security program, but there are some modifications for the other programs. For Unemployment Insurance the amount paid by the employer in payroll taxes is a function of employee salaries. A major difference between this program and Social Security is that for the Unemployment Insurance program, the tax is paid by employer alone; there is no employee contribution. The Workmen's Compensation program is also paid by the employer. The Unemployment Insurance program and the Workmen's Compensation program illustrate that social insurance does not necessarily call for benefits to a worker in proportion to his contribution to the program. The benefits, however, are in proportion to the contribution made by the employer. For all three social insurance programs, the benefits are paid by the employer or employee and not by the general public.

If the social insurance approach to income maintenance were interpreted as insurance against loss of earnings without respect to who pays for the insurance, it would be reasonable to consider financing the programs out of general federal and state funds. With respect to Social Security, such a shift could be defended on the grounds that it would eliminate the payroll tax which has some regressive characteristics. However, any such gain must be balanced against possible losses. At present the Social Security program receives much support because people feel that the recipients have earned their benefits by previous contributions in the form of the payroll tax. In other countries social insurance is sometimes financed out of general revenues and sometimes by a payroll tax. The benefits tend to be higher in those countries in which the program is paid for by a payroll tax. This suggests that if a change were made in the Social Security program so that it would be financed out of general federal revenues, it is possible that there would be increased opposition to efforts aimed at increasing the level of benefits.

There are arguments for and against the use of social insurance as a strategy against poverty. In some cases the same data are used to argue in support of social insurance by some people and against it by others. Due to differences between the alternative programs, some arguments are more relevant to one program than to another.

The following are arguments in support of social insurance programs:

Social insurance programs transfer more money to the poor than do all other income maintenance programs combined. In 1961, approximately 55 percent of all income maintenance payments to the poor came from the Social Security program and another 7 percent came from the Unemployment Insurance program. As a comparison, 16 percent of income maintenance payments to the poor came from the Public Assistance programs.

The social insurance approach to income maintenance has a broad base of political support. A broad base is assured by making the benefits available to a wide segment of the population including many of the poor. The popularity of the Social Security program is due largely to the fact that it is financed by a payroll tax that is paid by the potential recipient and his employer. Individual contributions are not made to Unemployment Insurance and Workmen's Compensation programs, but both of these programs are paid by employers. It is the employer and not the general public that pays for the program. All three of these social insurance programs have the politically attractive characteristics that they are not paid out of general tax revenues.

The administrative cost of social insurance programs is generally low. The administrative cost of Social Security is less than 3 percent of the benefits paid. This can be contrasted with the 18.5 percent administrative cost of the AFDC program.

There is very little social stigma associated with the recipient of social insurance benefits. This is particularly true of the Social Security program. The low social stigma is due in part to the generally held notion that the benefits are earned benefits. The argument is strongest in the case of the Social Security program because most recipients have paid a Social Security payroll tax for many years previously. For the Unemployment Insurance program and the Workmen's Compensation program the argument is somewhat weaker. The worker has not himself make a contribution to the program, but his employer has. Stigma is minimized by avoiding dependence on public funds for the payment of social insurance benefits.

Criticisms of the social insurance strategy are:

Many of the poor are ineligible for social insurance benefits. In 1965, 21 percent of the aged poor were excluded from Social Security benefits.[27] Most families with an employed worker are covered by at least one social insurance program, but many poor households do not include an employed worker. In 1969, the head of household was unemployed for the entire year in 44 percent of poor households. Of the poor who are employed, many are excluded from social insurance benefits because they are engaged in work that is not covered by social insurance. The poor constitute a substantial proportion of workers in occupations that tend not to be covered by social insurance such as farming, domestic work, and casual labor.

Many people remain poor even though they receive social insurance benefits. Social insurance benefits are generally so low that many of the recipients remain below the poverty line. In 1965, 59 percent of Social Security recipients had incomes that would have been below the poverty line without these benefits. When the benefits were taken into consideration, only 32 percent remained below the poverty line. While this represents a substantial reduction in the percentage of recipients in poverty, it also indicated that a substantial proportion remain in poverty. In 1961, 24 percent of Unemployment Insurance recipients remained below the poverty line despite their benefits.

Social insurance programs do not adequately take into consideration variation in needs among recipients. Workers who have higher earnings prior to retirement receive higher Social Security benefits even though the economic need is generally greater for the worker who has a low income prior to retirement. In the computation of Social Security benefits, accumulated wealth and unearned income (e.g. the return on invested money) are not taken into consideration. Neither Unemployment Insurance nor Workmen's Compensation takes into consideration accumulated wealth or unearned income. In these programs benefits are also based on prior earnings. A worker who becomes unemployed during an economic recession will find it more difficult to locate another job than the worker who becomes unemployed during a period of economic expansion, but such differences in the state of the economy are generally not taken into consideration in determining the length of time for which Unemployment Insurance benefits are available.

There are some ways in which social insurance programs do take into consideration variation in the individual needs. In the Social Security program there is an income test for all recipients under age 72. Benefits decrease as outside income increases. The income level at which the Social Security payment is eliminated altogether is higher for those recipients who are eligible for higher benefit levels. In 1969, the maximum Social Security benefit for a single individual was $218 per month; a person who was eligible for a benefit of this size had his benefit reduced to zero if he had an earned income in excess of $4,900 per year.

Social Security benefits are also designed to replace a specified fraction of what the worker's average earnings had been prior to his loss of earnings. The formula used to compute benefits is designed so that workers who had low earnings have a larger share of their earnings replaced than those who had higher earnings. In 1969, a recipient who had average monthly earnings of $75 prior to loss of earnings had about 75 percent of his earnings replaced. A worker with average monthly earnings of $400 had about 40 percent of his earnings replaced.

Another respect in which individual need is taken into consideration in the Social Security program is that recipients with dependents get higher payments than those without dependents, assuming that employment records are identical in both cases. In most states, as a contrast to the Social Security program, neither Workmen's Compensation nor Unemployment Insurance programs provide added benefits to recipients with dependents. But the benefits from the Workmen's Compensation program are related to the severity of the disability and thus to potential earning capacity. In periods of prolonged recession, Congress has extended the length of time for which Unemployment Insurance benefits could be received. This action takes into consideration the greater difficulty the unemployed have in locating new jobs during such periods.

It is possible for social insurance programs to take into consideration some variations in individual needs and still retain their identity as insurance programs. But it is sometimes argued that if they go too far in this direction, they will cease to be insurance programs because the benefits will not be associated closely enough with the size of the individual contribution. A weakness of this argument is that there already exist some social insurance programs for which there is no direct recipient contribution. But Social Security, which is the largest and most popular of our social insurance programs, does base benefits on the extent of individual contribution.

A high percentage of social insurance benefits go to the non-poor. In 1961, 37 percent of Social Security benefits and 64 percent of Unemployment Insurance benefits went to those who would have had incomes above the poverty line even without their social insurance benefits. In contrast, only 7 percent of Public Assistance benefits went to those whose income for the year fell above the poverty line.

As a response, it is sometimes asserted that social insurance programs are designed for both the poor and the general population. There is a broad base of political support for this approach, which in turn has contributed to the periodic increases in social insurance benefit levels. In this context, benefits paid to those who are not poor cannot be used as evidence of inadequacy in the approach. If social insurance programs are to be evaluated for their welfare impact, the focus should be on how much money rather than what percentage of the money goes to the poor. On this score the social insurance programs do well. Social Security alone provides more cash payments to the poor than all other income maintenance programs together.

Social insurance is not an effective way to help those who have been poor for a long time to escape poverty. Social insurance acts to replace income that is lost due to involuntary removal from the labor force, but the amount replaced is generally quite substantially below the prior income. A worker who has been poor for an extended period is likely to be ineligible for social insurance. The poorest segment of the labor force includes many workers who are excluded from social insurance benefits due to their irregular employment records or employment in those jobs that are exempted from participation in social insurance programs. Even when a poor worker is eligible for social insurance benefits, it is likely that his benefits will provide an income below the poverty line. Social insurance is much more effective as a means to keep workers with a strong employment record out of poverty than it is as a means to help workers with poor employment records to escape poverty.

There is substantial variation among the states in the size of benefits for several of the social insurance programs. This criticism is based on the assumption that persons in comparable situations should receive comparable benefits. In 1969, the variation between states in the average payment for the Unemployment Insurance program was from $32 to $56 per week. Some of this difference can be attributed to variations in wage levels between states. In 1966, the range of difference between the states for the maximum Workmen's Compensation payment for temporary total disability was from $32 to $150 per week. The Social Security program benefits are computed in the same way for workers in all states. There is some variation between the states for the Social Security program, but it is due to differences in wage levels rather than differences in procedures for computing benefits.

For several of the social insurance programs there is marked variation among states in the percentage of workers covered. This criticism is directed primarily at the Unemployment Insurance program and Workmen's Compensation program. In 1967, the range of differences between the states in percentage of nonagricultural workers covered by Unemployment Insurance was from 59 to 100 percent. There was also a wide range for the Workmen's Compensation program because casual laborers and agricultural workers are often excluded. The number of workers in these and other frequently excluded categories varies from state to state.

Social Security, Unemployment Insurance, and Workmen's Compensation are only three of many possible programs that would be consistent with the general strategy of providing cash assistance to specific categories of the population based on participation in an employment related social insurance program. Many of the arguments for and against the various existing programs would not necessarily hold for all possible programs consistent with the general strategy.

The following are some modifications in the existing programs that would invalidate a number of the criticisms that have been made of these programs:

Expand the coverage of the social insurance programs to include a larger segment of the labor force. Suppose a law could be passed requiring that all jobs be covered by social insurance programs. The law would be very difficult to enforce because some jobs, such as domestic work, are transitory. In transitory jobs, particularly those involving a small number of employees, the paper work involved would discourage compliance with the law. Another possible change would be to extend social insurance coverage to all workers in currently covered occupations. At present many workers are not eligible for social insurance benefits because they have not put in a specified amount of time on the job. The eligibility rules could be changed so that workers would be covered as soon as they arrived on the job. An expansion of labor force coverage would help the poor because many of the poorest workers are either in occupations that are not covered or do not yet have the required number of calendar quarters of covered employment.

Increase social insurance benefit levels. An increase in benefit levels would reduce the number of families living in poverty. If the benefits for Social Security were to be increased substantially, it is likely that there would be an increase in the payroll tax. The increase in the payroll tax that would be required would, of course, make it difficult to generate the political support necessary to raise the benefits to the level at which all recipients would be above the poverty line. The rise in costs to employers required for the Workmen's Compensation and Unemployment Insurance programs would also make it difficult to get support for the increase in benefit levels that would be necessary to assure recipients an income at or above the poverty line.

A related change would be to reduce or eliminate the discrepancies in benefit levels that occur due to differences in earnings during the period of covered employment. In 1969, the retirement benefits for the Social Security program ranged from $55 to $218 for a single individual. By reducing the discrepancies between the highest and lowest benefit level, the benefits of the poorest recipients would be increased.

Take variations in individual needs into consideration in the determination of social insurance benefits. At present the Workmen's Compensation and Unemployment Insurance programs do not take into consideration the number of dependents a recipient has. The Social Security program does supplement payments for up to two dependents, but even with this program there is room for liberalization in this respect.

A means test could be introduced which would consider personal wealth and unearned income as well as any earned income and reduce social insurance benefits accordingly. This would free funds to provide larger benefits to those who had the greatest need. Such a change would, however, increase the administrative cost of the program.

At present, the Social Security program replaces a higher percentage of the earnings of a low income worker than of a high income worker, but still the low income worker ends up with a very low benefit. By reducing the discrepancy between the highest and lowest benefit level, the needs of the worker with a poor earnings record would be taken into consideration more adequately than at present.

Restrict social insurance benefits to the poor. At present a substantial fraction of the benefits paid by social insurance programs go to those who are not poor. The benefits of these programs could be restricted to the poor. This change would require the introduction of a means test. This in turn would add to the administrative cost of the program. The reduction in the number of individuals eligible for benefits would make it possible to provide greater benefits to the eligible poor. But if enough of the less needy were excluded, the base of political support for the approach would be eroded. The result would be resistance to increases in benefit levels and, in the long run, the benefits to the poor might be lower than they would be under the present social insurance programs.

Eliminate between-state differences in eligibility requirements and procedures for computation of social insurance benefits. The Social Security program uses the same procedures in all states for computation of benefits and eligibility determination. But there are marked between state differences for the Unemployment Insurance program and the Workmen's Compensation program. Even if these changes were made, there would still be variations in average payments due to the differences in average salary rates.

Combine the existing social insurance programs into one program. At present some workers are covered by one social insurance program, some by two or more programs, and still others are not covered by any social insurance program at all. Depending on the state in which a worker lives and the employer he works for, there are marked variations in benefits available to him. If the programs were combined, the benefits available to workers in comparable situations could be made more equitable.

Even if the preceding modifications in the existing social insurance programs were made, some problems would remain that are implicit to the social insurance approach.

Some and possibly many of the poor would still be ineligible for any benefits. This would occur when no member of the family had recently been in the labor force. In 1969, 44 percent of heads of poor households were unemployed for the entire preceding year. Few if any of these families would be helped by expanding the coverage of the social insurance programs or increasing their benefits.

There would still be little help to the chronically poor. As long as benefits are employment related, many of the poor would not receive any benefits at all. Some poor families would be eligible for Social Security benefits, but their benefits would be too low to keep them out of poverty. As long as benefits are based on prior earnings, those with a poor earnings record will get less help.

The two preceding limitations of the social insurance approach assume that social insurance programs will continue to be employment related. It is possible to conceive of a program that would be similar in many respects to existing social insurance programs but would not be work related. An example of this is the provision that all persons age 72 and over are eligible for Social Security benefits regardless of prior labor force participation. This distinction could be extended so that all needy people would be assured benefits regardless of prior labor force participation. Such a program would resemble a negative income tax program. In some respects a negative income tax program can be viewed as an universalistic social insurance program. We will explore this point further in Chapter 6.

Notes

1. The unemployed parent component of the program is sometimes designated AFDC–UP. Much of the descriptive information presented in this section has been drawn from President's Commission on Income Maintenance Programs, *Background Papers,* (Washington, D.C.: U.S. Government Printing Office, 1969), pp. 272-278; and from *Report of the President's Commission on Income Maintenance Programs, Poverty Amid Plenty,* Ben W. Heineman, Chairman. (Washington, D.C.: U.S. Government Printing Office, 1969), pp. 114-126.
2. For more detail on the eligibility requirements see *Background Papers,* p. 273 and Heineman, *Poverty Amid Plenty,* pp. 115-116.
3. Some people prefer to consider the tax rate on gross income (i.e., earned income plus AFDC payments). When looked at this way the tax rate comes out closer to 20 percent. See *Background Papers,* p. 277.
4. David B. Eppley, "The AFDC Family in the 1960's," *Welfare in Review* 8, 5(1970): 8-26.
5. If we make the unrealistic, but conservative assumption that there were no administrative costs in 1960 and if we use the estimate that administrative costs come to 18.5 percent of AFDC payments (see Heineman, *Poverty Amid Plenty,* p. 123), more than 70 percent of the increase could be attributed to increased payments and increases in the number of recipients. A more realistic estimate would be that administrative costs have increased at the same rate as the number of recipients (138 percent). Under this assumption, roughly 93 percent of the increase in cost of AFDC could be attributed to the increase in payment levels and number of recipients. (Calculations based on data presented in *Social Security Bulletin* 33, 6(1970): 41.)
6. Between 1960 and 1969 there was an increase from 4.5 to 5.4 million female-headed families. But most of these families were not poor. Between 1959 and 1969 there was actually a slight decrease from 1.9 to 1.8 million female-headed poor households. See U.S. Bureau of the Census, *Statistical Abstract of the United States: 1970* 91st ed. (Washington, D.C.: U.S. Government Printing Office, 1970), p. 35; U.S., Bureau of the Census, *Current Population Reports,* Series, P-60 No.76, "24 Million Americans," Poverty in the United States: 1969, (Washington, D.C.: U.S. Government Printing Office, 1970), p. 6.
7. Eppley, "The AFDC Family in the 1960's." The median family size actually decreased slightly from 3.1 in 1960 to 3.0 in 1969.
8. *Poverty Amid Plenty,* p.121. David Gordon, Income and Welfare in New York City." *Public Interest* 16, (Summer, 1969): 64–88.
9. For a more detailed discussion of the factors that have contributed to the growth of the AFDC population. See Heineman, *Poverty Amid Plenty,* pp. 121-122.

10. Robert J. Meyers, "Administrative Expenses of The Social Security Program," *Social Security Bulletin* 32, 9(1969): 20-27.
11. Sydney E. Bernard, "The Nixon Family Assistance Plan: How It Will Fail And Why I Support It," *Poverty and Human Resources* 5, (1970): 5-13.
12. U.S. Department of Health, Education, and Welfare, Social and Rehabilitation Service, National Center for Social Statistics, *Preliminary Report of Findings-1969 AFDC Study,* March 1970, p. 23, (hereafter referred to as *Preliminary Report of Findings-1969 AFDC Study).*
13. Joel F. Handler and Ellen Jane Hollingsworth, "How Obnoxious is the 'Obnoxious Means Test'?" *Wisconsin Law Review* 1(1970): 114-135.
14. The following are reports on the two experimental studies (1) State of Colorado, *The Incentive Budgeting Demonstration Project, Final Report,* Colorado State Department of Public Welfare and the Denver Department of Welfare, December, 1961, (2) Cuyahoga County Welfare Department and Community Action for Youth (Cleveland), *Employment Incentives and Social Services: A Demonstration Program in Public Welfare,* 1965. In the Denver study AFDC recipients were allowed to keep $25 and were taxed at a rate of 75 percent of additional earned income. A similar study was conducted in Cleveland. Another study has been carried out on the willingness of AFDC versus non-AFDC women to take on casual work. The finding was a greater willingness on the part of non-AFDC women, who do not face the high marginal tax rate faced by AFDC women. See S. E. Bernard, *Fatherless Families: Their Economic and Social Adjustment* (Waltham, Massachusetts: Brandeis University, 1965).
15. The increase in full-time employment was from 4.6 to 7.5 percent. There was an increase in the number of persons employed full-time and a decrease in the number employed part-time. The Work Incentive Program was not actually started until 1968 so data for the 1967 to 1969 period can be used to check for its impact. The number of persons employed full-time increased from 6.6 to 7.5 percent but the number employed part-time decreased from 7.1 to 5.8 percent. The net result was a slight decrease rather than an increase in the percentage of AFDC women working. See Eppley, "The AFDC Family in the 1960's."
16. *Preliminary Report of Findings-1969 AFDC Study,* p. 35; Eppley, "The AFDC Family in The 1960's"
17. The reform of English poor law in 1834 was actually a step backward in generosity. The reform was in response to rapidly increasing English poor taxes.
18. For 1969 the median length for the current enrollment was 23 months. See Eppley, "The AFDC Family in The 1960's."
19. Christopher Green, *Negative Taxes and The Poverty Problem* (Washington, D.C.: The Brookings Institution, 1967), p. 20.
20. Leonard J. Hausman, "Potential for Financial Self-Support Among AFDC and AFDC-UP Recipients," *The Southern Economic Journal* 36, 1(1969): 60-66. The estimate is for the AFDC population in 1965.
21. In 1969 there were approximately 11 million Public Assistance recipients almost all of whom were poor and there were 24 million poor persons in the overall population. On the basis of these estimates it follows that 46

percent of the poor received Public Assistance benefits. But there are always some people who receive Public Assistance who are not poor so the actual level would be somewhat below 46 percent. See "24 Million Americans"; *Statistical Abstracts of the United States: 1970,* p. 297; Green, *Negative Taxes and the Poverty Problem,* p. 20.

22. Lester Salaman, "Family Assistance: The Stakes in The Rural South," *The New Republic* 164, 8(1970): 17-18.
23. There are several forms of social insurance that are not considered in the present discussion. The Railroad Retirement program is a social insurance program that is similar to Social Security; it provides benefits to employees of the railroad industry. Four states have introduced Temporary Disability Insurance programs; these programs are generally operated as extensions of the Unemployment Insurance programs. There are also retirement pension plans for federal civilian employees. The Veterans Compensation program is a major social insurance program. It provides benefits for Armed Service connected death or disability. For more information on these programs, see Heineman, *Poverty Amid Plenty,* pp. 108-112. Also see *Background Papers,* Chapters 3 and 4.
24. Blanch D. Coll, *Perspectives in Public Welfare* (Washington, D.C.: U.S. Government Printing Office, 1969), p. 75.
25. Benefits are available to the surviviors of workers who were covered for 6 out of the 13 quarters prior to death. For disability benefits, a worker must have been covered for 40 quarters including at least 20 of the 40 quarters preceding the disability.
26. There is no reduction for earnings below $1,680 per year. There is a reduction by 50 percent of earned income between $1,680 and $2,880 per year. Above $2,880 the benefit is reduced by 100 percent of earnings until the benefit is reduced to zero. The point at which the benefit is reduced to zero depends on the size of the benefit which may range from $55 to $434 per month. There is no earnings test or reduction of benefits due to earned income for recipents age 72 and over.
27. See Mollie Orshansky, "The Shape of Poverty," *Social Security Bulletin,* 31, 3(March 1968): 3-32, Table 19. This figure can be compared with the 25 percent of all aged persons not receiving benefits in 1965. See *Social Security Bulletin* 33, 6(1970): 53, Table Q-4.

3

Family Allowance And Negative Income Tax

In this chapter we shift to a consideration of the proposed alternatives to current programs, the family allowance and the negative income tax. We will first discuss the Vadakin, Schorr and McGovern family allowance proposals. Several negative income tax proposals will then be presented. The chapter concludes with a comparison between alternative income strategies and an evaluation of the income strategy more generally.

FAMILY ALLOWANCE

Family allowances have been adopted in 62 countries including Canada and all the European countries. The United States has never had such a program. A family allowance program provides cash payments to families based on the number of dependent children in the family. For this reason it is sometimes referred to as a children's allowance. Family allowance programs differ from AFDC because the benefits are generally not restricted to families with low incomes. The goal of family allowance programs is to improve child welfare.

In the 1870s certain private companies in France began to supplement the regular wages of workers with families. By the 1920s such programs were widespread in France and Belgium. These programs were private, covered only certain industries, and provided benefits only to families of employed workers. The first national family allowance program was introduced in Belgium in 1930.[1] Today many of the family allowance programs remain employment related, but in some countries all families are covered. In most countries benefits are paid to all children, but in some they are paid only for the first few, and in others only for those above a specified number.[2]

In some countries a means test is associated with the family allowance; in these countries the program is more analogous to the AFDC program in the United States. Some countries use a progressive scale in paying benefits; that is, a larger allowance is paid for each additional child. There is no country that pays less for each subsequent child. But some do set limits on the number of children the allowance is available for; this is equivalent to a zero payment for all children beyond the specified number.

A number of family allowance proposals have been made for the United States. A common characteristic is that the allowance benefits would go to families of all incomes, not just to poor families. The proposals by Vadakin, Schorr, and McGovern are among the most frequently cited. The family Assistance Plan (FAP), which has been proposed by the Nixon administration, has some characteristics in common with a family allowance plan, but it has more in common with a negative income tax plan. For that reason it will be considered with other negative income tax proposals. Brazer has also proposed a program which would combine features of both the family allowance and negative income tax approach.[3]

Vadakin's Proposal James Vadakin has proposed a family allowance to all families of $10 per month for each child under the age of 18 years. This source of income to the family would be taxable. The present income tax exemptions for children would continue unchanged. The gross cost (cost before the reduction in cost due to taxation on the added income) of the proposal is estimated at $8 billion for 1969. Of this approximately $1 billion would have been recovered as federal income tax payments. Of the $8 billion in benefits, only $1 billion would have reached the poor. There would have been an estimated 144 million persons living in recipient families and 16 million of these would have been poor. A very similar proposal was introduced to the House of Representatives in 1967 by Congressman John Conyers, Jr., but it was not enacted.[4]

Schorr's Proposal Alvin Schorr has proposed a family allowance plan he refers to as a pre-school allowance. This program would provide benefits of $50 per month for each child under the age of 6 years, but it would not pay any allowance for older children. The goal of this program would be to provide more support during the pre-school years, when it is most difficult for the mother to be employed, and the present income tax exemptions for children would be eliminated. The pre-school allowance would be taxable. The estimated gross cost of this proposal for 1969 is $13 billion; of this a substantial fraction would have been recovered as federal income tax payments. Of the $13 billion, $2 billion would have gone to poor families. There would have been a total of 111 million persons in recipient families and of these 13 million would have been poor.[5]

McGovern's Proposal As part of his human security plan, Senator George McGovern has proposed a children's allowance of $50 per child per month for all children under 18 years of age. The existing income tax exemptions for children would be eliminated and the allowance would count as taxable income. One estimate is that the program would have had a net cost (cost after taxes) of $28.5 billion in 1965. In 1965 the program would have raised 64 percent of poor families out of poverty; these families would have included 77 percent of all poor children. The impact of this program, as with all family allowance programs, would be greatest for large families. In 1965, it would have raised 30 percent of poor one child families out of poverty, 71 percent of poor three child families out of poverty, and 96 percent of poor families with 6 or more children out of poverty.[6] The estimated gross cost of this proposal for 1969 is $42 billion of which a substantial fraction would have been recovered in the form of income tax payments. Of the $42 billion, $6 billion would have gone to the poor. There would have been 144 million persons in recipient families and 16 million would have been poor.

Evaluation Of The Family Allowance Strategy There are some respects in which all three of these family allowance proposals differ from family allowance programs as they exist in at least some other countries. The preceding proposals for the United States would not require the participation of a family member in the labor force. In the Vadakin, Schorr and McGovern proposals benefits would be independent of the income of the family (in some countries the family allowance is based on the family's income).[7] The family allowance would be paid out of general revenues and not as in some countries, using a payroll tax.

The evaluation that follows is restricted to family allowances of the type that have been proposed for the United States. A family allowance is often viewed as a possible alternative to the present AFDC program or to a negative income tax program. For this reason, comparisons to these approaches are frequently made. Many of the comparisons with a negative income tax are delineated in more detail in the section on negative income tax proposals. Family allowance strategy can be supported by the following arguments:

A family allowance program would reduce the extent of poverty and deprivation experienced by children living in poor families. This is seen as a desirable goal firstly, because children cannot be held responsible for their poverty; they are clearly the innocent victims of circumstances. Secondly, childhood in poverty is likely to lead to a less productive adult life. An investment during childhood might more than pay for itself in the lifetime productivity of the recipient child.

It would reduce work incentives to a lesser extent than the AFDC program. For AFDC and most negative income tax proposals, there is a high marginal tax rate on earnings for the poor. Since 1967, AFDC recipients have been allowed to keep 33 percent of their earnings; this means that their earnings are subjected to an implicit 67 percent tax rate. Most negative income tax proposals call for a tax on earnings in the 50 to 70 percent range. The Nixon administration's FAP proposal calls for a tax of 67 percent of earnings. There would be no change in the tax structure with a family allowance program. For many poor families, this would mean that they would be taxed at a rate nearer the 14 percent minimum, if they were taxed at all. While common sense would suggest that far fewer people will work when there is a high marginal tax rate, conclusive evidence is not available to make such an assertion. What evidence is available from the Graduated Work Incentive Experiment currently being conducted in New Jersey suggests that a marginal tax rate of 70 percent does not have a worse disincentive effect on employment than does a 30 percent marginal tax rate.[8]

There would be less social stigma associated with being a family allowance recipient than there is with being an AFDC recipient. One factor contributing to the reduction in stigma is that the benefits would go to rich and poor alike; the receipt of benefits would not be a sign of poverty status. The elimination of the means test that is necessary with the AFDC program would also work towards a reduction of the present social stigma. With a family allowance, careful scrutiny of personal finances and other aspects of a recipient's personal life would not be necessary as a precondition for the receipt of benefits. In a negative income tax program, there would be an income test and benefits would be paid only to those with low incomes.

It would have a larger base of political support than does the AFDC program. This argument is based on the political popularity of Social Security. The Social Security program provides benefits to many who are not poor as well as to many who are. The inclusion of those who are not poor broadens the base of political support for the program. In addition to transferring substantial funds to the nonpoor, Social Security gives more money to the poor than all other income maintenance programs combined. However, the large recipient population is only one of several factors that contribute to the popularity of the program. Another major factor is that the benefits are viewed as having been earned by the recipients; this factor would not be present with a family allowance program. While it is likely that a family allowance program would be politically more popular than the AFDC program, it is possible that it would be less popular than the Social Security program. To the extent that the base of political support is determined by the number of recipients, a family allowance program would have a larger base than a negative income tax program. Family allowance benefits would be available to between 55 and 71 percent of the population depending on the proposal. In contrast, negative income tax benefits would be available to between 11 and 42 percent of the population depending on the proposal.

The administrative cost of a family allowance program would be lower than that of the AFDC program. It is likely that the administrative cost of a family allowance program would be similar to that of the Social Security program which is about 3 percent. The cost would be substantially below the 18.5 percent administrative cost of the AFDC program because there would be no need for the elaborate means test procedures that are used to determine eligibility for AFDC benefits. Between 50 and 70 percent of AFDC administrative costs are due to eligibility determination.

It would not require a means test. The AFDC program requires a means test to determine whether an applicant is sufficiently poor to warrant support. The means test is a substantial expense. It is also a source of social stigma. Both of these aspects of the AFDC program would be eliminated with a family allowance program. However, this gain is not made without a cost as substantial benefits are transferred to others who are not poor. In some cases small poor families with a great economic need would receive less support than large rich families with very little need. Also, while it is generally assumed that the means test is a source of substantial displeasure to the recipients of AFDC, there is some evidence that this is not always the case.[9]

It would provide benefits to a wider segment of the poor than currently receives AFDC benefits. In 1968 AFDC benefits went to an estimated 29 percent of the poor, but an estimated 67 percent of the poor lived in families with dependent children.[10] A family allowance program would have meant that approximately 70 percent of the poor had some assistance from the program. Many negative income tax programs would do even better as they would extend benefits to 100 percent of the poor.[11]

The benefits from a family allowance program would be more equitably distributed than are AFDC benefits. Due to variation in eligibility criteria and payment levels, the same family would be treated quite differently from one state to another by the AFDC program. But a family of a specified size would always get the same benefits from a family allowance program.

A family allowance program would provide less incentive for father's absence than does the AFDC program. It is generally difficult for a family to receive AFDC benefits when there is an able-bodied father in the home. As discussed earlier, if the father is unemployed or employed at a very low wage level, it is often to the economic benefit of the other members of the family if he leaves. Often the other members of the family then become eligible for AFDC. This would not be true for a family allowance program. The benefits would depend only on the number of children in the family. Since the money would be where the children were, there would actually be an economic incentive for the father to remain with the children.

It would be more effective than a social insurance program for helping many of those who have been poor for a long time to escape poverty. Family allowance benefits would not depend on the recipient's prior work record; the benefits would be just as large to a family with a poor record as to a family with a strong work record. Many poor families that would not be eligible for social insurance benefits would be eligible for family allowance benefits. But there are categories of the poor, such as the aged, who would be ineligible for family allowance benefits, yet eligible for social insurance or Public Assistance benefits. Due to the existence of such groups, it is not possible to say that all poor families would fare better under a family allowance program. The current AFDC payments in some states are higher than the benefits that would be paid by many family allowance plans. McGovern's proposal is the most generous of the family allowance proposals that have been made, but it would provide a mother and three children with only $1,800 per year. This is substantially less than the current AFDC payment to a comparable family in many states.

In addition to the preceding arguments that have been made in support of the family allowance approach to income maintenance, there are a number of arguments that have been made against the approach, such as the following:

A family allowance program would increase fertility in poor families. The fear is that a family allowance would make it possible for the poor to provide for as many children as they can have at a level of subsistence they are used to. Not only would this lead to an increase in the total population, but of even greater concern is the possibility that it would increase the size of the dependent segment of the population.

In reply, it is possible to point out that family allowance programs already exist in 62 countries. Efforts have been made to measure the impact of these programs on the birth rate. Such efforts have been unsuccessful in demonstrating that a family allowance program has ever caused fertility to increase. However, these efforts also failed to demonstrate that a family allowance program has never had an impact on fertility. In short, the historical data available make it difficult, if not impossible, to determine how much of any change in fertility was due to the introduction of the family allowance program. Efforts have been made to use family allowances as a way to increase fertility. Here too the results were inconclusive.[12]

It would lead to a reduction in work effort among the poor. A family allowance would provide families with children a guaranteed minimum income. Workers with unattractive jobs could stop working and live on the guaranteed minimum income.

In reply to this criticism it is important to note that even under McGovern's proposal the guaranteed annual income for a family of five would be only $1,800. There are not many families of this size which would consider such an income sufficient reason for not working. It is likely that at least some people would work less if a family allowance were introduced, but in many cases they would have legitimate medical reasons for doing so. At present many of the poor who are in poor health work despite the high personal cost; it is not obvious that a reduction in the number of persons in this category would be undesirable. No evidence had been presented showing that the introduction of a family allowance in another country has led to a reduction in economic productivity.

The family allowance benefits, which are paid to the parents, would not be spent on the children. The fear has been expressed that irresponsible parents would use the family allowance benefits unwisely. The suggestion has been made that it might be spent on alcohol, gambling, and so on instead of food and clothing for the children.

In Canada efforts were made to determine how family allowance benefits were spent. They found that the allowance was sometimes earmarked for a special need of the child, but was more generally combined with other sources of family income. The parents were generally not able to say how much of the allowance had gone to meet the needs of the children. In one study 38 percent of small families and 46 percent of large families reported that they had spent the entire allowance on the children. The percentage of families reporting that they had spent none of the allowance on the children ranged from 44 percent for small families to 28 percent for large families.[13] There are obvious limitations to such self-report data. The parents could say they spend the money on the children and actually spend it on themselves.

From the available evidence it seems that family allowance payments generally go to increasing the family's living standard which benefits both the children and the parents. There have not been reports of extensive misuse of family allowance funds for gambling and so on.

A family allowance program would depress wages. When family allowances were first introduced, they were financed by employers. In some countries employers pay part (e.g., Austria) or all (e.g., Argentina) of the cost of the program today. But there are other countries (e.g., Australia) in which the family allowance program is financed completely by the national government out of general operating revenues.[14] It is this type of financing procedure that has been suggested for the United States. None of the proposals for the United States have suggested that the program be financed in part or full by a special tax on employers. If a family allowance program were to be financed by a tax on employers, it is possible that the program would tend to depress wages. But if a family allowance program is financed out of general revenues, then there is less reason to expect any adverse effect on wages. However, it is possible that the existence of a family allowance program would weaken the position of those advocating increases in the minimum wage, Social Security, and the like.

A large proportion of family allowance benefits would go to those who were not poor. Some of the benefits would even go to the very rich. This criticism assumes that the welfare goal of a family allowance would be most adequately met if all or most of the money went to the poor. This argument has a certain plausibility, especially if the assumption is made that there is a fixed amount of welfare money to be distributed. But if it is assumed that the mechanism used to distribute welfare money is a determinant of the total amount of money that is available for distribution, then the preceding conclusion does not necessarily follow. In 1969, the Social Security program transferred an estimated $16 billion to the poor while the Public Assistance programs transferred approximately $6 billion to the poor.[15] This difference may in part be due to the tendency not to view the Social Security program as a form of welfare. Any program that transfers all or most of its funds to the poor is likely to be viewed as a welfare program. A family allowance program that transfers money to both the poor and others may be sufficiently more attractive politically that it could be used to transfer more funds to the poor than a similar program, such as the Nixon administration's Family Assistance Plan, that was restricted to the poor.

A family allowance program would not adequately take into consideration variation between recipient families in the extent of economic need. Families of the same size, but with very different degrees of economic need, would receive the same size benefit. It can be countered that a family allowance program would not completely replace the present Public Assistance program. It would be necessary to retain at least a small welfare program to help the poorest families through emergency situations. A family allowance program would reduce the number of families dependent on welfare, but there would still be some families that would need more support than the family allowance provided. Even the most generous family allowance proposals offer benefit levels that are substantially below the current Public Assistance payment levels of many states. It would be possible to create a family allowance program which would, for all practical purposes, replace the Public Assistance program; but the added cost of such a program would substantially reduce its political feasibility.

Many families receiving family allowance benefits would remain in poverty. Even with McGovern's proposal of allowances of $50 per month per child, many families without any other source of income would remain in poverty. A reply to this criticism is that a family allowance program would supplement rather than replace existing welfare programs. The family allowance program would keep many families out of poverty thus reducing the load on the Public Assistance program. The reduced welfare load might facilitate increases in benefit levels.

A family allowance program would further complicate the welfare system with yet another program. The criticism is that a family allowance program would not be able to replace the existing Public Assistance programs. Since it would have to be supplemented by some additional programs, much of the administrative cost and complexity of the existing public welfare system would remain.

NEGATIVE INCOME TAX

In 1962 Milton Friedman presented a proposal for what he called a negative income tax.[16] The proposal is described as a negative income tax (hereafter NIT) because it would extend the income tax schedule below the zero tax point; that is, it would be used to pay out rather than to collect money from families and individuals in the lowest income brackets. The suggestion to utilize the tax system as a vehicle for income maintenance was an innovation, as was the proposal that income maintenance be made available to all families and individuals with incomes below a specified level.[17]

There is some disagreement as to the goals of the NIT approach; the following are a few for which there is the most consensus. (1) A primary goal is to increase the equity of the welfare system. A NIT program would be more universalistic than the present welfare system. It would provide benefits to all persons with incomes below a specified level, not just specific categories of those with incomes below this level. (2) Another goal is to deliver a higher proportion of the welfare dollar to the recipient; that is, to cut down on administrative expenditures. In part this would be achieved by providing cash benefits rather than goods and services. There would also be a shift to simpler procedures for determining eligibility. (3) Another goal is to provide an economic incentive for the recipient to seek work. This is achieved by avoiding the implicit 100 percent tax rate on outside income that was until recently (1967) associated with the AFDC program. If welfare benefits are reduced $1 for each $1 in outside earnings, there is an implicit tax rate of 100 percent. Under a NIT program the recipient would always be allowed to keep some fraction of any earned income. (4) Another goal is to reduce the social stigma that is presently associated with being a recipient of welfare. This would in part be accomplished by making the NIT payments automatic when the individual or family income drops below a specified level; it would not be necessary to apply for special status as a welfare recipient. Checking up on people would involve an extension of the same procedures used to check up on income tax returns; some of the more humiliating procedures sometimes used to check on welfare recipients would be dropped.[18]

The two basic components of any negative income tax proposal are (1) a guaranteed minimum income and (2) a tax schedule specifying the tax rates on other income. Using the two basic components, it is possible to calculate the other frequently mentioned component of a negative income tax proposal, (3) the point at which the net allowance is zero (the breakeven point). If the preceding components are used in conjunction with a federal income tax schedule, it is possible to calculate (4) the point at which the net tax liability under the NIT is equal to the net income tax liability under the existing federal income tax system. Each of these components will be considered in turn.

Several alternative procedures have been suggested for calculating the guaranteed minimum income. Friedman suggests that it be set equal to 50 percent of the sum of income tax exemptions and deductions for the family or individual. For a family of four this came to $1200 in 1962. The most frequent alternative to Friedman's procedure is to base the guaranteed minimum income on the Social Security Administration's poverty line. The poverty line, $3970 for a family of four in 1970, is adjusted yearly for increases in the cost of living. Some proposals suggest a level at a fraction of the poverty line, some at the poverty line, and some a specified amount above the poverty line. Not all guaranteed minimum income levels are stated in terms of a poverty line; some specify a flat per person minimum allowance without attempting to justify the amount in terms of some external standard. In all NIT plans the guaranteed minimum income is adjusted for family size; in some plans an upper limit is set on the number of family members for whom benefits will be provided, but any such limit is generally quite high (e.g., eight persons).

The second basic component of a NIT plan is the tax schedule for other income. In Friedman's proposal the tax rate on outside income would be taxed at a rate of 50 percent. That is, if a man with no income other than the allowance were to obtain some income from another source such as a job, his income from the job would be taxed at a rate of 50 percent until the tax on his earnings was equal to his guaranteed minimum income. Often this procedure is described as reducing the magnitude of the allowance, but it is equivalent to taxing outside income. Some NIT proposals suggest tax rates lower than Friedman's and some suggest higher tax rates. Tax rates ranging from 33 to 90 percent have been proposed. Some proposals specify a proportional tax rate; that is, the same tax rate for the entire range below the breakeven point. Some proposals call for a progressive tax schedule and others call for a regressive tax schedule. In addition, there are those proposals which specify that a certain amount of income such as $1500 per year should be exempt from taxation. This is equivalent to a progressive tax schedule in which a zero rate of taxation is used for the first $1500 in outside income.

The point at which the tax on outside income and the guaranteed minimum income equals zero is referred to as the breakeven point. According to Friedman's proposal, in 1970 a family of four with an outside income of $3600 would be at the breakeven point; that is, the net income after being taxed and receiving the guaranteed minimum income would exactly equal the outside income. Families with incomes above this point would pay a net tax, and families with incomes below this point would receive a net allowance. People with incomes above this point are paying for the benefits to those below the point. The breakeven point generally occurs at an income level which under the present income tax system would call for a net income tax. For this reason the negative income tax rate is sometimes extended above the breakeven point to a higher income level at which the net liability under the negative income tax program is equal to the net liability under the present income tax system. The reason that such a point can be reached is that the rate of taxation utilized in a NIT plan is generally higher than the tax rates at the bottom of the existing tax schedule (which start at 14 percent). Extending the NIT plan in this way makes it possible to utilize the existing tax system for upper income levels.

Several negative income tax proposals are described below. Some are included because they are frequently cited; others are included because they illustrate the range of variation that is possible using the NIT approach. The proposals by Friedman, Theobald, Schwartz, Tobin, the President's Commission on Income Maintenance Programs, the Nixon Administration, and The National Welfare Rights Organization have been actively advocated. Both Lampman and Green describe a wide range of NIT proposals; the proposals attributed to these authors are not necessarily the ones they would most strongly advocate. The Office of Economic Opportunity and the Institute for Research on Poverty at the University of Wisconsin are conducting experimental studies of several NIT proposals which are actually variations of one basic design; none of these proposals have been singled out for endorsement.

Friedman's Proposal The guaranteed minimum income for this proposal is equal to one-half of a family's income tax exemptions and deductions. For a family of four, Friedman's guaranteed minimum income came to $1200 when it was proposed in 1962, but due to changes in the tax laws it came to $1775 in 1970.[19] The rate of taxation on any other source of income is 50 percent until the allowance due the family or individual is reduced to zero; that is, until the income from other sources reaches the breakeven point. For a family of four the breakeven point would have been $2400 in 1962 and $3550 in 1970. The estimated cost of this proposal for 1969 is $4 billion and of this $3 billion would have gone to the poor.[20] There would have been 23 million persons in recipient families and of these 19 million would have been poor. Friedman would have estimated a net saving to the federal government because he saw his proposal as a replacement for the existing federal, state, and local welfare programs which cost $33 billion in 1961 and would have cost substantially more in 1969.[21] Among the programs that Friedman would eliminate are Public Assistance, Social Security, and public housing to name only a few. Friedman viewed his proposal as a way to spend less money on welfare. The actual cost of a NIT program would also be influenced by any effect the subsidies had on work incentives.

Theobald's Proposal The guaranteed minimum income for this proposal is $3200 per year for a family of four; this is based on a guarantee of $1000 for each adult and $600 for each child in the family.[22] The proposal calls for a 90 percent tax rate on any outside income. The breakeven point for this plan is $3,555 per year. The guaranteed minimum income specified is supposed to be adequate for minimum subsistence and thus it is reasonable to expect upward adjustment with increases in the cost of living. The proposal was originally made in 1963. By 1965, Theobald had already revised his suggested guaranteed minimum income upward to $3400 per year.[23] The estimated cost of the $3400 version of this proposal for 1969 is $9 billion and of this $7 billion would have gone to the poor.[24] There would have been 26 million recipients and 22 million of these would have been poor. Theobald refers to his proposal as a Basic Economic Security program. Although he never refers to his proposal as a negative income tax plan, there is no reason that he could not do so. He prefers to emphasize the guaranteed minimum income aspect of the program.

Schwartz's Proposal The guaranteed minimum income for this proposal is $3,000 per year for a family of four; the exact procedure for adjusting this figure for other size families is not specified. The proposal calls for a progressive tax on outside income with a 60 percent tax for the first $1000, a 70 percent tax for the second $1000, and 80 percent for the third $1000, and a 90 percent tax for the fourth $1000. The breakeven point for the proposal is $4,000 per year. The estimated cost of this proposal for 1969 was $10 billion and $7 billion of this would have gone to the poor. There would have been 29 million persons in recipient families and 22 million of these would have been poor.[25]

Tobin's Proposal For the first six members of a family the guaranteed minimum income would be $400 per person; the next two members would increase the allowance by $150 each, but there would be no increase for additional members. For a family of four the guaranteed minimum income would be $1600 per year. The tax rate on the other income would be 33 percent until the net tax liability under the proposal (the guaranteed minimum income less one-third of outside income) was equal to the net income tax liability under the existing income tax system. At $4,800 the net payment under Tobin's proposal would be reduced to zero. The 33 percent tax rate would be extended above this point until the resulting tax liability would be equal to the tax under the existing tax schedule. This would occur at $6,289 in 1965. Above that point the regular income tax schedule would be utilized. The estimated cost of this proposal for 1969 is $6 billion and $4 billion of this would have gone to the poor.[26] There would have been 37 million recipients and 22 million of those would have been poor.

Commission's Proposal This proposal is presented in the 1969 report of the President's Commission on Income Maintenance Programs. The guaranteed minimum income for this proposal is $2400 for a family of four; there would be a guarantee of $750 for each adult and $450 for each child. It calls for a 50 percent tax rate on this allowance until the allowance is reduced to zero at the breakeven income of $4,800 per year. The estimated cost of this proposal for 1969 is $11 billion and $8 billion of this would have gone to the poor.[27] There would have been 41 million recipients and 23 million of those would have been poor. The proposal does not call for the elimination of any existing Public Assistance programs; but the point is made that the number of persons qualifying for Public Assistance would be reduced due to the allowances from the NIT program. The commission that prepared the proposal recommends that the level of benefits be increased when it becomes politically feasible.

National Welfare Rights Organization's Proposal This proposal was introduced as a Senate Bill in 1970 by Senator Eugene McCarthy.[28] It is basically the same as the National Welfare Rights Organization proposal which they have been advocating for some time and for this reason will be referred to as the NWRO proposal. The guaranteed minimum income for this proposal is $5,500 for a family of four. The guarantee is $2,000 for the filer, $1,500 for the second member of the family unit, and $1,000 for each additional member of the unit. The actual benefits would be adjusted for variation between regions of the country in the cost of living. The benefits would also be adjusted for yearly increases in the cost of living. The guaranteed minimum income is based on the U.S. Bureau of Labor Statistics' "low standard budget."[29] The tax rate on outside income would be 67 percent in McCarthy's version of the proposal. A modification that is suggested in some Welfare Rights Organization literature is that the tax rate be 50 percent on income up to 25 percent of the guaranteed minimum income. The breakeven point with a 67 percent tax rate and a guaranteed minimum income of $5,500 is $8,250. A unique feature of this NIT proposal is that it calls for a wealth test. Any wealth in excess of $10,000 (excluding equity in a house) would be counted as income in the computation of benefits. Our estimate is that this proposal would have cost $52 billion in 1969 and $25 billion of this would have gone to the poor. There would have been 84 million recipients and 29 million of these would have been poor. The National Welfare Rights Organization estimates that the proposal would cost $50 billion per year, but an analysis reported by Ulmer estimates a cost of $71 billion above present welfare expenditures.[30] Recently, the level of the guaranteed minimum income for this proposal had been increased to $6,500 per year. It is likely that the NWRO will continue to increase the size of the guaranteed minimum income to take into consideration increases in the cost of living.

Lampman's Proposals

Proposal 1: The guaranteed minimum income would be $187.50 per person; for a family of four this would come to $750 per year. The tax rate on the first $1,500 in outside income would be zero; the tax rate on the next $1,500 in outside income would be 50 percent. The breakeven point for the proposal would be $3000 per year. The proposal was made in 1969.[31] It has been estimated that the proposal would have cost $5 billion in 1964.[32]

Proposal 2: The guaranteed minimum income would be $500 per person; for a family of four this would be $2,000 per year. The tax rate would be 75 percent on the first $2,000 in outside income and 33 percent on the next $1,500. The breakeven point would be $3,500 per year. The preceding proposal is a slightly modified version of a proposal originally presented by Lampman in 1965.[33]

Graduated Work Incentive Experiment This study often referred to as the Graduated Work Incentive Experiment or as the New Jersey Negative Income Tax Experiment is sponsored by the Office of Economic Opportunity and run by the Institute for Research on Poverty at the University of Wisconsin. It began in 1968 and continued through 1972 costing more than $5 million. The results will be most applicable to urban families with an income below 150 percent of the $3300, 1967 poverty line, with an employable adult family member, with at least one dependent, and with a male between the ages of 18 and 58 who is not disabled or in school. The families selected for the experiment were assigned either to a control group in which they were periodically interviewed, but receive no NIT benefits; or they were assigned to one of the eight experimental conditions.[34] Four different guaranteed minimum income levels were considered; they range from 50 to 125 percent of the 1967 poverty line. Three different levels of taxation were considered, 30, 50, and 70 percent. Each of the experimental conditions has its own breakeven point. Cost estimates from some, but not all of the experimental conditions are available. Kershaw estimates that a program with a guaranteed minimum income equal to one-half of the poverty line and a 50 percent tax rate would cost from $5 to $8 billion per year. He estimates that a program with a guaranteed minimum income equal to the poverty line and a 50 percent tax rate would cost $20 to $25 billion per year. A program with a guaranteed minimum income equal to the poverty line and with a 30 percent tax would cost $50 billion per year.

Green's Proposals

Proposal 1: The guaranteed minimum income is taken to be $3,000 for a family of four which is an approximation of the poverty line for such a family. The tax rate on outside income is 33 percent. The breakeven point is $9,000. The proposal was presented in 1967. Green estimates that the program would have cost $41 billion in 1964.[35]

Proposal 2: The guaranteed minimum income would be equal to $3,000 for a family of four. The tax rate on outside income is 100 percent up to the breakeven point of $3,000 per year. This proposal illustrates the fill-the-gap approach. If the family's income falls below the poverty line, the difference between the family income and the poverty line is paid in an allowance. Green estimates that the proposal would have cost about $12 billion in 1964.[36] This plan is a limiting case of a negative income tax rate in that the marginal tax rate below the breakeven point is 100 percent rather than some smaller percentage. Because the tax rate is not below 100 percent, the proposal would generally not be referred to as a negative income tax.

Family Assistance Plan The guaranteed minimum income for the Nixon Administration's proposed Family Assistance Plan (FAP) was originally $1,600 for a family of four, but this was subsequently increased to $2,400. The present discussion is based on the revised version of this proposal submitted to the 92nd Congress. There would be a guarantee of $800 per year for the first 2 members, $400 for the next 3 members, $300 per year for the next 2 members, and $200 for the eighth member. States would be free to supplement these benefits, but there would be no incentive through matching federal funds for them to do so. There would be no tax on the first $720 of a recipient family's income from other sources, but there would be a marginal tax rate of 67 percent on any income above that level. The breakeven point would be $4320 for a family of four. The proposal would require able-bodied recipients to register for training or employment unless they had adequate reasons for being exempt from this requirement. Our estimate is that in 1969 the proposal would have cost $7 billion and $6 billion of this would have gone to the poor. There would have been 23 million persons in recipient families and 14 million of these would have been poor. The administrative cost of the FAP proposal has been estimated at 7 percent of benefits paid.[37]

The Family Assistance Plan shares with family allowance proposals the characteristic of being restricted to families with dependent children. Since universality is considered essential to the concept of a negative income tax, a case can be made that the FAP proposal should not be classified as a negative income tax. But the FAP proposal does share many characteristics with other NIT proposals and for this reason it will be classified as a categorical NIT proposal.

Comparing Negative Income Tax Proposals The following comparisons can be made between the preceding NIT proposals.

For a family of four the magnitude of the guaranteed minimum income ranges from $750 for Lampman's proposal 1 to $6,500 for the NWRO's proposal. In those proposals specifying a guaranteed minimum income below $3,000 per year the goal is generally to fill a fraction of the gap between a family's income and the poverty line. For those proposals with a guaranteed minimum income of $3,000 to $3,500 per year, the goal is generally to assure each family and individual an income at least as great as the poverty line; most of these proposals were made at a time when the poverty line was below $3,500. In most cases it is safe to assume that the authors would want their proposals modified in view of more recent poverty line figures.

The guaranteed minimum income of $6,500 specified in the NWRO's proposal is clearly an effort to assure a minimum income substantially above the minimum subsistence implicit in the poverty line income.

Strong arguments can be made for using programs that specify a guaranteed minimum income equal to the poverty line to replace the present Public Assistance program, and possibly other welfare programs, but the argument for replacing the present system with a NIT program that calls for a guaranteed minimum income substantially below the poverty line is much weaker. The implications of this difference are important. In one case, the NIT program would end up being yet another welfare program increasing the total number of such programs; in the other case, the NIT program could be used to reduce the total number of different welfare programs.

Another important distinction between proposals is whether or not the guaranteed minimum income is stated in terms of the poverty line or some fraction thereof. In Friedman's proposal the guaranteed minimum income is stated in terms of income tax exemptions and deductions—consequently it would not be adjusted yearly for increments in the cost of living. The proposals being tested in the Graduated Work Incentive Experiment are all stated in terms of the Social Security Administration's poverty index which is adjusted yearly for any increases in the cost of living.

The rate of taxation on outside income (e.g., income from a job or interest on money in a savings account) ranges from 33 percent in Tobin's proposal to 90 percent for Theobald's proposal. The goal of a high tax rate is to minimize the cost of the program given the specified guaranteed minimum income. The goal of a low tax rate is to minimize any work disincentives. These two goals necessarily conflict: it would be desirable to use a high tax rate if it were possible to do so without reducing work incentives. The preliminary results from the Graduated Work Incentive Experiment suggest that the reduction in work effort is not greater when the tax rate is 70 percent than it is when the tax rate is 30 percent.[38] But it is still possible that at a higher tax rate such as 90 percent there would be a substantial drop in work effort.

Each NIT proposal calls for either a progressive, proportional, or regressive tax schedule for income below the breakeven point. In a progressive schedule the tax rate increases as income increases. This approach is designed to minimize work disincentives at lower income levels. The tax schedule specified in Schwartz's proposal is progressive. A proportional tax rate remains constant up to the breakeven point. The goal of this approach is to keep the work disincentives due to rate of taxation constant up to the breakeven point. Friedman's proposal includes a proportional tax rate. In a regressive tax schedule the tax rate decreases as income increases. The approach aims to minimize work disincentives at incomes near the breakeven point at the cost of somewhat greater work disincentives at lower income levels. Lampman's proposal 2 includes a regressive tax schedule. At present there is no evidence on which to base a choice between a progressive and a regressive tax schedule. This can be used as a rationale for choosing the simpler proportional tax schedule, but the other alternatives cannot be ruled out until the relevant experiments have been conducted.

Some proposals, such as the Family Assistance Plan and Lampman's proposal 1, specify that a recipient can make a certain amount of outside income without any reduction in the allowance. This is done to provide a strong positive incentive for the recipient to seek at least some employment. The hope is that for at least some of those seeking casual part-time work, more long-range employment opportunities will open up.

The breakeven points for the proposals that have been considered range from $2,400 for Friedman's original proposal to $9,000 per year for Green's proposal 1. Each proposal specified a redistribution of income in which people with incomes above the breakeven level pay for benefits to those with incomes below the breakeven level. For a specified guaranteed minimum income level, the higher the breakeven level the greater the cost of the program.

The cost estimates for the proposals that have been considered range from $4 billion for Friedman's proposal to $52 billion for the NWRO proposal. Generally the procedures for arriving at the estimated cost have not been specified in sufficient detail to allow exact comparisons between cost estimates.[39] One point that most authors do not make clear is the extent to which they have reduced their cost estimate by assumed reductions in the cost of other existing welfare programs. To compare the cost of alternative NIT proposals, it is best to consider cost estimates by using the same assumptions for several alternative proposals.[40]

EVALUATION OF THE NEGATIVE INCOME TAX STRATEGY

Sometimes negative income tax programs have been proposed to replace existing welfare programs; at other times they have been proposed to supplement existing programs. The potential advantages of a negative income tax program are often presented as improvements over the present Public Assistance programs, particularly the AFDC program. Arguments for and against the NIT approach will be considered; those in favor of the approach are discussed first:

A negative income tax program would be universalistic; it would provide benefits to all poor persons. In contrast, the categorical programs such as Public Assistance, social insurance, and the family allowance would only provide benefits to specific categories of the population. The argument is valid for all those programs that have been proposed as NIT programs. However, the other characteristics of a negative income tax plan could be included in a categorical income maintenance program. The Nixon Administration's Family Assistance Plan is an example of a categorical negative income tax program. It would provide benefits only to families with dependent children. While this program would be more universalistic than the present AFDC program, it would not provide benefits to all poor persons.

It would provide greater work incentives than are provided by the AFDC program. Originally the payment to an AFDC recipient was reduced $1 for every $1 of earned income. In 1967, the rules were liberalized so that the working AFDC recipient could keep the first $30 per month and 33 percent of any income above that level. This resulted in a marginal tax rate of 67 percent for most employed AFDC recipients.

A major stimulus to the creation of NIT proposals was the 100 percent tax rate implicit in the AFDC program prior to 1967; the introduction of the 1967 modifications has made the comparison between the NIT approach and AFDC less dramatic. Tobin's NIT proposal calls for a tax rate of 33 percent which is substantially below the current 67 percent marginal tax rate. But Theobald's NIT proposal calls for a tax rate of 90 percent which is substantially above the 67 percent tax rate. Many NIT proposals suggest a tax rate of approximately 50 percent which is below the tax rate for AFDC recipients, but not by much. Several NIT proposals are currently being tested experimentally. The preliminary results suggest that a 70 percent tax rate does not reduce work incentives any more than does a 30 percent tax rate.[41] If this finding holds up, the trend in the future may be to suggest NIT proposals with higher tax rates.

A negative income tax program would reduce the incentive for father absence that is implicit in the AFDC program. For a negative income tax program benefits would be paid to poor families even when there was an able-bodied father present. Under the AFDC program most families with an able-bodied father present are not eligible for benefits even if he is unemployed or has earnings below the poverty line (the AFDC-UP program provides benefits to some families with an unemployed father). Sometimes it is economically to the family's advantage for the father to move out and maintain a separate residence so that his wife and children can receive AFDC benefits.

While a negative income tax program would quite likely contribute less to family instability than does the AFDC program, it is possible that the program would still contribute to family instability. The existence of a negative income tax program with its implicit guaranteed minimum income could lead to the father feeling that he was not essential for the support of the family. This in turn could lead to friction and instability in the marital relationship.

There would be less social stigma associated with being a recipient of negative income tax benefits than there is with being a recipient of AFDC benefits. One reason for this is that the present AFDC means test procedure would be eliminated. Due to it being administered in person, due to its exhaustiveness, and due to the frequency with which it is administered, the AFDC means test reflects a high degree of distrust towards recipients. With a NIT a much less exhaustive income test would be used to determine eligibility. Spot checks would be made as they are with tax returns. Another reason that there would be less stigma is that it would not be necessary to apply for a special status as a welfare recipient. All persons with incomes below a specified level would be eligible to receive the benefits. In such a situation it is less likely that it would be considered a moral virtue to forgo puplic support.

While there would be less social stigma associated with the receipt of NIT funds than is associated with the receipt of AFDC funds, it is possible that there would still be some social stigma. It is likely that upper income groups would feel a certain amount of contempt for those who were receiving public support, and this would result in some stigma being associated with the receipt of NIT benefits.

A negative income tax program would have lower administrative costs than does the Public Assistance program. It has been estimated that the administrative cost for the Public Assistance program is approximately 16 percent of benefits paid. This figure can be contrasted with the 3 percent administrative cost for the Social Security program. It is likely that the administrative cost of a negative income tax program would be similar to that for the Social Security program because the eligibility determination procedures are similar. If a NIT program were to completely replace the Public Assistance program, it is likely that there would be a substantial reduction in the administrative costs involved.

It would provide a stronger incentive for saving money than is provided by the present Public Assistance program. The means test currently used with the Public Assistance program requires that any savings above a specified small amount be deducted from benefits. A NIT would not take into consideration accumulated wealth in the determination of benefits; for this reason there would be no savings disincentive.[42]

It would be more equitable than the present Public Assistance program. With the Public Assistance program there are differences in benefit levels between states. There are also arbitrary differences in benefit levels between the various categorical Public Assistance programs. With a negative income tax program the benefits would not vary from one part of the country to another or from one category of recipient to another. In the NWRO proposal there would be differences in the benefits for different regions of the country.

Negative income tax benefits would not be used for social control of the poor. With the present AFDC program which combines social services with income payments it is possible to use the money as a means for social control. The money can be used to induce the recipient to utilize social services which in turn are likely to reflect middle class values about sexual morality, personal responsibility for poverty, the importance of hard work, and so on. The welfare liberal is likely to view the social control aspect of the AFDC program as undesirable, but the welfare conservative is likely to see this as one of the advantages of the program. The use of AFDC payments as a form of social control would be eliminated if a NIT program were to completely replace the AFDC program. In some areas there have been reports of Public Assistance benefits being witheld in order to restrict the political participation (voting) of blacks. The federal control of a NIT as opposed to local control of Public Assistance would eliminate such forms of coercion.

The negative income tax approach appeals to a wide range of the political spectrum. To the welfare conservative the approach is viewed as a means to simplify the present welfare system by substituting one program for a number of the existing programs. An anticipated consequence of this reform is less welfare spending. The welfare liberal sees in the negative income tax approach a way to extend welfare benefits to all poor persons; this is in contrast to the present welfare system which provides benefits only to specific categories of the poor. The welfare liberal also sees in the negative income tax approach a mechanism for gradually increasing the income floor (that income level below which no person can fall) so that eventually poverty as it exists today will cease to exist. While both welfare conservatives and welfare liberals can support the negative income tax approach, there will still be conflict when it comes to deciding on a specific program. The welfare liberals may compromise with the conservatives by agreeing upon a modest program to start with. But eventually any efforts to increase the income floor will be actively opposed by welfare conservatives. As Marmor points out, a NIT with a high guaranteed minimum income is a very different program than one with a low guararanteed minimum income even though they share certain structural characteristics and are administered in the same way.[43]

Opposition to the NIT approach to income maintenance center on the following arguments:

A negative income tax program would reduce work incentives for the working poor. This argument is directed at persons who are currently employed, but have incomes below the breakeven point for a specified NIT program. The size of this group would vary with the level of the breakeven point, which could range from $3,000 to $9,000 per year for a family of four. There would be more families below even a low breakeven point than there are presently on Public Assistance. While most NIT programs would increase work incentives for those on Public Assistance, they would decrease work incentives for those workers not on Public Assistance who are earning a wage that is below the poverty line.

There are two components of a NIT program that have potential for reducing work effort. One is the level of the guaranteed minimum income; the other is the tax rate on outside income below the breakeven point.

The best source of data for the impact of guaranteed minimum income on work incentives comes from the preliminary findings of the Graduated Work Incentive Experiment. Considering only the families in the experimental group, the difference between families with a high guaranteed minimum income (100 or 125 percent of the poverty line) and the families with a low guaranteed minimum income (50 or 75 percent of the poverty line) is not significant. Looking at the trend, there is evidence that there is, if anything, less of a decrease in work effort for the families in the high guaranteed minimum income condition.[44]

The best source of data for the impact of the tax rate component of a NIT program on work effort also comes from the Graduated Work Incentive Experiment. The difference between the 30 and 70 percent tax rate conditions in the extent of decrease in work effort is not statistically significant. Since most NIT programs suggest rates of taxation below 70 percent, this evidence suggests that the tax rate component of most NIT proposals is not likely to reduce work effort.

A negative income tax program would have less flexibility than do the Public Assistance programs for dealing with variation in the extent of need for economic assistance. Most NIT proposals would provide the same benefits to all families of the same size with the same income. But families of the same size and same low income can differ substantially in extent of economic need. If some families have property, savings, and other such sources to draw upon, they have less economic need than do families without such resources. The means test that is used with the Public Assistance program is designed to channel support to those families with the greatest economic need; it does so by taking not only income, but also a wide range of other possible economic resources into consideration.

The NWRO negative income tax proposal illustrates that it is possible to take variation in need into consideration when determining NIT benefits. Benefits for this program would be based on "available income." Available income would include 10 percent of "net usable wealth." The "net usable wealth" is the family's assets minus certain specified deductions. This would keep benefits from going to families with substantial wealth. In the computation of available income a number of deductions would also be allowed. Deductions would be allowed for medical expenses, alimony, business losses, and child care services when needed to allow a parent to work. While most NIT plans would have less flexibility than Public Assistance in dealing with variations in need, the NWRO proposal illustrates that this would not be true for all NIT plans.

A negative income tax program would leave much room for inequity. This criticism is very similar to the preceding criticism. Some families and individuals would receive payment-in-kind from relatives or some other source. These payments would not show up as income and would not be considered in the computation of the NIT payment for most NIT plans. Another source of inequity would be differences in wealth for families with similar incomes. A family whose income is due primarily to earnings on invested capital may have less economic need than a family with the same income due entirely to salary.

Some suggestions have been made for dealing with these sources of inequity. One possibility is to set an upper limit on the net worth a family can have and be eligible for NIT payments. Another suggestion is to compute an "imputed income" to all sources of family wealth. The imputed income would be the income the family's net wealth could be expected to return if it were invested in some low risk security. The NWRO proposal requires that 10 percent of a family's net usable wealth be counted as income. This procedure has the effect of setting a limit on the amount of wealth a family can have and still receive benefits. It also has the effect of reducing the size of the benefits in proportion to family wealth. While it is possible to take wealth into consideration in the determination of NIT benefits, to do so is to give up some of the administrative simplicity of the original proposals which required only information on the recipient's income. With any increase in administrative complexity there would be a parallel increase in administrative cost.

A negative income tax program would allow substantial leakage to those who are not poor. A NIT plan is designed so that the benefits are reduced over a wide range as income increases. For most NIT proposals there would be some benefits to persons with incomes above the poverty line. This would be one source of leakage to less impoverished groups. But most of this money would be going to families with incomes near the poverty line. The real needs of a family just above the poverty line are similar to those of a family just below the poverty line; for this reason, leakage to these groups is not as much of a problem as leakage to the rich. Another source of leakage to those who are not poor is that for most NIT plans differences in wealth are not taken into consideration. This allows some persons with a low income, but substantial wealth, to receive NIT payments. The NWRO proposal illustrates that it is possible to design a NIT plan that does take differences in wealth into consideration.

A negative income tax program would destroy the progressive nature of the present income tax structure. The 1970 income tax structure called for no taxation on an income below $3,600 for a family of four; it called for a tax rate of 14 percent on income above this level and below $4,000 per year. In contrast, a NIT program would specify a tax rate of from 33 to 90 percent for income in most or all of this range, depending on the proposal considered. For example, in Friedman's proposal there would be a tax rate of 50 percent on income below $3,600 per year for a family of four and at $3,600 the tax rate would abruptly shift to 14 percent. The tax rate would then increase progressively with increasing income in accordance with the existing income tax structure and eventually reach 70 percent. Thus the marginal income tax rate would start at 50 percent, decrease to 14 percent, and then gradually increase to 70 percent. This pattern is inconsistent with the philosophy of a progressive negative income tax structure.

One reply to the preceding argument is that if the total amount of income paid in taxes is considered, rather than the marginal rate being paid at a specific income level, there would be less curvilinearity. The tax rate would start at 50 percent and would decrease somewhat when the marginal tax rate dropped to 14 percent on the income above $3,600, but the amount of income paid in taxes would not drop to 14 percent because the much higher 50 percent tax rate had been paid on all income below $3,600 per year. If the total percentage of income paid in income taxes were considered, there would still be a curvilinear trend as income increased; but the curvilinearity would be less marked than is the case with marginal tax rates.

The progressive income tax structure is based on the principle that persons with higher incomes should pay a higher percentage of their income in taxes than persons with lower incomes. Since a NIT program would change the existing income tax structure in this fundamental respect, it is reasonable to examine what justification is given for the change.

One justification is that there is an important distinction between taxing the income of a person who is receiving public support and taxing the income of a person who is not receiving public support. When the income of a person receiving public support is being taxed, it is possible to view the tax as reducing the public support rather than his income. Assume that a NIT plan calls for a guaranteed minimum income of $2,000 and a tax rate of 50 percent on earned income. If a man has an earned income of $1,000, his net income would be $2,500. This can be interpreted as a 50 percent tax on his earned income or as no tax at all on his earned income, but a $500 reduction in the extent of his public support. Such an interpretation would be justified on the grounds that the man is still taking home more, not less than his salary. It would be possible for the NIT recipient to view the situation in this alternative way, but it is highly unlikely that he would do so. The most probable way to view the situation would be in terms of the net increase in income that could be obtained by increasing time at work. From this perspective the tax rate is 50 percent, not 0 percent, and the income tax structure is curvilinear, not progressive. Another justification that is given for the curvilinear income tax structure that would be required with a NIT plan is that it would not require any change in the income tax structure at higher income tax levels. It would require changes only at the bottom of the income tax structure. Sometimes the argument is given that it would be unwise politically to require a revision in the entire income tax structure as a precondition to the introduction of a NIT program. The elimination of the concept of a progressive federal income tax is a high price to pay to obtain the political support that would be necessary to introduce a NIT program.

A negative income tax program would provide incentives for higher fertility, especially among the poor. One incentive would be the availability of a guaranteed minimum income with which to support a family. Another would be the increase in the size of the guaranteed minimum income for each additional child. The Graduated Work Incentives Experiment will yield some information relevant to this issue, but its short three year duration is a serious limitation for the study of fertility shifts. Many countries in the world have family allowance programs that provide an income based on family size. There have been instances in which the birth rate has increased soon after the program was introduced or after the benefits were substantially increased, but these have always coincided with many other changes relevant to an increase in fertility. It is not possible on the basis of available evidence to determine whether or not a family allowance program has ever increased a country's birth rate.[45] Even if there was an increase in the birth rate with the introduction of a NIT program, it is possible that the increase would be temporary. In a short time most people would adjust their level of consumption so as to reflect their newly acquired income. In many poor families little or no effort is made to limit family size. It is unlikely that an increase in family resources will increase the fertility in those families that do not plan their family size in the light of available economic resources.[46]

A negative income tax program would encourage social instability. The argument is that the assurance of a guaranteed income would lead many people to give up unattractive jobs. People would drift around the country living off the guaranteed income. The family would not be as dependent on the father for support and this would increase the frequency of desertion. People would stop working and spend their time either drifting from one place to another, or by getting into trouble.

When people are attached to one place, the opinions of other people in the community often exert a social pressure that can be used to control behavior, but such controls break down in an anonymous situation. Many of the counter culture groups that are emerging in the United States today, hold values about work, family responsibility, and the use of drugs, that those who oppose NIT fear would become even more widespread. The preliminary results of the Graduated Work Incentives Experiment do not show any tendency for families receiving a guaranteed minimum income to be less stable than families without a guaranteed minimum income. But the argument can be made that these people might behave differently if they knew that the guaranteed income would be available indefinitely. The general expectation is that a NIT program would have the greatest impact on the poorest segment of the population. But many of those who are a part of the counter culture are from a middle class background.[47] This suggests that the impact of a NIT program might be greatest on the young middle class segment of the population.

A negative income tax program could not provide adequate welfare benefits at a politically feasible cost. Welfare costs have been increasing at such a rapid rate in recent years that it is quite possible that a program which would not be politically feasible today would be quite feasible in a few years. The Nixon Administration's Family Assistance Plan has an estimated yearly cost of $7 billion. This would suggest that any NIT program that would cost this much or less would be politically feasible as far as cost is concerned. Thus a NIT program with a guaranteed minimum income of $2,400 per year and a 50 percent tax rate would be politically feasible. However, such a program would leave many recipient families substantially below the poverty line. An alternative program that would provide a family of four with a guaranteed minimum income of $4,000, a figure approximately equal to the 1970 poverty line ($3,968), would have a net cost of approximately $27.5 billion per year. This program would keep most families above the poverty line, but its cost is not in a range that could be considered politically feasible today. The evidence suggests that the criticism is soundly based; at present it would not be politically feasible to introduce a NIT program that would provide an adequate standard of living for all.

A negative income tax program would just add another layer to the total welfare system. This argument is based on the preceding criticism that no NIT program that was politically feasible would provide an adequate standard of living. NIT programs within the range of political feasibility, such as one that would provide a guaranteed minimum income of $2,400 per year for a family of four, would have to be supplemented by other welfare programs. It would be possible to reduce the number of persons requiring support from Public Assistance, Social Security, and other such programs; but there is nothing in the NIT approach which would justify eliminating any of these programs. While it is possible that some of these categorical programs would be eliminated, it is unlikely that this would happen.

If any were eliminated, there would be some people who would be worse off under the new system than they were under the old one. For example, the Nixon Administration's Family Assistance Plan calls for the elimination of the AFDC program. But it also allows states currently providing benefits above $2,400 per year to a family of four, to supplement the FAP payments. While the AFDC program would be eliminated in name, it is possible that the programs used to supplement the FAP program would resemble the current AFDC programs in many respects.

If the assumption that Public Assistance and the other categorical income maintenance programs would not be eliminated is valid, many of the arguments that are made in support of the NIT approach are substantially undermined. It has been argued that a NIT approach would reduce the social stigma associated with being a Public Assistance recipient; but if it were necessary to retain the Public Assistance program to supplement the NIT program, social stigma would still be associated with being a recipient of the supplementary benefits. It is likely that the present means test procedure would be retained in much its present form. Although the cost of administering the Public Assistance program would be reduced, the cost of administering the smaller Public Assistance program in addition to the NIT program would substantially reduce the savings that might have been achieved had the Public Assistance program been entirely replaced by the NIT program. The continuation of the Public Assistance program and other categorical programs would mean the continuation of arbitrary differences between states in payment levels. It might also mean arbitrary differences in treatment for various categories of the poor; that is, some of the poor might be eligible to have their NIT benefits supplemented by a categorical program, and others might not. The continuation of the Public Assistance program would also involve a continuation of the social control of the poor by mixing social services and welfare benefits.

In defense of the NIT approach, it is necessary to point out that the long run impact on the complexity of the welfare structure might be much more favorable than the short run impact. While it is unlikely that a NIT program that would be politically feasible would do much to simplify the overall welfare structure, it is possible that in the long run, such a program could replace many of the existing welfare programs. In recent years there has been a tendency to liberalize the welfare system. This has been accomplished by adding new programs such as AFDC-UP and WIN. If this trend continues, the welfare system will continue to grow in complexity. There is also a trend toward higher benefit levels. The simplicity of a comprehensive NIT program is likely to become increasingly attractive and the high benefit levels that would be needed to replace existing programs are likely to appear increasingly reasonable.

COMPARING ALTERNATIVE INCOME STRATEGIES

The sections which follow serve to integrate the discussion of the family allowance and negative income tax strategies with our discussion of Public Assistance and social insurance in the preceding chapter. Consideration is first given to assumptions implicit in the income strategy for dealing with poverty. We then consider several of the advantages as well as limitations of the income approach. The chapter concludes with a comparison of 14 of the preceding income strategies on the basis of 28 dimensions of which 26 are the standard dimension used throughout the book.

Assumptions Implicit In The Income Approach One of the most fundamental implicit assumptions of income strategies is that many of the undesirable consequences of poverty can be alleviated or at least mollified by increasing the income available to the poor. Income maintenance benefits increase the quantity and quality of food, medical care, housing, and clothing as well as other essential goods and services available to the poor. Income programs generally increase the economic security of recipients and have other benefits related to this increase.

Another implicit assumption is that the poor are capable of allocating family income economically and of deciding what expenditures are in the family's best interest. This is in contrast to those who advocate income-in-kind as an alternative, on the grounds that the poor are likely to waste family income on gambling, alcohol, drugs, and the like. While it is feasible to meet some of the needs of the poor with income-in-kind programs, it would be very uneconomical to use them in meeting all needs. For example, it would be reasonable to provide medical care, housing, and some other goods and services through income-in-kind programs, but there would always be certain needs (e.g. haircuts) which would occur too infrequently or would involve too low a dollar volume to justify an additional income-in-kind program. The voucher principle (e.g. food stamps) could be used to extend the income-in-kind approach.

Also involved is the assumption that certain basic economic needs must be satisfied before an individual will be in a position to take full advantage of the various programs which are designed to increase long run economic self-sufficiency. If a child lives in a family which does not have sufficient funds to assure an adequate diet, it is unlikely that he is going to be able to take full advantage of an educational program designed to improve his long-term employability. A similar argument can be made for the extent to which the father in such a family would be able to take advantage of a job training program.

An underlying assumption in most income strategies is that some categories of the poor are deserving of public support, and others are not. Of those who are considered deserving some are assumed to be deserving of more support than others. Most maintenance programs and proposals are categorical; that is, they call for benefits to certain categories of the poor and exclude others. For example, those poor families headed by an able-bodied employed male are excluded from virtually all categorical income programs. The negative income tax (NIT) is generally considered a universalistic strategy because it calls for benefits to all categories of people with incomes below the breakeven line. But for NIT strategies in which the breakeven point is below the poverty line (e.g., Friedman's proposal), all poor persons with incomes between the breakeven point and the poverty line would be excluded. Thus, even the NIT is not necessarily universalistic with respect to all categories of the poor. Of those who are eligible for NIT benefits, there is variation in the size of the benefits provided. Assuming the same size family, those with lower incomes are eligible for greater NIT payments. With other strategies such as Public Assistance, there is also considerable variation in the size of benefits between categories of recipients. In some states a couple eligible for Old Age Assistance may receive payments almost as great as those received by a family of four on AFDC.

The preceding are assumptions common to all or most income strategies; the assumptions which follow are generally specific to particular programs. An implicit assumption of the AFDC program is that the poor are likely to be dishonest in reporting their economic circumstances unless closely policed. Most people who file an income tax return receive a personal visit from the Internal Revenue Service once every few years. In contrast, many AFDC recipients have their eligibility checked four times a year by an unannounced personal visit of a social worker. In recent years, however, there has been a liberalization in the investigation procedure. For instance, in some states, eligibility redetermination in the past included a check with all savings banks in the area as a measure to verify the accuracy of the recipient's statement of her financial situation. Today such checks are not made unless there are grounds for believing that the recipient is not honestly reporting personal assets.

An underlying assumption of the Unemployment Insurance program is that the worker who is fired or laid-off deserves support for a reasonable length of time while he seeks employment. The benefits are often available for several months, but never for as long as a year. The benefits are frequently available for a longer period for the worker who has been employed for more time prior to unemployment. The assumption is that workers who have had a stronger work record deserve more time to locate a new job.

An implicit assumption of the Workmen's Compensation program is that workers who are disabled on the job deserve at least a modest level of support from the employer for as long as the disability continues. Actually, the employer pays for the necessary insurance rather than the benefits directly. It is also assumed that the level of benefits paid should be a function of the extent of the disability.

An assumption of the Social Security program is that both employers and employees need to be forced to invest in social insurance. If the workers had the choice, many who were poor would choose to forgo the investment in social insurance. Money that currently is deducted as an insurance premium would instead be spent in the effort to meet more short run economic needs. The requirement that Social Security taxes be taken out of payroll taxes forces the employee to cover himself with social insurance. The stipulation that the employer make a matching contribution forces him to help pay for social insurance on behalf of his employees.

An implicit assumption of the family allowance approach is that it is possible to increase the welfare of children by increasing the overall welfare of the family. Studies which have been done tend to support this assumption. In some families there is a tendency to use the funds explicitly for the children, but it is more common that the family allowance payments go into a common fund out of which all family needs are met.

An underlying assumption of the NIT approach is that all people with incomes below the breakeven point should be given income maintenance benefits, regardless of the reason or reasons why their incomes are so low. For some NIT proposals (e.g., the NWRO proposal) the guaranteed minimum income is above the poverty line; an implicit assumption for proposals in this category is that all persons should be assured an income which is equal to, if not greater than, what is now considered the poverty line. Other proposals (e.g., the Commission's proposal), call for a guaranteed minimum income below the poverty line and a breakeven point above the poverty line. Implicit to proposals in this category is the assumption that all of the poor should receive at least some benefits. A third category includes those proposals in which the breakeven point is below the poverty line (e.g., Friedman's proposal). There is no assumption for proposals in this category that all of the poor should receive benefits, but the assumption that all of those with incomes below the breakeven point should benefit still holds.

Another assumption in all NIT proposals is that there should be an economic incentive for the poor to work. While AFDC taxed earned income at a rate of 100 percent prior to 1967, no NIT proposal calls for such a high rate of taxation on earned income. Since the AFDC amendments of 1967, which called for a reduction in the tax rate for AFDC recipients to 67 percent, this work incentive characteristic of a NIT is less useful for distinguishing NIT proposals from AFDC. Despite the effort to provide a work incentive as part of the NIT, the rate of taxation is generally quite high (often in the range of 50 to 70 percent), leaving the approach open to the criticism that despite the effort to provide a positive work incentive, the potential for a substantial work disincentive does exist. The 33 percent tax rate specified in Tobin's NIT proposal is below that of any other NIT proposal, but it is still substantially above the 14 percent used in the lowest federal income tax bracket.

Evaluation Of The Income Strategy In this section arguments are considered which apply to all or most income strategies. The goal is to summarize both the advantages and the limitations of the income approach as a general strategy for reducing the extent of poverty. The advantages of the income strategy are considered first.

The income strategy can be used to meet immediate needs. When a family has an acute need for food, medical care, housing, clothing, and so on, income benefits can help meet the need immediately. While manpower and education programs may help in the long run, they generally do not offer as quick a response to acute family needs as does an income program.

The income strategy gives the recipient freedom of choice. In so doing it enables recipients to decide for themselves which of their many pressing needs have priority. This advantage is most evident when the income approach is compared with the in-kind approach.

There is no uncertainty as to whether the recipient will benefit. At the end of an educational or job training program, the recipient may or may not be able to realize the benefits of the program by obtaining a better job. But with an income program there is never any such uncertainty. Money almost always contributes to family welfare; education and training more frequently fail to do so.

Benefits are generally quite accessible. There is some variation among income programs in the accessibility of the benefits. The Unemployment Insurance program, for instance, does require that the recipient show up in person at a central location, on a weekly basis. But others, such as Social Security, carry out all the necessary transactions by mail. With the income approach, benefits can be delivered to remote areas by mail. This makes the benefits more accessible than those available through an educational or manpower training program. Such programs require the recipient to appear in person, and many are inaccessible to those in rural areas.

Administrative costs tend to be low. This is not so for all income programs; the AFDC program being one of the most noteworthy exceptions. Most income strategies call for direct disbursement of cash benefits with a minimum of bureaucracy. In contrast, a program which seeks to provide the poor with housing, education, or job training will generally involve much more administrative complexity and expense. The administrative cost of an income program tends to be low because the approach is simple compared to those programs which provide goods and services.

Most of the money spent on the program goes to the poor themselves. This argument is closely related to the preceding argument. With a program designed to provide housing, medical care, education, or job training, substantial sums go into salaries and profits of those who provide these goods and services. The argument is sometimes made that even the recipient of a cash benefit contributes to the profits of other sections of society when he goes to purchase his goods and services on the open market. But this argument does not take into consideration that the government could itself take the place of the venders and provide the goods and services at cost.

The strategy is effective even during periods of economic decline. A program which is designed to increase the employability of the poor or find jobs for the poor is generally less effective when there is a slump in the economy. When the economy weakens and earnings decline, the benefits from many income programs increase. However, if the goal is taken to be keeping income above the poverty line, then even the income strategy is less successful when there is an economic decline. The benefits paid do increase, but generally there is a net reduction in the recipient's disposable income because the benefits replace only part of the income loss.

The following are some of the limitations of the income strategy:

The income strategy encourages long-term economic dependency. While some income programs such as Unemployment Insurance specify a definite limit on the length of time for which benefits can be received, as a general rule most income programs increase the opportunities for long-term dependence on public support. The rationale is that many people have a legitimate need for support over an extended period of time. In many cases the alternative to long-term public dependency is a life for an equally long period at an even lower standard of living.

The approach does not deal with the causes of low income. Manpower and educational programs are designed to provide the skills that are needed to escape poverty over the long run. An income program does not directly enable the recipient to acquire the skills that he will need to escape poverty. It can, however, be pointed out that a person must have certain immediate needs met before he will be able to take advantage of programs designed to increase long-term self-sufficiency. These needs can better be met by an income program than by a training program. However, it remains true that income strategies are generally short run. Supplementation in some form is necessary if the recipient is to become self-sufficient.

Some recipients do not use their income benefits in such a way as to maximize family welfare. Of greatest concern are those families in which the parents use income maintenance benefits for gambling, alcohol, or drugs rather than for the provision of an adequate family diet. While there have always been isolated instances of such flagrant misuse of income benefits, the frequency is quite low.

Income maintenance without work is inconsistent with the work ethic. The argument is that people should be required to work for their money. If they are given public support, it will undermine the desire to work. Not only will this reduce the amount a person works, but it will also have undesirable consequences on his character. For those who do not hold the work ethic in high regard, this is not a compelling argument. Many who would be income maintenance recipients are either incapable of working or incapable of earning an income above the poverty line, given the wage scales for the jobs open to them. The emphasis on the value of hard work tends to place the responsibility for poverty on the poor themselves and ignores the part played by the social and economic system.

The approach provides support with less dignity than the alternative of offering an opportunity to earn a decent living.

For men and increasingly for women, paid work is connected with self-concept. When a person is deprived of a job, he or she he is denied a positive self-concept, in addition to being denied an adequate income. An income program helps mollify problems related to the income deficit, but it does not come to grips with the need for a positive self-image.

The approach tends to reduce work incentives. Most of the income programs and proposals call for relatively high rates of marginal taxation on earned income for those who continue working or return to work. A related argument is that a program which provides a guaranteed income undermines the incentive to work by reducing the need for employment. The validity of these arguments is open to question. They are not consistent with the preliminary results of the Graduated Work Incentive Experiment.

Comparing Income Strategies In this section, 14 of the income strategies are compared on the basis of ratings along 28 dimensions. Some of the programs and proposals considered earlier are not included in the ratings made here for various reasons. In some cases the information needed to make the ratings was not available. In other cases the ratings would have been redundant with other similar strategies which were rated. This is the basis for the exclusion of several of the NIT proposals.

In Table 3.1, the following 14 strategies are compared: (1) AFDC, (2) Social Security, (3) Unemployment Insurance, (4) Workmen's Compensation, (5) Vadakin's family allowance proposal, (6) Schorr's family allowance proposal, (7) McGovern's family allowance proposal, (8) Friedman's NIT proposal, (9) Theobald's NIT proposal, (10) Schwartz's NIT proposal, (11) Tobin's NIT proposal, (12) the Commission NIT proposal, (13) the NWRO's proposal, and (14) the FAP proposal.

A total of 28 dimensions are used to compare these strategies. The first 26 are the standard dimensions defined in the Appendix. Dimension 27 (administrative cost) and dimension 28 (fertility incentive) are defined below.

Dimension 27, administrative cost, is a measure of the proportion of all funds spent on the program that go into various administrative costs. For our purposes administrative costs include all expenditures that are not income benefits to recipients. Thus, the cost of casework counseling and rehabilitation programs included as part of the AFDC program are counted as administrative expenses. A rating of 5 indicates that the administrative cost of the program is up to 3 percent of benefits paid; a rating of 3 indicates that the administrative cost is between 3 and 10 percent; and a rating of 1 indicates that the administrative cost is over 10 percent of benefits paid.

TABLE 3.1

RATINGS FOR COMPARING ALTERNATIVE INCOME STRATEGIES

DIMENSION FOR THE RATING* INCOME STRATEGY BEING RATED**

	1	2	3	4	5	6	7	8	9	10	11	12	13	14
1	3	5	3	3	3	3	4	3	4	4	3	4	5	4
2	3	5	3	3	3	3	4	3	4	4	3	4	5	4
3	3	3	3	3	3	3	3	3	3	3	3	3	5	3
4	1	4	2	3	3	3	3	3	3	3	3	3	5	3
5	1	4	4	4	4	4	4	4	4	4	4	4	5	5
6	1	5	1	1	1	1	1	1	1	1	1	1	1	2
7	1	3	1	3	3	3	3	2	1	2	2	2	1	1
8	3	3	3	3	3	3	3	3	3	3	3	3	3	3
9	3	3	3	3	3	3	3	3	3	3	3	3	5	3
10	3	3	3	3	3	3	3	3	3	3	3	3	3	3
11	5	5	5	3	3	3	3	5	5	5	5	5	5	5
12	1	5	1	1	5	5	5	5	5	5	5	5	5	5
13	5	3	3	1	1	1	1	4	4	4	4	4	5	4
14	5	1	1	1	5	5	5	5	5	5	5	5	5	5
15	5	5	5	5	5	5	5	5	5	5	5	5	5	5
16	3	5	3	5	5	5	5	5	5	5	5	5	5	5
17	1	1	1	1	1	1	1	1	1	1	1	1	1	1
18	1	5	5	5	1	1	1	5	5	5	5	5	5	3
19	3	5	5	5	3	3	3	1	1	1	1	1	1	3
20	3	5	5	5	3	3	3	3	3	3	3	3	5	5
21	3	3	2	2	4	4	4	4	5	5	5	5	5	4
22	3	3	3	3	5	5	5	5	5	5	5	5	5	5
23	5	3	1	1	1	1	1	3	3	3	3	3	1	3
24	2	3	2	2	5	5	5	3	3	3	3	3	4	3
25	5	5	3	3	5	5	5	5	5	5	5	5	5	5
26	4	5	4	4	4	4	5	4	4	4	4	4	5	4
27	1	5	3	3	5	5	5	5	5	5	5	5	5	3
28	2	4	5	5	1	1	1	3	3	3	3	3	3	3

* Dimensions 1-26 correspond to the 26 standard dimensions presented in the Appendix; 29 is administrative cost; 28 is fertility incentive.

** The numbers used to identify the 14 income strategies are to be interpreted as follows:

(1) AFDC
(2) Social Security
(3) Unemployment Insurance
(4) Workmen's Compensation
(5) Vadakin's Family Allowance Proposal
(6) Schorr's Family Allowance Proposal
(7) McGovern's Family Allowance Proposal
(8) Friedman's NIT Proposal
(9) Theobald's NIT Proposal
(10) Schwartz's NIT Proposal
(11) Tobin's NIT Proposal
(12) The Commission NIT Proposal
(13) The NWRO NIT Proposal
(14) The FAP Proposal

Dimension 28, fertility incentive, is a measure of the extent to which the program provides a fertility incentive by making benefits proportional to the number of children in the family. A rating of 5 indicates that the size of the benefits are not influenced by the size of the family; a rating of 4 indicates that family size influences the size of the benefit, but in a minor way; a rating of 3 indicates that family size is a major determinant of the size of the benefit, but family income is also a major determinant; and a rating of 1 indicates that the benefits are solely determined by the number of dependent children in the family with benefits increasing as the size of the family increases.

By way of summary a comparison will be made among the ratings of the fourteen income strategies considered above. Some dimensions are excluded because they would, to some extent, represent double counting; others are deleted because it was not clear that either a high or low rating would necessarily be a desirable characteristic. For example, some would argue that a high rating on dimension 23, percentage of benefits going to the non-poor, would be desirable because it would indicate minimal leakage to other sections of society. On the other hand, a case can also be made that a low rating would be desirable because programs which provide substantial benefits to those who are not poor are more likely to receive the political support that would be needed. For example, the Social Security program provides more income to the poor than any existing income program, but a substantial fraction of the benefits from the program actually go to those who are not poor. For the purposes of the present analysis, a subset of 18 out of the original 28 dimensions has been selected. The following dimensions were selected: 2–9, 11–12, and 14–21. For each of these dimensions the assumption is that a rating of 5 is high (positive) and that a rating of 1 is low (negative). In Table 3.2 the total number of high and low ratings as well as a difference score is presented for each of the fourteen income strategies.

If the income strategies are divided into existing programs (1–4) and proposals (5–14), it is clear that the proposals tend to receive higher ratings. This difference is most likely due in part to actual differences between the approaches and in part to the lack of full knowledge about the problems that would arise were any of the proposed programs introduced.

Of the existing programs Social Security receives by far the highest rating. One factor leading to this high rating is that it distributes far more in the way of benefits to the poor and those on the borderline of poverty than any other income program does. Another factor is that it encourages economic self-sufficiency; benefits are based on contributions the recipient has made to the program over a period of years in the form of a payroll tax on wages. Compared to the other programs, there is much more equity in the level of benefits for Social Security.

Of the existing programs, AFDC receives the lowest overall rating. Some of the factors that contribute to the low rating of this program relative to other programs are the social stigma associated with being a recipient, the tendency to encourage family instability, and the relatively high administrative cost of the program.

The NIT proposals are generally rated higher than the family allowance proposals. They tend to have more high ratings and about the same number of low ratings. The FAP proposal falls at the lower end of the range for NIT proposals which is consistent with its combining characteristics of both the NIT and the family allowance.

The NWRO negative income tax proposal receives the most high ratings and the most low ratings of any income proposal considered. It has the highest overall rating of any income proposal considered. This strategy would have a greater impact on the distribution of in-

TABLE 3.2

SUMMARY OF RATINGS FOR ALTERNATIVE INCOME STRATEGIES ON SELECTED EVALUATIVE DIMENSIONS

SUMMARY OF THE RATINGS*	INCOME STRATEGY BEING RATED**													
	1	2	3	4	5	6	7	8	9	10	11	12	13	14
HIGH	3	9	5	5	5	5	5	6	7	7	7	7	13	7
LOW	7	2	5	4	3	3	3	3	4	3	3	3	4	2
DIFFERENCE SCORE (HIGH-LOW)	-4	7	0	1	2	2	2	3	3	4	4	4	9	5

* The summary is based on dimensions 2-9, 11-12, and 14-21 of Table 3.1; the row marked HIGH is a summary of the total number of times the specified strategy received a rating of 5 in Table 3.1; the row marked LOW is a summary of the total number of times the specified strategy received a rating of 1; the DIFFERENCE SCORE is obtained by subtraction.

** The numbers used to identify the 14 income strategies are to be interpreted as follows:

(1) AFDC
(2) Social Security
(3) Unemployment Insurance
(4) Workmen's Compensation
(5) Vadakin's Family Allowance Proposal
(6) Schorr's Family Allowance Proposal
(7) McGovern's Family Allowance Proposal
(8) Friedman's NIT Proposal
(9) Theobald's NIT Proposal
(10) Schwartx's NIT Proposal
(11) Tobin's NIT Proposal
(12) The Commission NIT Proposal
(13) The NWRO NIT Proposal
(14) The FAP Proposal

come than any other income proposal presented; as will become more evident in Chapter 6, it would also have a greater impact than any of the other 62 strategies considered in this book. Related to this impact on the distribution of income would be a greater impact on the distribution of political influence, a greater contribution to a positive self-concept, and a greater reduction of the gulf between social classes. Once introduced, the proposal would be quite invulnerable to funding cutbacks, unless it proved to be highly inflationary or led to massive voluntary unemployment. But the proposal would be strongly opposed by the upper income groups who would end up paying for it. This opposition would be sufficiently intense so that the proposal cannot at present be considered politically feasible. This high rating for a politically unfeasible proposal illustrates a limitation of our rating procedure.

In the preceding discussion the comparisons between the 14 income strategies are based on a consideration of 18 dimensions, each of which is weighted equally. A similar analysis might have been carried out with a smaller or a larger set of dimensions. It would have been possible to reverse the direction of some dimensions. Another possible modification would have been to weight some dimensions more heavily than others. While the preceding ratings offer considerable flexibility for making comparisons, it is important to keep in mind that any such comparisons are necessarily restricted to the relatively small number of dimensions. For each program and proposal presented, there are a number of characteristics, both positive and negative, which do not lend themselves to such comparisons.

Credit Income Tax The credit income tax is a special case of the negative income tax. Here we will describe the credit income tax and briefly indicate how it differs from other negative income tax proposals.

What has come to be called the credit income tax was first proposed thirty years ago in England by Lady Rhys-Williams.[48] Her plan called for a "social dividend" to be paid by the government to every man, woman, and child in the country. The program was to be financed by a proportional (flat) tax on all personal income.

In this country Earl Rolph was the first to propose the approach.[49] Subsequently, Tobin, Rainwater, and Van Til have also outlined credit income tax proposals.[50] The approach received relatively little attention prior to the 1972 Presidential primary campaign. George McGovern proposed a credit income tax plan as his answer to welfare reform.[51] His proposal calls for a payment of $1,000 to every man, woman, and child in the country. The program would be financed by a proportional tax of 33 percent on all personal income. The breakeven point for a family of four would be $12,000. Below $12,000 the family would receive a net payment from the government; between $12,000 and $20,000 the family would pay a net tax, but the tax would be lower than under the existing tax structure; and a family of four with an income above $20,000 would face a greater tax burden than under the existing tax structure. McGovern's proposal came under heavy attack causing him to withdraw his support for the idea well before the end of the 1972 Presidential campaign.

All credit income tax proposals include two components: (1) the first is a system of tax credits which are sometimes referred to as a demogrant; these credits are the equivalent to the guaranteed income component of other negative income tax proposals; (2) the second component is a flat (proportional) tax on all other sources of personal income allowing no exemptions and substantially reducing the number of available deductions. Below the breakeven point the credit income tax is identical to any other negative income tax proposal. But above the breakeven point it differs from the other negative income tax proposals we have considered. It will be recalled that with the other NIT proposals there is a point at which the tax liability under the NIT is equal to the tax liability under the existing income tax structure; for incomes above that point the existing progressive income tax structure is retained. But with the credit income tax approach the entire tax structure is revised; there is no shift to the existing tax structure. The net effect of the proportional tax called for is actually somewhat progressive due to the tax credits (guaranteed income). For example, with McGovern's proposal the effective tax rate on a family of four with an income of $12,000 would be 0 percent (no net tax); but the effective rate for a family of four with an income of $24,000 would be 17 percent (there would be a $4,000 tax credit and a tax of 33 percent of $24,000 which is $8,000; the net tax would thus be $4,000 and the effective tax rate would be $4,000/$24,000 or 17 percent).

Lidman points out that the credit income tax program would involve an extensive redistribution of income in favor of large families. For example, a family of six earning $20,000 would pay approximately the same tax as a single person earning $5,000.[52] To deal with this inequity Rainwater proposes that the size of the tax credit (guaranteed income payment) increase with the age of the child. One of the proposals he considers calls for a tax credit that starts at 10 percent of the adult credit and increases with age to 100 percent of the adult credit at age 25. McGovern was also concerned that the payment be carried out in such a way as to provide roughly equivalent standards of living. The distinction he suggests is between those who are single, married, or dependents; citing Pechman he indicates that the size of the tax credit could be in the ratio of 75:100:25 so as to assure approximately the same standard of living for each of these three categories of recipients.

The strengths and weaknesses of the credit income tax are basically those of other negative income tax plans. One added strength is that the effective income tax structure would be progressive and not curvilinear as is the case with other NIT proposals. Another strength is that it would greatly simplify the whole federal income tax system and remove numerous inequitable loopholes. A liability of the approach is that it calls for a much more radical tax reform than is called for with other NIT proposals. If achieved this would be a plus, but it could well delay for several years the introduction of a guaranteed income program; the result would be a loss in social welfare benefits to the poor for a few and possibly many years. A second limitation is that it calls for a reduction in the progressiveness of the existing tax structure at higher income levels. To deal with this issue Watts has proposed that a progressive tax schedule be used as an alternative to the flat tax that is generally considered central to the concept of a credit income tax.[53] Incomes under $50,000 would be taxed at a rate of 33 percent; those between $50,000 and $100,000 would be taxed at a rate of 40 percent, and those above $100,000 per year would be taxed at a rate of 50 percent. Another limitation is that most credit income tax proposals make no provision for increasing the guaranteed income implicit in the tax credit as a function of rising incomes in the general population and inflation. To remedy this problem Gans proposes that the tax credit be set equal to 60 percent of the median income.[54] This would provide a mechanism for increasing the size of the credits as the median income rises over the years.

Notes

1. For more about the history of family allowances see James C. Vadakin, *Children, Poverty and Family Allowances* (New York: Basic Books, 1968), Chapter 3.
2. In Tunisia allowances are only paid for the first four children; in U.S.S.R. they are only paid for the fourth and subsequent children. In Chile allowances are paid for dependent adults as part of the same program. See Vadakin, *Children, Poverty and Family Allowances.*
3. Harvey E. Brazer, "The Federal Income Tax and The Poor: Where Do We Go From Here?" *California Law Review* 57, 2(1969): 422-449. His proposal calls for an allowance of $1,400 per year for the first child, $900 for the second, $600 for the third, and $400 for each additional child. The proposal calls for a reduction in the size of the allowance according to a marginal tax rate of between 30 and 40 percent depending on family income and family size.
4. Vadakin, *Children, Poverty and Family Allowances,* Chapter 7. Vadakin specifies that all families would be eligible for this allowance as long as the children's attendance in school was satisfactory. He estimates that the gross cost of the program would have been $8.6 billion in 1968 and of this $1.3 billion would have been recovered through income taxes.
5. Alvin L. Schorr, *Poor Kids* (New York: Basic Books, 1966), Chapter 9. Schorr estimates that the gross cost of the proposal would have been $14.9 billion in 1964 and that $9 billion would have been recovered in taxes. The discrepancies between estimates cited in the text and estimates in the footnotes are because the estimates in the footnotes are for different years.
6. See George McGovern, "A Human Security Plan," (an address before Citizen's Committee for Children, New York, N.Y., Jan. 20, 1970). Also see "Background Material on Senator McGovern's Human Security Program," (Office of Senator McGovern, n.d.). The data as to the proportion of the poor raised out of poverty is from Mollie Orshansky, "Who Was Poor in 1966," *Research and Statistics.* Note No. 23 (1967), Office of Research and Statistics, Social Security Administration, Department of Health Education and Welfare, Tables 18-21.
7. A family allowance program has been proposed for the U.S. which includes a steep progressive tax on other income, which would be used to reduce the size of the allowance. See Brazer, "The Federal Income Tax and The Poor." The Nixon Administration's Family Assistance Plan (FAP) is basically a family allowance plan with a special tax on earnings until the allowance is reduced to zero.
8. Harold W. Watts, "Adjusted and Extended Preliminary Results from the Urban Graduated Work Incentive Experiment," (Discussion Paper 69-70

revised, Institute for Research on Poverty, University of Wisconsin, 1970).

9. Joel F. Handler and Ellen Jane Hollingsworth, "How Obnoxious is the 'Obnoxious Means Tests'?" *Wisconsin Law Review* 1, (1970): 114-135.

10. The estimate of 29 percent of the poor receiving AFDC was made under the assumption that all AFDC payments went to the poor. This somewhat overstates the percentage of the poor receiving benefits because some AFDC benefits go to the nonpoor. The calculation is based on data from U.S. Bureau of the Census, *Statistical Abstract of the United States: 1970* 91st ed. (Washington, D.C.: U.S. Government Printing Office, 1970) pp. 297,328. In 1963, 70 percent of the poor lived in families with dependent children. At that time 18 percent of the poor living in families were in families without any dependent children. Assuming that 18 percent of the poor living in families were in families without dependent children in 1968, the calculation can be made that 67 percent of the poor lived in families with dependent children in 1968. In short, there is little evidence of any change between 1963 and 1968. See Mollie Orshansky, "Counting the Poor: Another Look At The Poverty Profile," *Social Security Bulletin* 28, 3(1965): 3-29.

11. A negative income tax program would extend benefits to all the poor if the breakeven point was above the poverty line. For many, but not all, proposals the breakeven point is above the poverty line.

12. In Germany a family allowance was used in the effort to increase fertility during the 1930s. There was an increase in the birth rate from 15 to 20 births per 1000 population, but so many other changes were being made in the effort to increase fertility that it is not clear how much of the increase can be attributed to the family allowance. At that time the sale of contraceptives was made illegal, abortion was suppressed, the distribution of birth control information was made illegal, taxes were made more favorable to large families, job preference was given to men with large families and the economy was improving. See Schorr, *Poor Kids,* p.72. and Vadakin, *Children, Poverty and Family Allowances,* p. 98.

13. Vadakin, *Children, Poverty and Family Allowance*, p. 104.

14. *Ibid.*, p. 60.

15. These estimates were made on the basis of 1969 figures for total spending for the Social Security program and total cash payments (this excluded medical payment-in-kind) to Public Assistance recipients. To make the estimate of the payment to the poor, the estimates by Green for the percentage of funds for each of these programs going to the poor in 1961 were used. See *Statistical Abstract of the United States 1970,* pp. 284,297, Tables 426 and 449. Also see Christopher Green, *Negative Taxes and the Poverty Problem* (Washington, D.C.: Brookings Institution, 1967), p. 20.

16. Milton Friedman, *Capitalism and Freedom* (Chicago: University of Chicago Press, 1962), p. 190-195.

17. The idea of a negative income tax had been discussed for several years prior to Friedman's proposal, but his was much more fully worked out. Stigler had discussed the idea of extending the personal income tax to include negative income tax rates in 1946. See George Stigler, "The Economics of Minimum Wage Legislation," *American Economic Review* 36, 3(1946): 358-365.

18. The Internal Revenue Service makes an exhaustive check on approximately 10 percent of income tax returns. Persons who have been involved with irregularities in the past are more likely to be checked.
19. In 1962 the exemptions for a family of four came to $2,400. In 1970 they came to $2,450. In 1962 there was no minimum deduction so that it would be zero for a family with no income. In 1970 there was a low income allowance that was effectively a minimum deduction of $1,100. Thus the total of exemptions and minimum deductions was $2,400 in 1962 and $3,550 in 1970.
20. Hildebrand estimates the cost of the proposal at roughly $10 billion on the basis of 1963 data. See George H. Hildebrand, "Second Thoughts on the Negative Income Tax," *Industrial Relations* 6, 2(1967): 138-154. His estimate is based on a guaranteed minimum income of $1,500 per year for a family of four in 1963. In another discussion he illustrates that cost estimates ranging from $1.5 billion to $11 billion are possible, depending on a number of assumptions. See George H. Hildebrand, *Poverty Income Maintenance and The Negative Income Tax* (Ithaca, N.Y.: New York State School of Industrial and Labor Relations, 1967),pp. 29-30.
21. Friedman, *Capitalism and Freedom,* p. 193.
22. Robert Theobald, *Free Men and Free Markets* (Garden City, N.Y.: Doubleday, 1963), pp. 155-163.
23. Robert Theobald, ed. *The Guaranteed Income* (Garden City, N.Y.: Doubleday, 1965), p. 18.
24. Vadakin estimates the cost of the proposal as between $25 and $30 billion. See James C. Vadakin, "A Critique of the Guaranteed Annual Income," *Public Interest* 11, (Spring, 1968): 53-66.
25. Edward E. Schwartz, "A Way to End the Means Test," *Social Work* 9, 3(1964): 3-12. Schwartz estimates the cost of the program at $11 billion per year in 1964. He also gives cost estimates for similar programs utilizing higher levels of guaranteed minimum income. At $4,000 per year the estimated cost is $23 billion and at $5,000 per year the estimated cost is $38 billion.
26. Tobin estimates the cost of his proposal for 1965 at $15 billion per year. This estimate does not take into consideration the savings in Public Assistance. The proposal as described by Tobin applies to a family of five. The breakeven point for such a family is $6,000 and the point at which the net tax liability equalled that under the existing system would have been $7,963. See James Tobin, "Improving the Economic Status of the Negro," *Daedalus* 94, 4(1965): 878-898. For a more recent and somewhat different proposal by Tobin, see James Tobin, Joseph A. Pechman, Peter Miezhowski, "Is a Negative Income Tax Practical," *Yale Law Journal* 77, 1(1967): 1-27.
27. The Commission estimates the net cost of the program for 1971 at $6 billion. This figure takes into consideration savings in Public Assistance and other federally supported programs which takes income into consideration in the computation of benefits. *Report of the President's Commission on Income Maintenance, Poverty Amid Plenty,* Ben W. Heineman, Chairman, (Washington, D.C.: Government Printing Office, 1969).
28. The bill is referred to as S.3780; it was introduced into the U.S. Senate in April 1970.

29. The Bureau of Labor Statistics prepares estimates of the amount of income that is necessary to live at various standards of living. The Social Security Administration's poverty line is based on the Department of Agriculture's Low-Cost Food Plan. Only one-fourth of those living at this level have nutritionally adequate diets. The low standard budget of the Bureau of Labor Statistics assures that a higher proportion of families would have adequate diets. But even at this higher standard of living some families will have inadequate diets because they choose to spend their money on other things. For a description of the low standard budget see S.3780 and U.S. Department of Labor, Bureau of Labor Statistics, *Bulletin* No. 1570-5, 1969.
30. See National Welfare Rights Organization, "Guaranteed Adequate Income: A Social Program for the 1970s," (n.d.), and "NWRO Proposals for a Guaranteed Adequate Income," (n.d.). For the $71 billion estimate see Melville J. Ulmer, "The Family Assistance Plan: Work and Welfare," *New Republic* 165, 1(1971): 12-14.
31. See Robert J. Lampman, "Expanding the American System of Transfers to do More for the Poor," *Wisconsin Law Review* 2, (1969): 541-549. This proposal is presented in Table 2.
32. Green, *Negative Taxes and the Poverty Problem,* pp. 127, 139, 141.
33. This proposal is a modified version of Plan II-D as described in Robert J. Lampman, "Negative Rates Income Taxation," (unpublished paper prepared for Office of Economic Opportunity, August 1965). Lampman's original proposal called for a 75 percent tax rate on the first $1,500 in outside income, and a 33 percent tax rate on the next $1,500 in outside income. These conditions are inconsistent with the $3,000 breakeven point he indicates. They also leave the tax rate between $3,000 and the actual breakeven point unspecified. The modification which has been introduced yields a breakeven point of $3,500 and specifies the tax rate at all incomes below this breakeven point.
34. The information presented here is drawn from the following two papers. Harold W. Watts, "Adjusted and Extended Preliminary Results from the Urban Graduated Work Incentive Experiment," (discussion paper 69-70, revised, Institute for Research on Poverty, University of Wisconsin, 1970); David M. Kershaw, "The Negative Income Tax Experiment in New Jersey," (paper presented at the conference on Public Welfare Issues, New Brunswick, N.J.: April 26, 1969).
35. Green, *Negative Taxes and the Poverty Problem,* pp. 139-141. This is Green's Plan D-2: Adjusted.
36. Green, *Ibid.,* pp. 140-141. This is Green's Plan E: Earnings not reduced.
37. Ulmer, "The Family Assistance Plan: Work and Welfare." He points out that the government estimate of the cost of the program is $6.5 billion. For a detailed discussion of the FAP proposal see Daniel P. Moynihan, *The Politics of a Guaranteed Income,* (New York: Random House, 1973)
38. Watts, "Adjusted and Extended Preliminary Results from the Urban Graduated Work Incentive Experiment." The lack of disincentive effect with a 70 percent marginal tax rate may be influenced by the recipient's knowledge that the experiment will last only three years. If the program were longer term, there might well be a substantial work disincentive with a 70 percent tax rate.

39. Cost estimates made by the present authors do not take into consideration any savings in other federal programs as a consequence of the introduction of a NIT. They assume no change in work effort or fertility. Separate calculations were made for families and unrelated individuals. The assumption was made that all families were the size of the mean family.
40. One such source is Heineman, *Poverty Amid Plenty,* p. 61. Other sources presenting cost estimates for several programs include Green, *Negative Taxes and the Poverty Problem,* p. 141; Hildebrand, *Poverty Income*; Robert J. Lampman, "Transfer Approaches to Distribution Policy," *The American Economic Review* 60, 2(1970): 270-279.
41. Watts, "Adjusted and Extended Preliminary Results from the Urban Graduated Work Incentive Experiment.
42. The NWRO proposal would take into consideration savings in excess of $10,000 but this is a sufficiently high limit that it would have little effect on most of the poor.
43. Theodore Marmor, "On Comparing Income Maintenance Alternatives," *American Political Science Review* 65, 1(1971): 83-96.
44. Watts, "Adjusted and Extended Preliminary Results from the Urban Graduated Work Incentive Experiment."
45. Schorr, *Poor Kids,* Ch. 5.
46. For a discussion of the difficulty the poor have in planning the size of their families see Lee Rainwater, *And the Poor Get Children,* (Chicago: Quadrangle, 1960). pp. 59, 167.
47. See Lewis Yablonsky, *The Hippie Trip,* (New York: Western Publishing Company, 1968).
48. Lady Juliette Rhys–Williams, *Something to Look Forward To* (London: MacDonald, 1943).
49. Earl R. Rolph, "The Case for a Negative Income Tax Device," *Industrial Relations* 6, 2(1967): 155-165.
50. See James Tobin, "Raising the Incomes of the Poor," in *Agenda for the Nation* ed. by Kermit Gordon (Washington: The Brookings Institution, 1968); Lee Rainwater, "Economic Inequality and the Credit Income Tax," *Working Papers for a New Society* 1, 1(1973): 50-61; and Arthur B. Shostak, Jon Van Til, and Sally Bould Van Til, *Privilege in America: An End to Inequality?* (Englewood Cliffs, N.J.: Prentice-Hall, 1973), Chapter 8.
51. George McGovern, "George McGovern: On Taxing and Redistributing Income," *The New York Review of Books,* (May 4, 1972). pp. 7-11.
52. Russell Lidman, "Costs and Distributional Implications of McGovern's Minimum Income Grant Proposal," Discussion Paper 131-72 (Madison, Wisconsin: University of Wisconsin, Institute for Research on Poverty, 1972).
53. Harold Watts, "Income Redistribution: How It Is and How It Can Be," unpublished paper for the Democratic Platform Hearings, June 17, 1972.
54. Herbert J. Gans, *More Equality* (New York: Pantheon, 1973), Chapter 6.

4

Income-In-Kind

Income-in-kind programs provide income in the form of basic goods and services. Our discussion focuses on four major categories of income-in-kind: housing, food, medical care, and social services. Before turning to a description of specific income-in-kind strategies, we will consider some assumptions that are implicit in this approach.

ASSUMPTIONS IMPLICIT IN THE INCOME-IN-KIND APPROACH

The present discussion is limited to those assumptions common to all or most income-in-kind strategies. Assumptions peculiar to individual strategies or programs are dealt with later.

The most basic assumption implicit in the income-in-kind approach is that due to ignorance, immaturity or immorality the poor are unable to make the decisions which would provide them with the basic goods and services required for their health and welfare. Thus, a number of subsidy plans have been devised all of which insure that basic goods and services, but not cash, are distributed directly to the poor.

Secondly, it is assumed that poverty is a temporary condition and income-in-kind is needed only until the poor cease to be poor and can afford to pay for these goods and services themselves. Most income-in-kind programs are not conceived as strategies to eliminate poverty but rather as a means of easing the effects of poverty until a particular family, individual, or group become upwardly mobile. This assumption may operate to limit the design, funding, and consequent impact of individual programs.

EVALUATION OF THE INCOME-IN-KIND APPROACH

In this section, arguments will be summarized which can be made regarding the advantages and disadvantages of the income-in-kind approach as a general strategy against poverty. We first consider the advantages of the income-in-kind strategy.

The income-in-kind strategy is a necessary corrective for a faulty private market system. Given the basic structure of our economic system scarcity is a fact of life. At any given point in time there is a fixed amount of resources which are distributed by the private market system according to ability to pay. Experience has shown that the private market mechanism has been unable to satisfy the basic needs of all people for such things as food, shelter, and health care. When this is the case, it is the responsibility of government to use its resources to correct this fault and to insure that all people's basic needs are met.

It circumvents the problem of faulty consumer choice. Some families, either due to ignorance or value preferences, do not choose to spend their income for the basic goods and services which adequate health and welfare require. Thus, income-in-kind programs are preferable to direct income payments because they ensure that families will receive the benefits that are most needed.

It meets the immediate needs of the poor. Food, shelter, health and equal justice are needs which cannot wait to be met. The income-in-kind approach to poverty is designed to meet these basic needs in an immediate way. This is not true of an approach such as education or economic development.

The following are some of the limitations of the income-in-kind strategy:

Most income-in-kind programs suffer from administrative difficulties. Determination of eligibility is usually a cumbersome process and often the actual administration of the benefits requires a separate delivery system with serious management and financial problems.

It often results in an inequitable distribution of benefits. Most income-in-kind programs involve a large measure of local control. One consequence of this is the lack of uniformity in benefit levels with large differences between regions, states, and even counties.

Participants in income-in-kind programs are often stigmatized. Participation in most income-in-kind programs encourages the labeling of people as "welfare families." This can occur through the procedures of establishing eligibility. It can result from the actual process of receiving the benefit (waiting in line), or it may be a function of using the benefit as when a family lives in a public housing project or shops with food stamps.

The quality of goods and services provided by income-in-kind programs is inferior. Goods and services produced and distributed in a non competitive environment are likely to be of lower quality and more expensive than similar products which are sold on a competitive market. Because there is a guaranteed market for the goods and services provided in these programs, many private entrepreneurs who are depended upon by the government to supply the necessary goods can take advantage of the program by charging higher prices for participation or by producing inferior products. Thus, local merchants have been known to raise their food prices when food stamps are distributed, landlords raise their rents to the maximum when they participate in the Leased Housing program, developers construct poor quality homes under the 235 Homeownership program, and public defenders make only a token effort when defending the poor.

Most income-in-kind programs encourage economic dependency. Income-in-kind programs encourage the formation of dependency habits. There are no mechanisms for helping people disengage from participation. There are no work incentives and some programs have a built in disincentive to work in the form of a sliding income scale to determine level of benefits. Thus, the amount of subsidy will decrease as income rises in most programs.

Freedom of choice is restricted by the income-in-kind strategy. Unlike direct income, manpower, education, and community development programs, income-in-kind programs do not enlarge the sphere of opportunity of poor people. They either restrict the poor to choose from a narrow range of goods and services or offer no choice at all except the decision of whether to participate or not.

HOUSING

This section deals with housing, perhaps the most basic of all income-in-kind strategies. The discussion is both descriptive and evaluative. The major programs, proposals and policies which have had or could have a significant impact on the supply of low income housing, its quality, and the housing choice of low income families are described. We examine the assumptions implicit in the housing approach and conclude with a comparison between alternative housing strategies along 26 dimensions.

The federal government has been actively involved in the housing field since the 1930s. However, evolution of a low-income housing strategy did not take shape until 1949 when the Housing Act of that year initiated basic revisions of the Public Housing program and the beginnings of the controversial Urban Renewal program. It was in this Act that the often repeated goal of the federal housing strategy was first made explicit: "The realization as soon as feasible of the goal of a decent home and suitable living environment for every American family."

Since 1949, federal low income housing policy has evolved rapidly with a variety of innovations and much controversy. Overall, however, the total effort has been rather small consisting of perhaps 2 percent of the existing housing stock. In general, it can be said that federal policy has been directed toward increasing the total housing supply and improving the existing stock A guiding assumption has been that the problem of housing for low income families is primarily one of an inadequate supply rather than a matter of ineffective demand. Critics of such an approach would choose to focus on the problem of demand and suggest that increasing the purchasing power of the poor would do more to improve their housing than all the existing subsidy and public housing programs. Two ways of doing this that have been suggested are the negative income tax and the national housing allowance proposal.

Conventional Public Housing:[1] Public Housing is the oldest and largest of federal housing programs. The Housing Act of 1937 created the program, but in its present form as a low income housing program it is primarily the result of the Housing Act of 1949. This legislation authorizes local housing authorities to develop, own and operate rental units for low income families.

Leased Housing:[2] Leased Housing was added to the Housing Act of 1937 as a part of the Public Housing program by the Housing and Urban Development Act of 1965. It authorizes local authorities to lease privately owned dwelling units and then make them available to low income tenants on the same terms as they would conventional units. Initially the program was intended to utilize only existing stock, but in practice a substantial number have been newly constructed.

Rent Supplement:[3] This program was authorized by Title 1 of the Housing and Urban Development Act of 1965. It consists of a subsidy which takes the form of a direct payment to the owner of a private unit, making up the difference between 25 percent of the tenant's income and existing market rentals.

235 Homeownership:[4] This program was initiated in 1968 by the

Housing and Urban Development Act. It represents the first effort by the federal government to extend subsidies to low income families for the purchase of homes. The program is designed to reach families within the $3,000 to $8,000 income range. The actual subsidy is known as an "interest subsidy" and goes to the private lender who finances the purchase. In actual practice the developer is the middleman who locates potential buyers, helps them to get certified by HUD, assists them in their dealing with the private lender, and is reimbursed for this entire package of services by the lending institution.

National Housing Allowance:[5] This is a proposed program which is in some respects similar to a negative income tax proposal. The federal government would provide a subsidy to low income households to be used to meet housing expenses. The subsidy would make up the difference between that fraction of family income that the typical family spends on housing (say 20 percent) and the actual cost of adequate housing in the specified area. The size of the subsidy would vary directly with family size and the cost of housing in the area and inversely with family income. The subsidy would take the form of a voucher or in some other way be restricted to meeting housing expenses. The proposal being considered would reach approximately 8 million households; it would cost $8 billion annually of which $7 billion would be disbursed as benefits and $6 billion would reach the poor.

Assumptions Implicit In The Housing Approach A basic assumption of housing as well as the income-in-kind approach more generally is that the poor are unable, due to certain individual shortcomings, to make decisions as consumers that will insure their basic health and welfare.

Another assumption which is implicit in the housing approach is that the poor have a fairly low value preference for housing relative to other consumer items such as automobiles and clothing. This is related to the economist's argument that the elasticity of demand for housing is low. The current supply approach to the low income housing issue is consistent with this assumption. The poor, in this view, cannot be depended upon to allocate enough of their resources to housing. Such an assumption is closely related to the first one mentioned above, though it does not carry the same moralistic overtones.

As federal low income housing policy has moved to acknowledge importance of residential location as an independent variable, two other related assumptions have become apparent. One states that poverty is more than a lack of money. It is also a way of life rooted in a particular physical, social and cultural milieu. Changes in this milieu are necessary if poverty is to be eliminated. In the case of the more recent housing strategies, these changes are not viewed as the result of community organization and renewal in low income areas, but of relocation of the poor into more affluent neighborhoods.

The second and closely related assumption implicit in the new housing policies is that opportunity is the key to understanding poverty. The assumption is made that the cause of poverty is not primarily individual inadequacy or failure, but the absence of opportunity structures such as quality jobs, schools, government, and public services which make a decent and fulfilling life possible. It is clear that the location of a person's residence is a crucial factor which must be dealt with when considering ways to eliminate poverty.

The housing allowance strategy operates with some, but not all, of these assumptions. It does not assume, for instance, that the poor are unable to operate effectively with cash in the private market for housing. However, this would be less true if such a program were over regulated and the poor were made to account for every penny spent and every decision made.

In addition, this strategy does not assume that poverty is a temporary condition, the effects of which must be eased until individuals can overcome them. The assumption is rather, that an unequal distribution of income and other basic resources is endemic to modern industrial societies, and that some permanent redistributive process must be established to correct the situation.

The assumption that the poor have a fairly low value preference for housing is operative in the housing allowance approach to the degree that program regulations insure that the allowance is allocated to housing. Conceivably, the program could be structured so that allowance recipients would be free to spend the money in any way they choose. However, it is more likely that a program which is politically feasible would regulate the process more closely.

Evaluation Of The Housing Strategy The following are some of the arguments that have been made in support of housing as an antipoverty strategy:

The private market system has failed to provide adequate shelter at a reasonable cost for a large minority of American households. Adequate shelter is a basic human need which is not being met through the private market for a very large percentage of the poor. The President's Commision on Urban Housing estimated that there were about 7.8 million "housing-poor" families in the United States in 1968. These are people who need some form of a subsidy in order to obtain a decent home. They include both the poor and the near poor. These noneffective demand households include families and individuals who would have to pay more than 20 percent of their income for adequate shelter in the absence of a subsidy. In 1960 dollars, the minimum income required to insure a family of four inside an SMSA standard housing was around $3,700. By 1973 that would be approximately $4,500.

There are important external benefits related to housing. Housing is more than shelter. An effective housing strategy could be the key to the elimination of poverty. The external benefits of the quality and location of a person's residence are very great. It has been found that density within dwelling units is related to emotional strain, the extent of social relationships outside the home, and the nature of the parent-child relationship. The location of one's home establishes certain limits to the quality of education available for one's children, the types and quality of education available to the adults, and the quality of other public services such as recreational facilities, police protection, trash and garbage collection, and public transportation. In short, where a person lives and what he lives in are basic determinants of his life chances.

Housing is perceived by the poor as their basic problem. When asked, the poor make it very clear that housing and matters related directly to housing are the problems of greatest concern to them. They feel and think and suffer a great deal in relation to housing. Core city dwellers have expressed dissatisfaction about many aspects of their lives but their dominant complaints have to do with cost and quality of housing and their relationship with their landlord.

Racial residential segregation is on the increase. Recent trends indicate that in our major metropolitan areas instances of increases in the extent of segregation substantially outnumber instances of reduction in residential segregation. Thirty-one percent of all non-whites were poor in 1969. It is clear that race is a more important determinant of where a person lives and the quality of his shelter than is income. Census data on housing and race used by Taeuber to construct a segregation index show that during the decade of the sixties when some progress was being made in closing the gap between income and educational levels of whites and non-whites, the housing market in at least one major city was functioning to increase segregation.[6] Without the intervention of government at some level this situation is not likely to be reversed.

The poor pay a large proportion of their income for housing. A recent survey showed that the elderly, who make up close to 30 percent of all the poor, were paying 34 percent of their income for rent in 1971. The GE TEMPO study suggests that most poor families are paying in excess of 20 percent of their income for rent or mortgage payments. One survey has shown that 70 percent of welfare recipients in a Washington, D.C. study spent from 25 to 55 percent of their total incomes for rent alone while 40 percent spent at least half.[7] This is as good an indicator as any of the central importance of housing in the lives of the poor. The average American family spends around 15 percent of its income for rent or mortgage payment. These comparative figures suggest both the importance of housing and the seriousness of the problem. Our national policies should include some method or set of methods that will both insure quality housing for low income families, and insure it in such a way that they will not have to spend more than 20 percent of their income for it.

The income elasticity of demand for housing is low. This argument states that as income increases a smaller proportion of total income is spent on housing. Thus, it is unlikely that income subsidies which are not tied directly to housing will be spent by the poor to improve their situation in this regard. Rather, the increased income might be diverted to other items such as clothing, a new car, or leisure time activities. Many people, including some economists, feel that this argument has never really been proven or, if once true, that it is no longer the case. Netzer suggests that it does not take into account the possibility that consumers' tastes have changed since the Second World War. He notes that for the most part, statistical evidence for the argument is pre-1950. People may be placing a higher value on adequate housing today than they did in the 1940s and before. Thus, housing expenditures are possibly becoming much more sensitive to increases in income, reflecting a kind of reordering of family priorities. A second problem with the low elasticity argument has to do with the interpretation of the data itself. The data is cross-sectional, which is to say that it takes households in the aggregate at a particular point of time and compares the housing expenditures of people in one income bracket with those in another. This type of data does not reveal how a particular household at a particular stage of the family and lifetime earning cycles changes its expenditures as it moves to the next stage of the family growth or earnings cycle.[8] Along this line, it is quite possible that stability of income rather than level of income, or long-range expectations of earnings rather than short range prospects are the crucial factors determining housing expenditures.

Political support for housing programs is generally good. Politicians of all persuasions will agree that the private housing market is unable, without some sort of federal or state assistance, to provide adequate housing for low income families. The issue is not whether the government should intervene, but how it should do so. Conservatives insist on providing only the bare necessities, in this case, shelter, and on bringing the private money and housing markets into the process. Liberals, for the most part, are willing to try anything that will get the job done, but are also interested in using the housing programs to pursue other goals such as integration.

The following are some criticisms that have been made of the housing strategy:

On the basis of performance our overall low income housing policy is a failure. In 22 years of intentional low income housing policy the federal government has managed to supply approximately 1 million units. This is less than 2 percent of the total housing stock. Poor families today make up about 12 percent of the population. The GE TEMPO study estimates that there were 7.8 million housing-poor families in the United States in 1968.

Low income housing programs are wasteful and benefit groups other than the poor. It appears that too frequently private developers and landlords take advantage of housing programs. Poor quality units have been constructed and rents kept at the maximum.

Housing programs have contributed to segregation by race and class. Conventional Public Housing accounts for 64 percent of the publicly assisted housing stock and an even higher percentage of low (rather than moderate) income units. These units are typically located in low income black ghettos in the core cities.

Housing programs are not equitable. The benefits of most housing programs are distributed unevenly among the poor. Rural areas, where the incidence of poverty is the greatest, are systematically excluded from the benefits of most programs. Taggart discusses several reasons for this, one of the most important being the relative absence of financial institutions with the capital and skills to take advantage of the various programs. Inequities are also apparent between areas of the country and between cities of different sizes. Areas and cities with high development costs are unable to take advantage of construction programs with rigid cost limits. Both the Rent Supplement and the 235 Homeownership programs have been confronted with this problem.

Comparing Housing Strategies In this section, the five housing strategies discussed above are rated using the 26 standard dimensions defined in the Appendix. In Table 4.1 the following strategies are compared: (1) Conventional Public Housing, (2) Leased Housing, (3) Rent Supplement, (4) the 235 Homeownerhip program, and (5) the proposed National Housing Allowance. The availability of comparative data was the primary consideration in the selection of which programs to rate. The housing allowance was chosen because it offers a basic alternative to present housing strategies.

In an effort to summarize the ratings presented in Table 4.1, we have selected 18 dimensions for evaluative comparisons. We have excluded some of the original dimensions to reduce redundancy and others because a high rating could not unambiguously be considered a positive rating.

Several observations can be made on the basis of the material presented in Table 4.2. The most obvious conclusion is that the three rental programs receive uniformly low ratings. As it turns out, of the 63 strategies rated in this book, these three receive the lowest rating.

TABLE 4.1

RATINGS FOR COMPARING ALTERNATIVE HOUSING AND FOOD STRATEGIES

DIMENSION FOR THE RATING*	STRATEGY BEING RATED**							
	HOUSING					FOOD		
	1	2	3	4	5	6	7	8
1	1	1	1	1	1	1	1	1
2	2	2	2	2	4	3	2	2
3	1	1	1	1	3	1	1	1
4	1	3	1	5	3	1	1	3
5	4	4	4	5	5	4	4	4
6	1	1	1	5	1	1	1	2
7	1	1	1	3	1	1	1	3
8	1	1	1	5	1	3	3	3
9	1	1	1	5	5	3	3	3
10	1	1	1	3	3	3	3	3
11	1	1	1	1	5	5	5	5
12	1	1	5	5	5	1	1	1
13	4	4	4	4	5	5	2	4
14	1	1	1	1	5	1	5	1
15	5	5	5	5	5	5	5	5
16	1	1	1	1	5	3	1	3
17	3	3	3	3	1	1	1	3
18	1	3	1	1	5	1	1	1
19	3	1	1	5	3	1	1	5
20	3	3	3	3	5	3	3	3
21	2	1	1	1	5	3	3	4
22	3	1	1	1	5	3	3	3
23	3	3	5	1	3	3	3	1
24	2	1	1	1	3	3	2	4
25	5	5	5	5	5	5	5	5
26	3	2	2	1	4	4	3	4

* Dimensions 1-26 correspond to the 26 standard dimensions presented in the Appendix.

** The numbers used to identify the 5 housing and 3 food strategies are to be interpreted as follows:

(1) Coventional Public Housing
(2) Leased Housing
(3) Rent Supplement
(4) 235 Homeownership
(5) National Housing Allowance
(6) Food Stamps
(7) Commodity Distribution
(8) School Lunches

The four existing programs are all rated lower than the national housing allowance proposal. The high rating for the latter suggests that it does offer an attractive alternative to existing housing strategies. Here, as throughout the book, caution must be exercised when comparing the ratings of programs with the ratings of proposals. It is likely that a number of unanticipated problems would arise were a proposal introduced as a program; consequently the rating indicated may be somewhat inflated.

The 235 Homeownership program has a substantially higher overall rating than any of the other existing housing programs. Among the factors contributing to its high rating are its positive impact on self-concept due to the psychic benefits people derive in the form of increased status and security when purchasing their own home; its encouragement of economic self-sufficiency; its impact with respect to racial integration; the equity in benefit levels; and its popularity among those who are not poor.

TABLE 4.2

SUMMARY OF RATINGS FOR ALTERNATIVE HOUSING AND FOOD STRATEGIES ON SELECTED EVALUATIVE DIMENSIONS

SUMMARY OF THE RATINGS*	STRATEGY BEING RATED**							
	HOUSING					FOOD		
	1	2	3	4	5	6	7	8
HIGH	1	1	2	8	10	2	3	3
LOW	11	11	12	6	4	9	9	4
DIFFERENCE SCORE (HIGH-LOW)	-10	-10	-10	2	6	-7	-6	-1

* The summary is based on dimensions 2-9, 11-12, and 14-21 of Table 4.1; the row marked HIGH is a summary of the total number of times the specified strategy received a rating of 5 in Table 4.1; the row marked LOW is a summary of the total number of times the specified strategy received a rating of 1; the DIFFERENCE SCORE is obtained by subtraction.

** The numbers used to identify the 5 housing and 3 food strategies are to be interpreted as follows:

(1) Coventional Public Housing
(2) Leased Housing
(3) Rent Supplement
(4) 235 Homeownership
(5) National Housing Allowance
(6) Food Stamps
(7) Commodity Distribution
(8) School Lunches

FOOD

There is clearly an inverse relationship between income and malnutrition. The Citizens' Board of Inquiry, after reviewing the available evidence and conducting field interviews of their own all around the country, concluded that the incidence of malnutrition in 1968 was highly correlated with income. They felt a conservative estimate would be that from one-third to one-half of all people living in families below the poverty line were affected by hunger and malnutrition. The nation wide Household Consumption Study conducted by the Department of Agriculture in 1965, found that the diets of 20 percent of all American families were "poor" according to the National Research Council standards. Further, it was found that 36 percent of households with incomes below $3,000 had "poor" diets, while nearly two-thirds of the poor, or around 20 million people, were eating less than a "satisfactory" diet according to these same NRC standards.

The effects of malnutrition are many. They may be direct or indirect. There is unambiguous evidence that malnutrition increases the risk of infant death and vulnerability to disease. While the argument is frequently made that malnutrition contributes to organic brain damage, there are authorities who argue that except in situations of extreme food deprivation, there is no evidence to support such a relationship. But, even though malnutrition as it occurs in the United States rarely results in organic brain damage, it does adversely affect school performance due to effects on the ability to learn, remember, and concentrate. Thus, in the long run, the malnourished child may fall several years behind in intellectual development. Studies clearly suggest too that there is a kind of vicious cycle of poverty—malnutrition—retardation—poverty. It seems clear that a comprehensive anti-poverty strategy must include some measures to assure every American an adequate diet.

The federal government sponsors several food programs for the poor. The three largest, and the ones which will be discussed here, are the Food Stamp program, Commodity Distribution, and the National School Lunch program.

These programs have come under severe criticism in the past five years. The Citizens' Board of Inquiry determined that in 1968 the Food Stamp and Commodity Distribution programs were reaching only about 18 percent of the poor. They found that neither had been adopted in more than one-third of the poorest counties in the United States. The School Lunch program, they noted, was benefiting about 2 million, or only one-third of all poor school children. Further, they noted that while malnutrition had risen sharply among the poor during the past decade, participation in government food programs dropped by about 1.4 million in the previous six years. Overall, the Board painted a rather bleak picture of lack of knowlege, interest, and commitment on the part of both the executive and legislative branches of our federal government.

Since the report of the Citizens' Board of Inquiry, a second critical study, this one of the National School Lunch program, has been made. In addition, the Select Committee on Nutrition and Human Needs of the United States Senate, chaired by Senator George McGovern, has conducted extensive hearings on the operation and impact of federal food programs. The result of all these efforts seems to have been to spur the government into increasing their efforts to make food programs reach the poor. In 1971, the government announced a new set of regulations for the Food Stamp program. The overall effect is expected to increase benefits and extend coverage. Even prior to this, the performance of the Food Stamp program had improved immeasurably since 1968. In 1971, there were 14 million persons benefiting from the Food Stamp and Commodity Distribution programs. This was a 40 percent increase over a year earlier and more than twice the number participating in 1968. The Food Stamp program alone accounted for 10 million of the total. The National School Lunch program has been expanded too. In 1968 it was estimated to be reaching approximately 20 million school children of whom 2 million were poor. In 1971, the Department of Agriculture announced that 7 million children received free or reduced price lunches, and a total of 24 million school children were participating. While it is true that not all of those receiving free or reduced price lunches were poor, it is likely the number exceeded by far the 2 million figure of three years earlier.

Assumptions Implicit In The Food Approach In this section some of the assumptions about the poor and the nature of poverty which are implicit in food strategies will be considered. It will be recalled that earlier two assumptions implicit in the income-in-kind approach were discussed. These are also applicable to food strategies. For example, such strategies assume that the poor are unable to use cash in the market place in such a way as to insure an adequate diet for themselves and their families. It is believed instead that the money will be channeled into other directions or spent on food items which are low in nutritional value. Secondly, food strategies have operated for many years with the assumption that poverty was a temporary condition and the purpose of food programs was to ease its effects until people were able to afford an adequate diet. There was no recognition that for many families poverty was a permanent way of life, and the need for a subsidy to insure against hunger and malnutrition was a long-term need. Thus, many of the poor could conceivably be shopping with food stamps or eating surplus commodities for the rest of their lives.

There are contradictions present in the Commodity Distribution program. On the one hand, food strategies assume the existence of faulty consumer choice and thus provide food directly to the poor or, in the case of food stamps, insure that the benefits will be converted into food. Yet, the commodity program is essentially a strategy to supplement existing diets and assumes that the poor will continue to spend the same amount of money on food subsequent to receiving commodities as they did prior to participation. If they do this, however, the poor are clearly acting contrary to the first assumption, which is that they cannot be depended upon to spend cash out of their own pocket for food, when they could stay alive on a minimal diet and devote the money to something else. It would seem that at least one of these assumptions is less than satisfactory.

Implicit in the Food Stamp program is the assumption as to the consumption levels necessary for families of a particular size and income level. For example, families of the same size in the same area do not receive equal benefits if one earns more than the other. While the family with the lower income will receive the largest subsidy, the family with the higher income will be required to purchase stamps with a higher face value. Thus, although they are of the same size and composition, they are assisted in spending different amounts on food. This practice is based on studies of consumer behavior at different income levels.

It is possible to derive more than one assumption from this procedure. Perhaps it is assumed that those who earn less require less nutrition. A second possibility is that those who earn less are thought to be more capable shoppers and, therefore, can convert fewer resources into an adequate diet. Finally, it may be that it is assummed poor people at different income levels have developed shopping habits and tastes for food that enable those with less money to obtain an adequate diet, not because they are more capable shoppers, but because they are willing to eat certain foods that others might find distasteful. In the absence of one or more of these assumptions it would seem that families of equal size and similar composition would be assisted in spending the same amount on food.

Evaluation Of The Food Strategy In this section, arguments which have been made regarding both the advantages and disadvantages of food programs will be presented. Those claiming its advantages are considered first.

Food programs meet the most basic of human needs. Without the commodities or food stamps or school breakfasts and lunches, the incidence of death due to diseases related to malnutrition among the poor would be higher.

We have the resources to eliminate hunger and malnutrition in the United States. There is no question that American agriculture is producing enough food to feed everyone. The question is how to insure a more equitable distribution of food. Neither the government nor the private sector has come up with a solution to this problem. The goals of the food strategy are much more within range than the goals of most other anti-poverty strategies. For example, the goal of adequate nutrition for all could be achieved more easily than adequate education or adequate housing for all.

An adequate diet is a prerequisite for the success of any anti-poverty effort. Nourishment is basic to adequate functioning and the poor will not be able to benefit from other anti-poverty programs such as education and manpower if they are malnourished. Thus, the effects of food programs reach far beyond the elimination of hunger.

Political support for food programs is generally good. While funding for food programs has not been over generous, it is true that at the federal level a basic commitment exists to do something in this area. This commitment seems to be growing as additional and less ambiguous evidence is being made available to legislators concerning the extent of hunger and malnutrition in this country and more knowledge is assembled regarding its effects. At the same time, such a commitment at lower levels of government is slower in developing.

Food strategies are effective during periods of economic decline. When unemployment rises and wages decline, the number of persons eligible for participation in food programs increases. The ability of these programs to meet such an increase in demand is fairly good.

The following are some of the criticisms that have been made of food strategies:

Existing food programs are used more as market support techniques than as anti-poverty programs. One of the stated objectives of food programs is to expand the market for certain domestic products. The secretary of Agriculture has the authority, which he often uses, to purchase items for the commodity programs as part of a market stabilizing program. The overriding goal is aid to agriculture. The secondary goal is aid to people who are hungry. This hierarchy of values will not lead to the elimination of hunger in the United States.

Existing food programs are made more impotent by decentralization of certification and of the decision to participate. Discrimination, lack of financial and administrative resources, and differing standards at the local level make administration of a comprehensive and equitable program for the entire country virtually impossible.

The food strategy does not deal with the causes of low income. While food strategies may relieve hunger and decrease malnutrition among the poor, they can do little to provide the skills and resources needed to escape poverty. They are designed to minimize the effects of poverty rather than to eliminate the causes.

Food strategies are designed to supplement rather than insure adequate diets for all the people. None of the existing food programs were created to eliminate hunger and malnutrition in this country. It has taken a long time for most public officials to acknowledge the problem as a serious one.

Participation in food programs is degrading. It would be more humane to provide the poor with money or work opportunities than to require them to use commodities or food stamps.

Benefits are not very accessible. The crucial decision to make food programs available is made at the local level. This has resulted in the *de facto* denial of benefits to many needy people. In participating areas, the process by which eligibility is determined often discourages or prevents the poor from using the program. Finally, participants in a program may discover that benefits are difficult to receive because of personal handicaps or the location and timing of distribution.

Commodity Distribution:[9] The Commodity Distribution program was initiated by the Agriculture Adjustment Act of 1949. The Secretary of Agriculture also has other funds at his disposal with which to purchase basic foods for distribution to poor families, charitable institutions and school children. One goal of the program is to improve the diets of school children, inmates in charitable institutions, and low income households. Another aim is to increase the market for domestic food products which have been acquired through the government's price support of surplus removal operations.

Food Stamps:[10] The Food Stamp program was created by the Food Stamp Act of 1964. It was designed to correct deficiencies in the Commodity Distribution program and is offered to states and localities as an alternative food strategy. It seeks both to improve the diets of low income households and to support the market for certain food items. The program is administered by state welfare agencies.

School Lunches:[11] The School Lunch program was authorized by the National School Lunch Act of 1946. The act was subsequently amended in 1962 and 1968. This act authorizes both purchase of commodities and cash grants for educational agencies at the state level. Its purpose is to insure the health of children and to expand domestic consumption of certain agricultural commodities.

Comparing Food Strategies In this section the three food strategies are rated using the 26 standard dimensions defined in the Appendix. In Table 4.1 the following strategies are compared: (6) Food Stamps, (7) Commodity Distribution, and (8) School Lunches.

In an effort to summarize the ratings presented in Table 4.1, we have selected 18 dimensions for evaluative comparisons. In Table 4.2 the total number of high and low ratings as well as a difference score is presented for each of the three food strategies.

An observation that can be made on the basis of the information in Table 4.2 is that the School Lunch program is rated considerably higher than the Food Stamp and the Commodity Distribution programs. The higher rating for the School Lunch program is the result of fewer low ratings; there is not much difference between the programs with respect to number of high ratings. One factor contributing to the higher rating is that in contrast to the other food programs, the School Lunch program does not stigmatize the recipient. The School Lunch program is less likely to encourage economic dependency and less likely to undermine work incentives. The School Lunch program is more responsive to recipient families. The program is also more popular with the general public than are other food programs.

MEDICAL CARE

For those who can pay, the United States provides the highest quality medical care available anywhere in the world. But those who cannot pay do not fare so well. One indicator of the quality of medical care received by the poor is the infant mortality rate. By this measure the United States ranks fifteenth in the world. While the infant mortality rate of the United States is not high in an absolute sense, it is high when the level of medical technology and per capita income are taken into consideration. The inferior medical care services available to the poor in the United States is due in part to a shortage of trained medical personnel, but a much more important factor is the inequity in the distribution of the presently available medical care services.

Medical assistance is particularly relevant as a strategy against poverty as it provides a needed basic service to the poor which they could not afford to pay for themselves. It is also relevant as a strategy for keeping the near-poor out of poverty. In this section four medical care strategies are considered: Medicare, Medicaid, Neighborhood Health Centers, and the proposed Kennedy-Griffiths National Health Insurance Plan. The Kennedy-Griffiths plan is the most controversial of these strategies because it would go furthest towards creating an equitable distribution of health care services.

Medicare:[12] Medicare is a medical assistance program for the aged which provides medical care benefits to those over 65. These benefits are related to the cost of health services not to the income of the aged. The main objective of Medicare is to provide hospital insurance protection for specified services to any person age 65 and older who is entitled to Social Security benefits. The program was created in 1965 as Title XVIII of the Social Securities Amendments Act. It is administered by the Social Securities Administration and is channeled through intermediaries such as Blue Cross and private insurance companies.

Medicaid:[13] The Medicaid program was enacted in 1965 as Title XIX of the Social Securities Act; it is administered by the Department of Health, Education and Welfare through the Division of Social and Rehabilitative Services. The program provides grants to the individual states to administer free medical services to Public Assistance recipients and to others at the option of the state. Title XIX states that services such as in-patient out-patient hospital services, laboratory and x-ray use, care by physician, and skilled nursing home care must be available in equal degree to all public welfare recipients and to indigent people and children whether or not they qualify for relief.

Neighborhood Health Centers:[14] The primary goal of Neighborhood Health Centers is to provide an easily accessible source of comprehensive health care services to residents of low income areas. The program includes provisions for active community participation in both the planning and the delivery of health care services. Neighborhood Health Centers were developed as part of Title II of the Economic Opportunity Act of 1964. The Comprehensive Health Plan of 1966 provides federal funding for community based health centers, and OEO provides advisory assistance to communities wishing to utilize these funds.

Kennedy-Griffiths National Health Insurance Plan:[15] The Kennedy-Griffiths National Health Care plan is a proposed system of comprehensive health care insurance which would provide health care services to virtually every resident of the United States. The recipient of the Kennedy-Griffiths plan would be free to choose a participating doctor, clinic, group practice or health care facility and to obtain the same quality and type of service as he does presently. The plan would not be free except for those unable to pay (present Medicaid recipients) and the elderly. (present Medicare recipients). Instead it would be financed in a manner similar to Social Security.

Comparing Medical Care Strategies In this section the four medical care strategies are rated using the 26 standard dimensions defined in the Appendix. In Table 4.3 the following strategies are compared: (1) Medicare, (2) Medicaid, (3) Neighborhood Health Centers, and (4) the Kennedy-Griffiths National Health Insurance Plan.

In an effort to summarize the ratings presented in Table 4.3, we have selected 18 dimensions for evaluative comparisons. In Table 4.4 the total number of high and low ratings as well as a difference score is presented for each of the four medical care strategies.

TABLE 4.3

RATINGS FOR COMPARING MEDICAL CARE AND SOCIAL SERVICE STRATEGIES

DIMENSION FOR THE RATING*	STRATEGY BEING RATED**							
	MEDICAL CARE				SOCIAL SERVICE			
	1	2	3	4	5	6	7	8
1	1	1	1	1	1	1	1	1
2	3	3	2	4	2	2	2	2
3	1	1	1	1	1	1	1	3
4	3	2	3	3	5	5	2	5
5	4	4	3	4	5	5	4	3
6	2	2	2	2	5	3	3	3
7	3	3	3	3	3	3	3	3
8	3	3	3	3	3	3	3	3
9	3	3	3	3	3	3	3	3
10	3	3	3	3	3	3	3	3
11	3	3	3	3	3	3	3	3
12	1	1	1	5	1	5	1	1
13	1	2	2	1	2	2	5	2
14	5	5	5	5	5	5	5	5
15	5	5	5	5	1	1	1	1
16	3	3	1	5	1	1	1	1
17	1	1	3	1	1	1	1	3
18	1	1	3	1	1	3	1	3
19	5	3	3	5	5	5	5	3
20	5	3	3	5	3	3	3	1
21	3	3	1	5	2	2	3	2
22	3	3	1	5	3	3	3	1
23	1	5	5	1	5	5	5	5
24	3	2	1	5	1	1	2	1
25	3	3	1	3	5	1	5	1
26	4	4	2	5	2	2	3	2

* Dimensions 1-26 correspond to the 26 standard dimensions presented in the Appendix.

** The numbers used to identify the 4 medical care and 4 social service strategies are to be interpreted as follows:

(1) Medicare
(2) Medicaid
(3) Neighborhood Health Centers
(4) Kennedy-Griffiths National Health Insurance Plan
(5) Day Care
(6) Family Planning
(7) Casework Social Services
(8) Neighborhood Legal Services

One observation that can be made on the basis of the information in Table 4.4 is that of the three existing programs Medicare receives the highest overall rating. One factor contributing to this is that it provides benefits to the general population as well as the poor. This increases its popularity and decreases its vulnerability to cutback in funding.

Another observation that can be made on the basis of the information in Table 4.4 is that the Kennedy-Griffiths National Health Insurance plan is rated substantially higher than any of the existing medical programs considered. The benefits for this plan would be more accessible than is the case with the existing programs; a higher proportion of the poor would benefit each year; and there would be more equity in the benefits provided. As has been mentioned before, caution must be exercised when comparing the ratings of programs with those of proposals.

TABLE 4.4

SUMMARY OF RATINGS FOR COMPARING MEDICAL CARE AND SOCIAL SERVICE STRATEGIES ON SELECTED EVALUATIVE DIMENSIONS

DIMENSION FOR THE RATING*	STRATEGY BEING RATED**							
	MEDICAL CARE				SOCIAL SERVICE			
	1	2	3	4	5	6	7	8
HIGH	4	2	2	7	5	5	2	2
LOW	4	4	4	3	6	4	6	4
DIFFERENCE SCORE (HIGH-LOW)	0	-2	-2	4	-1	1	-4	-2

*The summary is based on dimensions 2-9, 11-12, 14-21 of Table 4.3; the row marked HIGH is a summary of the total number of times the specified strategy received a rating of 5 in Table 4.3; the row marked LOW is a summary of the total number of times the specified strategy received a rating of 1; the DIFFERENCE SCORE is obtained by subtraction.

**The numbers used to identify the 4 medical care and 4 social service strategies are to be interpreted as follows:

(1) Medicare
(2) Medicaid
(3) Neighborhood Health Centers
(4) Kennedy-Griffiths National Health Insurance Plan
(5) Day Care
(6) Family Planning
(7) Casework Social Services
(8) Neighborhood Legal Services

SOCIAL SERVICES

In this section four somewhat diverse social service strategies are considered: day care, family planning services, casework social services, and Neighborhood Legal Services. Each of these strategies deals with the delivery of a specific type of social service. A wide range of other social services might well have been included. The day care strategy is selected because it offers the opportunity for many poor families to increase their income by having the mother enter the labor force. Family planning offers the poor an opportunity to limit the size of their families; in many cases a family would not be classified as poor were it not for the number of children in the family. The social casework approach has received considerable emphasis from public and private welfare agencies for many years. The Neighborhood Legal Service is included because it offers an opportunity to look at some of the possible advantages of providing more in the way of legal services to the poor.

The social service approach has two major goals. The first is to provide the poor with important services which they would not otherwise be able to afford. The second goal is to provide those services which the poor will need in order to become economically self-sufficient in the long run. The emphasis has generally been on the second of these two goals. It is obvious that if the poor were consulted, the priority they would give to various social services would not correspond to the priority indicated by the present funding levels.

Day Care:[16] Day Care programs were set up by the Social Security Act of 1962, which allowed for allocation of federal funds for the development and improvement of day care programs as a child welfare service. The purpose of most day care facilities is to provide care for children outside their homes, when one or both of their parents are unable to look after them because of employment, education or other training commitments. Programs can also provide care for children under other circumstances, for instance, if physical or mental illness of either parent requires the child's absence from home, or a generally undesirable home life.

Family Planning:[17] Family Planning projects attempt to make family planning services available to persons living in low income or poverty areas. The projects are administered by the Office of Economic Opportunity and vary widely in comprehensiveness of service and size of facilities. Services provided may range from counseling, planning services, and medical attention available a few hours weekly to full-time comprehensive family planning care. Size of facilities range from store-front offices to family planning components of large urban health clinics and hospitals. Generally, family planning projects provide information to poor people about family planning and contraception. Program services include clinical, educational, and counseling components, and also may have outreach and referral facilities.

Casework Social Services:[18] This program provides for welfare recipients services which, for the most part, relate to the encouragement of economic self-support, family stability, child care, and general counseling and referral. The nature of the services provided is usually determined by the circumstances of the particular beneficiary as well as by the qualifications and objectives of the agency and the personnel which provide them. Generally, casework social services attempt to provide individualized guidance to welfare recipients with the purpose of strengthening family relations, helping families to become self-supporting, rehabilitating dependent people, and preventing delinquency. The final goal of these services is to reduce the number of people requiring Public Assistance.

Neighborhood Legal Services:[19] This program provides legal assistance to residents of low income communities. The projects attempt to give the poor and those on the borderline of poverty, quality legal representation, assistance, and advice on an immediate, individual level, while at the same time attempting to make laws more responsive to the needs and circumstances of the poor. Neighborhood Legal Services were enacted as part of the Economic Opportunity Act of 1964. The projects provide attorneys to represent those clients unable to pay for lawyer's services; eligibility criteria are set by local offices. Neighborhood Legal Services are limited by statute to the consideration of civil cases.

Comparing Social Service Strategies In this section the four social service strategies are rated using the 26 standard dimensions defined in the Appendix. In Table 4.3 the following strategies are compared: (1) day care, (2) family planning, (3) casework social services, and (4) Neighborhood Legal Services.

In an effort to summarize the ratings presented in Table 4.3 we have selected 18 dimensions for evaluative comparisons. In Table 4.4 the total number of high and low ratings as well as a difference score is presented for each of the four service strategies.

It is evident from the information in Table 4.4 that family planning is the social service strategy with the highest overall rating. Equally noteworthy is the relatively low rating for the casework social service strategy which has for many years received the most emphasis. The recent upswing in emphasis on day care and family planning seem justified on the basis of our ratings.

Notes

1. For discussion of the Public Housing program see Robert Taggart III, *Low-Income Housing: A Critique of Federal Aid* (Baltimore: Johns Hopkins Press, 1970), pp. 21-39; *Report of the President's Committee on Urban Housing, A Decent Home* (Washington, D.C.: U.S. Government Printing Office, 1968), pp. 60-61; *More Than Shelter: Social Needs in Low and Moderate-Income Housing,* A report prepared for the consideration of the National Commission on Urban Problems (Washington, D.C.: U.S. Government Printing Office, 1968); U.S. Department of Housing and Urban Development, *1969 HUD Statistical Yearbook* (Washington, D.C.: U.S. Government Printing Office, 1969).
2. Taggart, *Low Income Housing,* pp. 41-51, 114; *1969 HUD Statistical Yearbook,* p. 194.
3. Taggart, *Low Income Housing,* pp. 53-62; *A Decent Home,* pp. 64-65.
4. Taggart, *Low Income Housing,* pp. 75-83; *A Decent Home,* p. 66; Dick Netzer, *Economics and Urban Problems* (New York: Basic Books, 1970), pp. 98-101.
5. *A Decent Home,* pp. 71–72; Richard F. Muth, "Urban Residential Land and Housing Markets," in *Issues in Urban Economics,* edited by Harvey Perloff and Lowdon Wingo, Jr. (Baltimore: Johns Hopkins Press, 1968).
6. Karl E. Taeuber, "The Effect of Income Redistribution on Racial Residential Segregation," *Urban Affairs Quarterly* 4, 1(1968): 5–14.
7. Patricia M. Wald, *Law and Poverty 1965,* a report to the National Conference on Law and Poverty (Washington, D.C.: The Conference, 1965), p. 13.
8. Dick Netzer, *Economics and Urban Problems* (New York: Basic Books, 1970), pp. 75–77.
9. Citizens' Board of Inquiry, *Hunger U.S.A.* (Boston: Beacon Press, 1968), pp. 50-56; *Report of the President's Commission on Income Maintenance Programs, Poverty Amid Plenty,* (Washington, D.C.: U.S. Government Printing Office, 1969), p. 136.
10. *Hunger U.S.A.,* pp. 57-67; U.S. Senate, Select Committee on Nutrition and Human Needs, *Hearings, Nutrition and Human Needs: Part 12—Welfare Reform and Food Stamps,* 90th Cong., 2nd. Sess. and 91st. Cong., 1st. Sess., 1969.
11. *Hunger U.S.A.,* pp. 67-68; U.S. Congress, Senate, Select Committee on Nutrition and Human Needs, *Hearings, Nutrition and Human Needs: Part 2—National School Lunch Program,* 91st. Cong., 2nd. Sess., 1970.
12. *Report of the President's Commission on Income Maintenance Programs, Background Papers* (Washington, D.C.: U.S. Government Printing Office, 1969), pp. 319-336; *Poverty Amid Plenty,* p. 133; Isadore S. Falk, "Beyond Medicare," *American Journal of Public Health* 59, 4(1969): 608-623; Alonzo

S. Yerby, "The Disadvantaged and Health Care," *American Journal of Public Health* 56, 1(1966): 5-9.

13. *Background Papers,* p. 324; Jay Brightman and Norman Allaway, "Evaluation of Medical and Dental Care Under the Medical Assistance Programs," *American Journal of Public Health* 59, 12(1969): 2215-2220; Sam Shapiro, "Ill Serving Medicaid Eligibles," *American Journal of Public Health,* 59, 4(1969): 635-642; Esther Spencer, "Medicaid: Lessons and Warnings," *Social Policy* 1, 5(1971): 47-51. Lowell E. Bellin and Florence Kavaler, "Policing Publically Funded Health Care for Poor Quality, Overutilization, and Fraud—The New York City Medicaid Experience," *American Journal of Public Health* 60, 5(1970): 811-820.

14. "Health and Community Control," *Social Policy* 1, 1(1970): 42-46; *Background Papers* pp. 335-336; David L. Cowen, "Denver's Neighborhood Health Program," *Public Health Reports* 84, 9(1969): 761-766; Robert C. Buxbaum, George A. Goldberg, and Fredrick L. Trowbridge, "Issues in the Development of Neighborhood Health Centers," *Inquiry* 6, 1(1969): 37-48; Ana Dumois, "Organizing a Community Around Health," *Social Policy* 1, 5(1972): 10-14; Edward J. O'Donnell and Marilyn M. Sullivan, "Service Delivery and Social Action Through the Neighborhood Center: A Review of Research," *Welfare in Review* 7, 6(1969): 1–12.

15. R.J. Bozell, "Health Insurance," *Science* 171, 3973(1971): 783-785; J. Ehrenreich and O. Fein, "National Health Insurance," *Current* 129, (May 1971): 24-31; R. Finch and R. Egeberge, "The Role of Prepaid Group Practice in Relieving the Medical Care Crisis," *Harvard Law Review* 84, 4(1971): 889-1001; T.J. Watson, Jr. "Health Service: Is the Next Step Socialism?" *Vital Speeches of the Day* 37, 8(1971): 249-251.

16. Lola Emerson, "The League's Day Care Project: Findings to Guide the Community in Providing Day Care Services," *Child Welfare* 48, 7(1969): 402-406; Gilbert Y. Steiner, "Day Care Centers: Hype or Hope?" *Transaction* 8, 9-10(1971): 50-57; Lydia Rappaport and Donna M. Cornsweet, "Preventive Intervention Potentials in Public Child Care Centers," *Child Welfare* 48, 1(1969): 6-13; Milton Willner, "Unsupervised Family Day Care in New York City," *Child Welfare* 48, 6(1969): 342-347; Marcella E. Upton, "The Impact of Day Care in a Poverty Area," *Child Welfare* 48, 4(1969): 231-234.

17. Lynn Landman, "U.S., Underdeveloped Land in Family Planning," *Journal of Marriage and the Family* 30, 2(1968): 191-201; Catherine S. Chilman, "Fertility and Poverty in the U.S.: Some Implications for Family Planning Programs, Evaluation, and Research," *Journal of Marriage and the Family* 30, 2(1968): 207-227; Fredrick S. Jaffe and Steven Polygar, "Family Planning and Public Policy: Is the 'Culture of Poverty' the New Cop Out?" *Journal of Marriage and the Family* 30, 2(1968): 228-235; Gitta Meier, "Implementing the Objectives of Family Planning Programs," *Social Casework* 50, 4(1969): 195-203; John B. Williamson, "Welfare Policy and Population Policy: A Conflict in Goals?" *Urban and Social Change Review* 4, 1(1970): 21-23.

18. *Poverty Amid Plenty,* p. 138; Michael S. March, "The Neighborhood

Center Concept," *Public Welfare* 26, 2(1968): 97-112; Max Siporin, "Social Treatment: A New-Old Helping Method," *Social Work* 15, 3(1970): 13-25; Wilbur J. Cohen, "The Developmental Approach to Social Challenges," *Children* 15, 6(1968): 210-213; Bernard Neugeboren, "Opportunity-Centered Social Services," *Social Work* 15, 2(1970): 47-52; Joel F. Handler and Ellen Jane Hollingsworth, "The Administration of Social Services and the Structure of Dependency: The Views of AFDC Recipients," *Social Service Review* 43, 4(1969): 406-420; *Background Papers,* pp. 303-306; Winifred Bell, "Services for People: An Appraisal," *Social Work* 15, 3(1970): 5-12.

19. Terry Lenzner, "Legal Services Fights for the Poor but Who Fights for Legal Services," *Juris Doctor* (February 1971); Lee Silverstein, "Eligibility for Free Legal Services in Civil Cases," in *American Bar Foundation Series for the Poor* (Chicago: The Foundation, 1967); Jane Handler, *Neighborhood Legal Services: New Dimensions in the Law,* Report prepared for the Office of Juvenile Delinquency and Youth Development, Department of Health, Education, and Welfare, (Washington, D.C.: U.S. Government Printing Office, 1966).

5

Manpower, Education Economic Development And Organization

In this chapter four anti-poverty approaches are considered: manpower, education, economic development, and organization. The manpower approach includes strategies which would increase the number and quality of jobs available to the poor. The education approach involves those strategies which would provide the education needed for the higher paying jobs. The economic development approach calls for strategies which would increase the number of jobs available to the poor as a consequence of local or national economic growth. The organization strategies encourage the poor to act together so as to increase their political influence, which in turn would lead to a wide range of economic and non-economic benefits to the poor.

MANPOWER

The programs and proposals described in this section are all consistent with the manpower anti-poverty strategy. The focus of this approach is on such matters as finding existing jobs, training for existing jobs, creating jobs, and minimum wage legislation.

United States Training and Employment Service (USTES):[1] The goal of this program is to assist employable adults in finding work, but since 1962, particular attention has been given to aiding the poor. This has been done through the expansion of counseling services and referral to job training programs. The origin of USTES was the United States Employment Service (USES), which was established in 1933 under the Wagner-Peyser Act. USTES's services are intended for all Americans seeking employment, its services are located in every state, and it is closely affiliated with other manpower programs in its referral capacities.

Opportunities Industrialization Centers (OIC):[2] This program is a nonprofit independently chartered manpower organization whose goal is to train the unemployed, under-employed and drop-outs (aged 17 to 70) for successful permanent employment. OIC was started in 1964 as a Negro self-help venture in Philadelphia by a black minister, but today it is an integrated organization.

Job Opportunities in the Business Sector (JOBS):[3] The goal of JOBS is to open up employment opportunities in the business sector to persons who are unemployed, under-employed, or poor and one of the following: under twenty-two or over forty-five; a minority group member; less than a high school graduate; or handicapped. Women have not substantially benefited from this program. JOBS promotes a "hire first" philosophy whereby a business hires a jobless adult over 18 and then provides any necessary pre-vocational or vocational training required by the new employee.

New Careers:[4] The goal of this program is to develop entry-level professional aide jobs with maximum upgrading opportunities for unemployed and underemployed persons age 18 or over. These jobs are to be in public and private nonprofit agencies, which deliver health, education, welfare, public safety, or neighborhood redevelopment services. In order for these aide positions to be created, the personnel or institutions involved have to agree to a certain amount of job restructuring.

Neighborhood Youth Corps (NYC):[5] This program is designed to assist poor youth on the secondary school level to continue their formal education or to participate in a program of work training. Presumably, either will enhance the enrollees' employability when they place themselves on the job market. This program was authorized by the Economic Opportunity Act of 1964. There are three components of the program. The first is the in-school approach, which is meant to provide work opportunities to youths from poor families who remain in school. The second is a summer program. The third is the out-of-school program which in many cases provides some remedial education, supportive services, and skill training.

Minimum Wage Legislation:[6] The mimimum wage was created by the Fair Labor Standards Act of 1938, and its basic goal was the elimination of substandard wages so as to improve the health, efficiency, and general well-being of workers. Between the passage of this act and the 1966 amendments to the act, the minimum wage was raised three times and coverage extended once. The 1966 amendments raised the specified minimum wage from $1.25 an hour to $1.40 starting in 1967 and $1.60 starting in 1968. At present 11.4 million workers are not covered by minimum wage legislation, including 3.6 million in retail trade, 4.6 million in the services, and 1 million in agriculture.

Concentrated Employment Program (CEP):[7] The Concentrated Employment Program was created to coordinate the various manpower provisions put forth in the 1966 Congressional amendments to the Economic Opportunity Act, to concentrate manpower resources on small poverty target areas, and to model itself after a pilot program in Chicago called Jobs Now, which provided prevocational training to the poor and then referred them to on-the-job training programs.

Jobs Corps:[8] The primary function of the Job Corps is to educate and train youths so that they will be able to live on a level superior to that offered the casual laborer. Not only is low income considered in screening applicants, but also school performance, unemployability, and low testing ability. The Job Corps was established in 1965 under the Economic Opportunity Act and included the goal of physically removing disadvantaged youths from their home environments for education and training experiences.

Work Incentive Program (WIN):[9] The proposed goal of the Work Incentive Program is economic independence for all employable persons aged 16 or over whose families receive Aid to Families with Dependent Children (AFDC). It is assumed that those persons receiving welfare who are physically able can be trained or educated for assimilation into the labor force—presumably in the private sector.

Manpower Development and Training Act (MDTA) Institutional Training:[10] This program is intended to provide participants with employment skills in a classroom setting. Originally, the program was designed to retrain men who were unemployed or about to be laid-off because of technological changes in the job market. During the 1960s, however, emphasis was placed on training the disadvantaged. The MDTA Institutional program was created by the Manpower Development and Training Act of 1962.

Government As Employer of Last Resort:[11] The proposed strategy of government as employer of last resort is based on the argument that a nation which emphasizes employment as a measure of self-reliance and individual worth has an obligation to assure every employable person a job. There is always a certain amount of frictional unemployment due to people temporarily out of work, but in addition there is a group of hard-core unemployed whose skill level is sufficiently low that they cannot find jobs in the private sector, even in a period of economic expansion. It is this group for whom the government would create jobs. Most proponents of the government of last resort proposal intend that the program be used as a last resort by the government, that is, all efforts should be made to stimulate the economy and encourage employment through normal competitive channels before the government turns employer. For the purpose of comparisons with other strategies, we will assume that the program being considered would provide guaranteed jobs to approximately 5 million persons and that the average income derived from these jobs would be $4,000 per year (this is roughly equal to the poverty line for a family of four). We estimate the cost at $20 billion for wages of which $16 billion would go to the poor. There would also be at least another $5 billion in cost of materials and administration.

Assumptions Implicit In The Manpower Approach In this section, some of the implicit assumptions of the manpower approach to poverty will be discussed. Some assumptions are common to all manpower strategies while others pertain to specific strategies.

One of the underlying assumptions of all manpower programs is that unemployment is a major cause of poverty and that if poor individuals can gain employment, the poverty problem will be substantially alleviated. Involved with this assumption are two other ideas: most of the poor are potentially employable, and potentially adequate job opportunities are available to accomodate the poor.

The manpower approach is also based implicitly on the assumption that the best way to integrate the poor into the mainstream of society is to place them in the work situation. Income maintenance programs provide considerable economic security, but they do not serve as a direct catalyst for placing the poor in the mainstream of society. Programs which combine these two benefits are superior.

The manpower approach also upholds the idea that society should not have to support the poor without some indication that they will ultimately assume financial independence. To this end, it is necessary to prepare the poor for economic self-support through work. Two assumptions connected with this idea are that the poor can make a decent living through work and that low paying jobs are better than unemployment. It should be noted, however, that many of the poor do work and yet do not make a decent salary. The need for minimum wage legislation is connected with this problem.

An additional assumption indigenous to the manpower approach is that there is a portion of the population, the unemployed poor, who are at a constant competitive disadvantage within the private labor market. The government must act as an agent to both elevate the employability of these people and encourage employers to assimilate them into the job market. This idea assumes that the government should help coordinate both the supply and demand sides of the labor market.

A primary assumption of the job finding assistance strategy is that sufficient job opportunities already exist to accomodate the unemployed poor. All that is necessary is matching people to the jobs. To this end, employment agencies and placement centers can work closely with employers and job-seekers in order to match them according to their respective needs.

Job creation programs involve the assumption that there are not enough jobs presently available to the disadvantaged to assimilate all of those needing employment. Either jobs presently closed to the poor must be opened to them or new jobs must be created. This goal has an implicit assumption that employers can be induced to hire high risk employees through the receipt of subsidies. JOBS assumes the business sector can use the services of disadvantaged persons and can benefit from this use even after subsidized training ends. NYC offers very low paying jobs and, until recently, jobs that did not require much skill. New Careers takes exception to the idea that any job is better than no job and attempts to create a stratum of paraprofessional jobs offering mobility within public service fields, such as health, education and welfare. In view of the relatively low pay offered by the program, there seems to be an underlying assumption that the poor do share middle class aspirations for a career in a profession; otherwise the program would have little appeal.

The government as employer of last resort proposal assumes that every person who seeks a job is entitled to one and that the job should pay at least the federal minimum wage. This proposal openly acknowledges and supports the American emphasis on work and its importance as a means of determining self-worth. Also implicit in this proposal is the assumption that some individuals cannot be absorbed into the private sector of the economy due to comparative disadvantages in marketability and due also to a constant amount of structurally-caused unemployment. Since wages would be paid by the government in such a program, the only real difference between this proposal and the guaranteed minimum income proposals is that a service would be performed both for society and for the individual's self-esteem.

Unlike other manpower strategies, minimum wage legislation assumes that employment in itself is not a solution for poverty. Indeed, this assumption is supported by the fact that so many poor persons do work and still remain poor. Another underlying assumption is that many employed persons can be lifted out of poverty if they receive a wage commensurate with wage increases taking place within the economy as a whole. However, in order for this strategy to be effective as a tool against poverty, several other factors must be assumed. First, the worker must be employed in a position which is covered by minimum wage legislation. Second, he must be employed full-time, that is 1800–2000 hours per year. Third, he must not have a large family, four at the most. If any of these conditions are not met, the value of the minimum wage legislation as a strategy against poverty is diminished. Also implicit in this strategy is the assumption that the benefits accruing to poor workers through increased wages will offset any harm done by unemployment due to an increased minimum wage. This assumption has proven to be valid on the aggregate level.

A primary assumption of the job training strategy is that the poor can become gainfully employed through increasing their employability. There are jobs for poor people; the solution is to train and coach the poor person in such a way that he will feel competent at work and will perform according to employer expectations. Job training aims solely at changing the supply side of the labor market, not the demand side.

Underlying this emphasis on elevating the employability of the poor is an implicit assumption that a deficiency in their preparation is the cause of their present unemployment (and poverty). Two programs, JOBS and New Careers, which have a job finding component as well as a job training component, are exceptions to this statement.

The on-the-job training strategy assumes that the poor need jobs which will provide an income while they are training. For this reason a "hire now, train later" philosophy permeates the programs in this category. Employers are subsidized for training enrollees. It is assumed that enrollees will feel it is in their interest to do a good job and that they will be company assets by the time they go on the regular unsubsidized payroll. A certain amount of good faith on the part of participating employers is assumed. Another assumption of on-the-job training is that even though enrollees receive training specific to a particular job, the employment experience itself will have a marketable value if and when termination takes place. For the most part, New Careers enrollees who have left their on-the-job training before six months have moved on to better paying jobs using the skills and experience acquired through the program. Enrollees in other job training programs, however, may not fare as well.

The institutional training strategy assumes that training of the poor should be prior to and removed from the employment experience. CEP with its pre-vocational training assumes that many disadvantaged persons must be given some work orientation before businessmen receive them as trainees. This involves the assumption that hiring the disadvantaged persons must be made as palatable and attractive as possible to private sector employers.

Individual institutional training programs involve assumptions of their own. The Job Corps has had an underlying assumption that poor youths can best be trained if they are physically removed from their home environment. The program carried this idea so far that enrollees were often sent hundreds of miles away for training. An underlying assumption of WIN is that many of the poor who receive Public Assistance can be encouraged to become economically independent when a program exists which tailors individual training opportunities. This involves the assumption that many of those persons receiving Public Assistance are potentially employable. OIC functions on the premise that the best way to guarantee employment for disadvantaged persons is to give them extensive pre-vocational training with particular emphasis on job expectations and personal orientation to the work setting and to tailor courses according to specific requirements made by particular employers within the local labor market. MDTA Institutional Training has recently come to assume that disadvantaged individuals benefit most from multi-occupational skill training, which offers them the opportunity to gain exposure to many skills without making a commitment to a specific long-term occupational training course. Because there is no effort on the part of MDTA personnel to place enrollees, it is apparent that an underlying assumption of this program is that once a person has skill training, he will be able to secure a job on his own.

Evaluation Of The Manpower Approach In this section arguments are presented both for and against the manpower approach as a strategy against poverty. The advantages of the manpower strategy are presented first:

The cost of the program is low relative to other strategies such as income maintenance. Even for programs like JOBS where subsidies average $3000 per enrollee, the overall cost cannot compare with the cost of providing a guaranteed minimum income to a sizable segment of the population. Many institutional training programs provide allowances for enrollees, but again the overall cost of these programs is not great. The one exception is the Job Corps with a per trainee cost averaging between $6000 and $8000 since the program's inception. This high cost is due to the many services offered enrollees such as food, shelter, medical care, vocational training, basic education, and an allowance. Congressional reaction to this high cost has caused the Labor Department to restructure the program in order to reduce expenses. Even the Job Corps may eventually conform to the low cost model presented by most manpower programs.

Helping a person gain employment through job development

or skill training prepares him for a life of economic independence. There is no question that this strategy represents an antithesis to income maintenance strategies. The focus is on improving the employability of the poor so that they can make a living for themselves thereafter. Minimum wage legislation is directed toward improving the financial situation of individuals who are already attempting to be economically independent.

Holding a job improves the poor person's self-image. By helping secure employment for the poor and by elevating their employability, manpower programs promote assimilation of the poor into the mainstream of American society. Not only do they participate in the work world, but they also benefit monetarily, which may help improve their self-image.

Most manpower programs have a positive effect on family stability. Those enrollees who work while training or who gain employment through training receive an income which enables them to take care of family financial needs or, in the case of unmarried enrollees, to be more financially independent of their families. Enrollees in programs offering allowances may not experience complete financial relief, but the allowances do help. Job Corps trainees have had all their living needs provided by the program thus improving their family's financial situation. NYC provides relatively low paying jobs, but these do serve as a source of income which reduces parental contributions. It is known that a good deal of friction within poor families is caused by anxiety and stress related to financial matters. Not only do families benefit from income gained through manpower programs, but the anticipation of a better life style in the future due to the increased employability of a family member may also reduce tensions.

The manpower strategy enjoys much support and popularity among the nonpoor. This strategy is regarded by most people as a short run device to enable the poor to compete in the job market. Costs are not great, and presumably enrollees can make their own way in the world as a result of their participation in these programs. Because this approach promotes self-reliance and elevated employability, the affluent can support it without feeling that they are enabling the poor to live a carefree, work-free existence. The government as employer of last resort proposal might be an exception as it would assume permanent responsibility for the unemployed. Since this is still a proposal and not widely discussed, its public acceptance is difficult to gauge.

Funding for the manpower strategy is not a problem since it is popular with politicians relative to other types of anti-poverty programs. Programs in this category experience a considerable amount of continuity and long run planning capability because budgets are usually approved by Congress with a minimum of problems. Congressmen know this strategy is well received among their constituents, and they also are products of a society which emphasizes the positive value of work.

The following are some of the disadvantages of the manpower strategy:

For some of the poor the manpower strategy is not enough to overcome their unemployability. Certainly employment and income are important factors in creating an improved life-style for the poor. However, some poor people have been so debilitated in mind and body that the acquisition of skill training and a job does not guarantee success. It is not a coincidence that most manpower programs have had to develop and improve counseling and other supportive services for enrollees. Many enrollees have such poor self-images and such feelings of alienation from the mainstream of society that they are unable to function successfully in the work situation.

The manpower approach is not available to all those within the poor population. Only potentially employable persons can benefit. For example, those who are disabled or mentally ill cannot avail themselves of this strategy. In addition, many poor people cannot afford a period of training. If a person has a job, yet is quite poor, he must choose between continuing in his low paying job and having some income, or enrolling in a training program which will improve his long-term financial situation but provide an allowance of less value than his already inadequate income. Some financial security is required before a poor person can think in terms of long-run improved employability. This is in contrast to a guaranteed minimum income, which would accomodate basic needs and enable action directed toward long-run improvements. Women who have young children and no means of child care cannot benefit from this strategy.

Many manpower programs are dependent on the state of the economy. Job finding assistance and job creation programs have difficulty in placing enrollees during a recession. Institutional training programs serve as buffers for unemployment during recessions, but ultimately these enrollees must face the market and compete with one another for jobs which may or may not materialize.

Manpower programs are to a large extent dependent on the goodwill of the business community, which is not always forthcoming. This is particularly true of job creation programs such as JOBS. It is true that many businessmen have an elevated social consciousness, but on the whole, decisions to hire the disadvantaged rest on economic feasibility. It is apparent from the small percentage of employers entering subsidy contracts that the government cannot make the poor attractive to businessmen, even with financial inducements. In other words, this program is dependent upon attitudinal changes. This dependence on attitudinal change is also true for New Careers. Again it does not appear that public service agencies are making genuine efforts to create a new level of subprofessional jobs. It is understandable that a Congress which supports manpower programs as a means of promoting self-reliance at a relatively low cost would also attempt to count on the private sector for assistance in carrying out the programs. The government does not want to become employer of last resort at this time, so manpower programs must to a considerable degree rely on help from the business community. Perhaps in the long run a consensus of values will emerge, but at present manpower strategies, and especially job creation and on-the-job training, are dependent on cooperation from sources not adequately committed to their goals.

The manpower strategy inadvertently supports the existence of unattractive jobs within the labor market. This situation occurs in part because of the strategy's assumption that any job is better than no job. Job development, training and placement are generally geared toward jobs that are either unfilled or so meaningless that they become available only through a subsidized program. Because the poor do not represent a highly educated segment of the population, little effort is made to provide them with jobs requiring much imagination or education. Consequently, enrollees in manpower programs usually obtain low skill jobs. In addition, employers tend to pay as little as possible to have these jobs done. Manpower programs as a rule are lending support to these low paying jobs by encouraging enrollees to accept them. Two exceptions are minimum wage legislation and the government as employer of last resort proposal. The minimum wage represents an attempt to keep a floor under the wage levels in the country, but it does not cover everyone and is kept at a fairly low level so as not to promote inflation. The government as employer of last resort proposal, if implemented, would serve as a competitive force within the labor market and cause private sector employers to make jobs as attractive as possible since jobs provided by the government would undoubtedly pay the national minimum wage. On the positive side, it should be mentioned that the Labor Department does not enter contracts under JOBS unless the locally accepted minimum wage is agreed to by the participating employer.

Many of the poor are not reached by the manpower strategy. Most manpower programs serve only a few thousand people, as opposed to a guaranteed minimum income or a family allowance strategy, which would reach several million poor persons. USTES is an exception to this since it services about 2 million disadvantaged individuals each year, but even this is low in comparison to Social Securi-

TABLE 5.1

RATINGS FOR COMPARING ALTERNATIVE MANPOWER STRATEGIES

DIMENSION FOR THE RATING*	MANPOWER STRATEGY BEING RATED**										
	1	2	3	4	5	6	7	8	9	10	11
1	3	2	2	2	2	3	2	2	2	2	5
2	3	2	2	2	2	3	2	2	2	2	5
3	1	3	1	3	1	1	1	1	1	1	5
4	4	5	4	5	3	4	3	3	3	3	5
5	5	5	5	5	3	4	4	3	3	4	5
6	5	5	5	5	5	5	5	5	5	5	5
7	5	5	5	5	3	5	3	5	4	5	5
8	3	5	5	5	3	3	3	5	3	3	3
9	3	5	5	5	3	3	3	3	3	3	3
10	1	1	1	1	1	3	1	1	1	1	3
11	1	3	1	1	1	1	1	1	1	5	5
12	1	1	1	1	1	5	1	1	1	1	5
13	1	2	2	2	2	1	2	2	2	2	1
14	1	5	1	1	1	1	1	5	1	1	5
15	5	1	5	5	5	5	5	5	5	1	5
16	3	1	1	1	1	5	1	1	3	3	5
17	1	5	1	3	1	1	1	1	1	1	1
18	1	3	3	3	3	5	1	3	1	1	1
19	5	5	5	5	5	5	3	3	5	5	3
20	5	3	3	3	3	5	1	1	3	3	1
21	3	1	1	1	1	3	1	1	1	1	4
22	3	1	1	1	1	5	1	1	1	1	5
23	1	3	3	5	5	3	3	5	5	1	3
24	3	1	1	1	1	3	1	1	1	1	3
25	1	3	3	5	3	5	1	3	3	3	5
26	3	3	3	2	3	1	3	3	3	3	5

* Dimensions 1-26 correspond to the 26 standard dimensions presented in the Appendix.

** The numbers used to identify the 11 manpower strategies are to be interpreted as follows:

(1) USTES
(2) OIC
(3) JOBS
(4) NEW Careers
(5) NYC
(6) Minimum Wage Legislation
(7) CEP
(8) Job Corps
(9) WIN
(10) MDTA Institutional Training
(11) Government as Employer of Last Resort

ty. Minimum wage legislation could theoretically affect the lives of many working poor, but there are limitations. Many poor workers are in labor categories not covered by minimum wage (farm and retail industries, for example). Many of the working poor cannot obtain full-time employment, so a minimum wage cannot alleviate their poverty to any sizable degree. Also, state minimum wage levels vary a good deal and some employers do not pay the legal minimum. Taking everything into consideration, it is hard to determine whether or not large numbers of poor people do benefit from minimum wage legislation.

Comparing Manpower Strategies In this section the manpower strategies are compared with respect to the 26 standard dimensions defined in the Appendix. In Table 5.1 the following strategies are compared: (1) USTES, (2) OIC, (3) JOBS, (4) New Careers, (5) NYC, (6) minimum wage legislation, (7) CEP, (8) Job Corps, (9) WIN, (10) MDTA Institutional Training, and (11) government as employer of last resort.

By way of summary, a comparison will be made among the ratings of the 11 manpower strategies considered above. We have selected 18 dimensions for evaluative comparisons. In Table 5.2 the total number of high and low ratings as well as a difference score is presented for each of the 11 manpower strategies.

The government as employer of last resort proposal is the manpower strategy with the highest overall rating. This proposal would have a greater impact on the distribution of income than any of the other manpower strategies considered. It would also go further toward increasing the political influence of the poor. The poor and near-poor would become less economically dependent on local employers and others in the local power structure. As a consequence, they would be more willing to support their own political interests. In addition, the benefits of such a program would be easily accessible, more equitably distributed than is the case with many existing manpower programs and there would be relatively little creaming. The strategy would contribute to a more positive self-concept for those recipients who would otherwise be unemployed. Another positive aspect of the proposal is that it would take up the slack in employment during periods of economic recession; that is, in contrast to many other manpower strategies, the number of job placements would increase during such periods. As we have often mentioned in earlier chapters, a high rating for any proposal, the government as employer of last resort being no exception, may in part be due to our inability to fully anticipate the problems which would arise were the proposal introduced as a program.

Among the existing programs, OIC receives the highest overall rating. Part of OIC's success is undoubtedly due to its localized goals and close relations with area businessmen. OIC reaches fewer of the poor than WIN and NYC do, but it has the same rating because of all three reach a relatively small segment of the poor. One factor contributing to the high rating of OIC is that there is less creaming than with several of the other manpower strategies. Another factor is that there tends to be more accountability to recipients and the community from which they are drawn. It is generally viewed as a self-help program and this contributes to a more positive self-concept than is the case for several other manpower programs.

The New Careers program receives a relatively high overall rating. Like OIC, it is a small program working closely with the local community and tailoring its assistance to the individual enrollee. Thus, it avoids some of the built in problems of larger manpower programs.

The CEP program receives the lowest overall rating. One reason for this poor showing is that CEP is primarily a referral agency and therefore impaired by problems indigenous to other manpower programs

TABLE 5.2

SUMMARY OF RATINGS FOR ALTERNATIVE MANPOWER STRATEGIES ON SELECTED EVALUATIVE DIMENSIONS

SUMMARY OF THE RATINGS*	MANPOWER STRATEGY BEING RATED**										
	1	2	3	4	5	6	7	8	9	10	11
HIGH	6	9	7	8	3	7	2	5	3	4	11
LOW	6	4	7	5	7	5	9	7	7	7	4
DIFFERENCE SCORE (HIGH-LOW)	0	5	0	3	-4	2	-7	-2	-3	-3	7

* The summary is based on dimensions 2-9, 11-12, and 14-21 of Table 5.1; the row marked HIGH is a summary of the total number of times the specified program received a rating of 5 in Table 5.1; the row marked LOW is a summary of the total number of times the specified program received a rating of 1; the DIFFERENCE SCORE is obtained by subtraction.

** The numbers used to identify the 11 manpower strategies are to be interpreted as follows:

(1) USTES
(2) OIC
(3) JOBS
(4) New Careers
(5) NYC
(6) Minimum Wage Legislation
(7) CEP
(8) Job Corps
(9) WIN
(10) MDTA Institutional Training
(11) Government As Employer of Last Resort

n whose cooperation it relies. The government's partial withdrawal of support before it was fully established as an independent force has contributed to its relatively poor performance.

It is interesting to note that JOBS, which enjoys strong Congressional support, has an overall rating only slightly above that of Job Corps, which has repeatedly undergone Congressional criticism. JOBS is popular because it embodies the concept of maximum participation by the private sector in solving employment problems, but this reliance upon private business cooperation has led to many of the administrative and job creation problems associated with the program. The Job Corps, on the other hand, is a costly program and therefore subject to Congressional criticism, but the high cost provides educational and training opportunities to poor youth, along with food, shelter, medical care and allowances.

EDUCATION

The programs and proposals described in this section are all consistent with the educational approach. A major objective is to provide the poor with the education they will need to obtain the jobs which will enable them to escape poverty permanently.

Head Start:[12] This program was established by Section 21.1 of the Economic Opportunity Act of 1965, to give poor childern pre-school training so that they will be able to compete with less disadvantaged students when they enter school. The program provides services and activities to stimulate the social and educational development of the child. There are two components of Head Start; short summer programs for children entering first grade and full year programs for pre-school children. The program operates on the premise that poor children enter school disadvantaged culturally as well as educationally. A wide range of medical, social, and educational benefits are provided.

Bilingual Education:[13] The Bilingual Education Act provides grants for the development and operation of innovative services and activities to meet the special educational needs of school age children who have limited English speaking ability. Most commonly, the program supports courses in English as a second language. More recently, broader bilingual curricula have been developed which are based upon academic subjects in the native tongue.

Adult Basic Education:[14] The purpose of this program is to give basic instruction to adults and to teach English to those who have some other mother tongue and who have not yet mastered english. The purpose is to help the participants reach a level at which they can take advantage of programs which will enhance their employability.

College Work Study:[15] Higher Education Work Study was authorized by the Economic Opportunity Act of 1964 and the Higher Education Act of 1965. College students who are in need of financial assistance may work up to 15 hours per week while in school and up to 40 hours during the summer. The federal government pays up to 80 percent of these earnings and also assists in paying some of the administrative costs. Any educational institution which offers at least a six month course to high school graduates is eligible for assistance under this program.

Open Enrollment:[16] This is a program whereby a university agrees to admit any student who has completed high school. Entrance requirements, previously of a competitive nature, are relaxed to include all high school graduates. City University of New York began such a program in the 1970-1971 academic year. A student's grade average in high school and the type of program he was in (academic, vocational or general) are not considered in admission, although they do determine which of the many City colleges he will attend. If a student does well in the community college, he may transfer to one of the other colleges after two years.

School Integration:[17] The initial impetus for national school desegregation came with the 1954 Supreme Court decision which declared the policy of separate schools for blacks and whites to be unconstitutional. Explicit in the Court's decision is the idea that blacks who are forced to attend segregated schools stand little chance of receiving an equal education. Title IV of the Civil Rights Act of 1964 authorized funds and specialized services to school districts and colleges to help effect integration. The Department of Health, Education and Welfare defines as integrated, a school in which the minority group enrollment is less than 50 percent. Thus the school which is 51 percent black would not be considered integrated whereas one that was 49 percent black would be.

School Vouchers:[18] A school voucher is basically a coupon with a specified cash value. One coupon would be issued to parents for each school age child in the family. These vouchers could be used as tuition to any school which had agreed to participate in the voucher program. The schools would cash in the vouchers with the state to obtain operating funds. Jencks describes a number of possible voucher schemes. Of these, the regulated compensatory model, which is the scheme considered here, is clearly intended to provide the poor with greater access to the benefits of the educational system. This proposal would award vouchers to all children, but increase the value of the voucher for poor children. Schools could not charge tuition above the vouchers, but could earn extra revenue by enrolling disadvantaged children.

Assumptions Implicit In The Education Approach A fundamental assumption implicit in educational strategies is that poverty cannot adequately be dealt with without provisions for the long run self-sufficiency of those who are poor. The compensatory programs, improvement of the schools and school reorganization, with very few exceptions, provide no immediate economic benefits. The goal is to encourage long run self-sufficiency, not just to provide for immediate financial needs.

A related assumption is that increased and improved education will enable the poor to compete successfully for employment. Success in the job market will in turn enable the poor to escape their present circumstances. Improved educational services will better prepare the poor to compete more successfully for higher paying jobs.

All the strategies considered here implicitly assume that the educational needs of the poor are not at present met adequately. A variety of approaches to correct this situation are offered, from early childhood to adult education. Basic to all is the idea that the condition of the poor is at least in part a result of the school system's deficiency in meeting its responsibility toward this segment of the population.

Education is assumed to be a right for all; the goal is to be universalistic. The approach is not universalistic in the sense that a negative income tax would be because in most instances it is restricted to the young. An exception to this generalization is adult education which represents an attempt to provide a basic education to adults who, for whatever reason, did not receive it as children. Within the basic target population, however, the need for an adequate education is considered to be universal; all children require and deserve an adequate education.

Many education programs assume that an effective program must take into consideration more than just educational needs. Several consider not only the poor's intellectual needs, but such needs as food, health care, income, as well as personal counseling. The assumption is that education is a total process; that is, attempts to improve the poor's education cannot separate intellectual growth from other aspects of the student's total environment. Often, if not responded to, problems in these other areas will impede scholastic progress.

The educational approach assumes that it is desirable to integrate the poor into the mainstream of society. The separation of the poor from the upper classes exists in much more than an economic sense. An equally serious problem for the poor is their political and social separation. An assumption made by the education strategies is that improved education will enable the poor to bridge the gaps which separate them from the mainstream in a number of ways. An important American ideal is the universality of education; the school experience is common to all, and equalization of the quality of education ideally should reduce the impact of many of the conditions which segregate the poor from the wider society.

Compensatory education seeks to make up for the deprivation suffered by the poor as a result of environmental conditions. These strategies assume that the poor come to the educational system deficient in cognitive development, social values and experience, the very tools which enable other children to progress through the system more successfully. This approach seeks to employ extra school programs to make up for these deficiencies. The compensatory education approach is particularly consistent with the view that the poor have their own sub-culture, characterized by political, social and psychological, as well as economic, segregation. This approach attempts to integrate the poor into the mainstream by offering programs of cultural enrichment and programs to compensate for their disadvantaged background.

Improvement of the facilities, curriculum and faculty, like compensatory education, assumes the inadequacy of the educational system in meeting the needs of the poor. This approach, however, sees the differences to be not in the poor themselves, but in the schools they attend. Such strategies as adult basic education and New Careers generally assume that educational neglect, and the resulting poverty are conditions reversible late in the academic career or even after a person has left the formal educational system.

Reorganization considers the nature of the balance of power in our educational system. This strategy assumes that the poor receive an inadequate share of our educational resources because of their position of powerlessness in our society. Integration and consolidation in the form of urban educational parks seek to change this by enrolling the poor in schools attended by other segments of society. This, it is held, will insure that the former receive the benefits of the best schools, teachers and educational programs. Decentralization and the proposal for school vouchers are attempts to redistribute power and access to the resources of the educational system. With these two approaches, it is held that giving the poor greater control over their children's education will result in improvements in its quality. Decentralization and vouchers are based on the value of parental involvement as an end in itself, leading not only to more effective school programs but to heightened self-esteem for the parents of poor children.

Evaluation Of The Education Strategy In this section a general evaluation of the education approach is considered. Arguments are presented which describe both the advantages and limitations of the approach. The advantages of the educational strategies are considered first:

There is a strong relationship between the level of education

and income. Those with some graduate work earn approximately three times as much as those who did not finish elementary school. It should be noted that the strong relationship which presently exists between level of education and income probably would not continue if all the poor were to substantially increase their level of education. Inflation in the level of education required for jobs no doubt would set in, resulting in discrimination against the poor for other, noneducational reasons. Jencks points out that to attribute all the difference in income between the most and the least educated segments of the population to education alone is to ignore all sorts of other differences. We cannot assume that these other differences would wash out if we were somehow able to get those who would otherwise be high school dropouts all the way through graduate school.

The education approach deals with a basic cause and not just a consequence of poverty. This argument is related to the first. Whereas the income and income-in-kind approaches may be viewed as stop-gap measures, the education approach is a fundamental attack on one of the causes of poverty. Much more than the short run strategies, education may be counted upon to produce meaningful and far-reaching changes in the lives of the poor. However, many radicals would argue that the educational system is a work force stratifier and, as such, an upward shift in the distribution of income would not necessarily benefit the poor. In short, many jobs already require much more education than is actually needed.

Education increases the political awareness and participation of the poor. There is a strong relationship between levels of education and various forms of political participation and political awareness. With increased education, the poor are more likely to recognize the significance of political issues and to engage in various forms of political activity on their own behalf.

Education is viewed favorably by the general population. The public generally views education as a chance to help the poor help themselves. Moreover, the need for education, at least on the elementary and secondary level, is considered so vital that few deny the appropriateness of measures to insure that the poor receive a decent education.

A major exception to this point concerns the reorganization strategies. While the public views education as a basic right, it is not so willing to accept drastic shifts in the balance of power in educational systems, as would occur with the strategies we have considered. Much more agreeable are strategies such as compensatory education, which are intended to help the poor, but do not really affect others.

Education encourages self-sufficiency. Successful educational strategies are likely to increase the desire of the poor to support themselves, as well as provide the necessary skills to enable them to do so.

The benefits of education are inter-generational. The self perpetuating cycle of poverty may be broken with education. The children of parents whose education allows them to compete for jobs and rise out of poverty are not so likely to experience that condition themselves. Instead, these children may be expected to profit from their parents' improved situation and economic security.

Education has a positive effect on the self-esteem of the poor. The education strategies improve the poor's perception of themselves. The social stigma attached to enrollment in many anti-poverty programs does not apply to the school system. Instead, the approach seeks to help poor children realize their potential. The following are some of the criticisms of the education approach:

The education strategies cannot guarantee that the recipient will benefit. Many intervening factors affect the relations between education, employment and elevation from poverty. Most notable among them are the structure of the economy and racial prejudice. While the education strategies may enable an individual to compete in the job market, they cannot provide any guarantee of success or future security. Jencks argues that there is little effect of school expenditure on school attainment. He also argues that the effect of school attainment on adult income is quite modest.

The value of improved education is not equal for all Americans. Blacks do not get as much advantage from increased education as whites do. The following statistics describe families in 1969 in which the head of household was at least 25 years old. Consider first those who had graduated from high school, but had not gone on for any college education. Of white families considered 5 percent were poor, whereas 17 percent of black families were poor. Considering families in which the head had only 8 years of education, 10 percent of white families and 24 percent of black families were poor. For those with between 1 and 3 years of college education, 4 percent of white families and 9 percent of black families were poor. At each of these education levels, blacks are more likely to be poor than whites.

Generally, the compensatory strategies and those similar in design give little indication of success. A major deficiency involves the absence of reliable educational models which are known to be effective with disadvantaged youth. It is generally accepted that the cognitive style and learning ability of the poor are marked by particular problems resulting from social and economic deprivation. Presently, however, educators have very little knowledge as to what these problems are and how they may best be approached through special educational activities. Without this knowledge, the education strategies which attempt to provide programs and services especially designed for the disadvantaged are destined, at best, to be minimally successful.

The education strategies are politically vulnerable. The reorganization strategies are most suspect in this respect. All of these plans, in varying degrees, would require a shifting of priorities, and their acceptance by politicians and the general public would probably be difficult to obtain. The federal education programs, while somewhat less controversial in nature, are still vulnerable because of their dependence on the national government for funding. Commitment to achieving the objectives of the educational strategies varies with political administrations, hence sufficient funding cannot always be counted upon.

Most of the education programs do not meet the acute immediate needs of the poor. With the exception of job related and some scholarship programs, the education strategies do not meet the poor's immediate need for food, shelter and clothing. While the emphasis placed on a long-range strategy is a favorable aspect of the approach, its disregard for the present must be viewed as a drawback. For the desperately poor, immediate needs are often the only concerns they are able to consider. Until these needs are met it is unlikely that the poor will take anywhere near full advantage of educational programs which exist or have been proposed.

All education strategies suffer from inequity in benefits. Equalizing the quality of education provided in different regions of the country is virtually impossible, as the commitment to achieving the goals of various strategies, as well as the availability of funding, differs substantially from area to area. Even within school districts, the quality of school programs is unlikely to be uniform.

The education strategies suffer from problems of accessibility. The major exception to this is the voucher program which if properly controlled by the Educational Voucher Agency would experience few problems of inaccessibility. Most of the education strategies, however, will encounter difficulties for a variety of reasons. Integration is restricted because of the political aspect of the issue. Financial limitations restrict the availability of most other programs in areas of the country where they are needed. In some areas there have been fundamental difficulties such as publicizing the programs among the poor.

A large amount of the money spent goes to other sections of society. Some of the strategies, such as integration, consolidation, and adult education are not directed exclusively toward the poor. For all the strategies, however, an important criticism is that a high percentage of the expenditures goes to pay the salaries of staff members and professionals who are not poor themselves. There is evidence that at least in some states the poor and working class end up subsidizing

TABLE 5.3

RATINGS FOR COMPARING ALTERNATIVE EDUCATION AND ECONOMIC DEVELOPMENT STRATEGIES

DIMENSIONS FOR THE RATING*	STRATEGY BEING RATED**											
	EDUCATION							ECONOMIC DEVELOPMENT				
	1	2	3	4	5	6	7	8	9	10	11	12
1	1	1	1	2	1	1	1	3	2	2	2	2
2	2	2	2	2	2	2	4	3	2	2	2	2
3	1	3	1	3	3	3	5	1	3	3	5	1
4	4	5	5	5	5	5	5	4	4	4	5	4
5	3	3	3	3	3	3	3	5	5	5	5	5
6	5	5	5	5	5	5	5	5	5	5	5	5
7	3	3	3	4	3	3	3	5	5	5	5	5
8	3	1	3	3	5	5	5	3	1	1	1	3
9	3	1	3	5	5	5	5	3	5	5	5	3
10	3	3	3	3	3	5	5	x	5	5	5	1
11	3	3	3	3	3	3	3	1	1	1	1	5
12	1	1	1	1	1	1	5	1	1	1	1	1
13	2	2	1	2	1	1	4	1	2	2	2	2
14	1	5	1	1	1	5	5	1	1	1	1	1
15	1	1	1	5	1	1	1	5	5	5	5	5
16	1	1	1	1	1	1	5	3	1	1	1	1
17	3	3	1	1	1	1	1	1	1	1	5	1
18	3	1	3	3	3	1	1	5	1	3	1	1
19	5	1	5	5	3	1	1	5	3	3	3	3
20	3	3	3	3	1	1	1	5	1	1	1	1
21	2	2	2	1	1	2	4	4	1	1	1	2
22	3	3	1	3	1	3	5	4	1	1	1	1
23	5	5	3	1	1	1	1	1	1	1	3	1
24	1	1	1	1	1	1	5	5	1	1	1	1
25	3	3	3	3	3	5	5	5	5	5	5	3
26	3	1	2	3	2	2	5	4	2	2	4	3

x Strategy not rated on specified dimension.

* Dimensions 1-26 correspond to the 26 standard dimensions presented in the Appendix.

** The numbers used to identify the twelve strategies are to be interpreted as follows:

(1) Head Start
(2) Bilingual Education
(3) Adult Basic Education
(4) College Work Study
(5) Open Enrollment
(6) School Integration
(7) School Vouchers
(8) Economic Growth
(9) Economic Opportunity Loan
(10) Cross' Black Capitalism Proposal
(11) CDC Proposal
(12) Public Works Programs for Area Redevelopment

the education of the middle class. Students from middle class families make more use of public education, particularly higher education, than do students from lower and working class families. Thus while the middle class families pay more in the way of school taxes, they actually use even more than they pay for.

Comparing Education Strategies In this section the education strategies are compared using the 26 standard dimensions defined in the Appendix. Table 5.3 presents a comparison of the following strategies: (1) Head Start, (2) Bilingual Education, (3) Adult Basic Education, (4) College Work Study, (5) open enrollment, (6) school integration, and (7) school vouchers.

By way of summary, a comparison will be made among these strategies. We have selected eighteen dimensions for these evaluative comparisons. In Table 5.4 the total number of high and low ratings as well as a difference score is presented for each of the seven strategies.

One observation that can be made on the basis of the information

TABLE 5.4

SUMMARY OF RATINGS FOR EDUCATION AND ECONOMIC DEVELOPMENT STRATEGIES ON SELECTED EVALUATIVE DIMENSIONS

SUMMARY OF THE RATINGS*	STRATEGY BEING RATED**											
	EDUCATION							ECONOMIC DEVELOPMENT				
	1	2	3	4	5	6	7	8	9	10	11	12
HIGH	2	3	3	5	4	5	8	7	5	5	8	5
LOW	5	7	6	5	7	7	5	5	9	8	8	7
DIFFERENCE SCORE (HIGH-LOW)	-3	-4	-3	0	-3	2	3	2	-4	-3	0	-2

* The summary is based on dimensions 2-9, 11-12, and 14-21 of Table 5.3; the row marked HIGH is a summary of the total number of times the specified strategy received a rating of 5 in Table 5.3; the row marked LOW is a summary of the total number of times the specified strategy received a rating of 1; the DIFFERENCE SCORE is obtained by subtraction.

** The numbers used to identify the twelve strategies are to be interpreted as follows:

(1) Head Start
(2) Bilingual Education
(3) Adult Basic Education
(4) College Work Study
(5) Open Enrollment
(6) School Integration
(7) School Vouchers
(8) Economic Growth
(9) Economic Opportunity Loan
(10) Cross' Black Capitalism Proposal
(11) CDC Proposal
(12) Public Works Programs for Area Redevelopment

in Table 5.4 is that the school voucher proposal is the most highly rated of the educational strategies considered. However, to repeat our earlier caution, it is always possible that our rating of a proposed program is somewhat inflated. The experimental studies of the strategy which have recently been undertaken will undoubtedly uncover at least some problems which have not been anticipated. One factor contributing to the high rating for this strategy is the tendency it would have to increase racial integration. It would also contribute to a reduction in the extent of the separation between social classes. By putting the funds used to finance education under control of parents and providing vouchers of greater value to low income parents, the influence of the poor with respect to the delivery of educational services is increased.

Among the existing programs, school integration receives the highest rating. One factor contributing to this rating is its positive impact on self-concept for poor blacks. Another important factor is that it contributes to a reduction in the extent of the separation between social classes. In many areas, the per pupil school expenditure and consequent quality of education in all black schools, is substantially below that in white schools. Integration generally leads to at least some improvement in the quality of the educational services delivered to blacks. Jencks, however, makes a compelling argument that the long term effects of segregation on achievement and adult income are quite modest.

One factor contributing to the relatively low rating of the bilingual education strategy is its limited scope. The strategy can only provide benefits to the non-English speaking segment of the poor. A related problem is accessibility; such programs can only be made available in areas with a relatively large concentration of non-English speaking residents. It is often argued that at least some of the educational difficulties of the poor, particularly poor blacks, can be related to differences between middle and lower class English, but the bilingual education programs at present are restricted primarily to the much smaller Spanish speaking segment of the poor.

ECONOMIC DEVELOPMENT

The programs and proposals considered in this section all call for some form of economic development as a means for dealing with poverty in America. The major objective of the approach is to generate the economic activity that is needed to provide many who are poor or potentially poor with jobs.

Economic growth:[19] This strategy calls for federal policies designed to keep economic growth at a rate of at least 3 percent per year. Proponents of the economic growth strategy point to the decrease in the size of the poverty population that has accompanied expansion of the economy. As the gross national product and disposable per capita income have increased, both the number and quality of available jobs have improved. Economic growth has increased tax revenues making it politically more feasible to create new public welfare programs and to increase the benefits provided by existing programs.

Economic Opportunity Loans (EOL):[20] The Economic Opportunity Loan program was initiated in 1964 under the authority of the Economic Opportunities Act of 1964. It was originally administered by the Office of Economic Opportunity, but in 1966 Congress shifted control to the Small Business Administration. The purpose of the program is to provide financial assistance to low income people for the expansion or establishment of small businesses in a low income high unemployment area.

Cross' Black Capitalism Proposal:[21] In his proposal Cross recommends the utilization of several mechanisms to attack the problem of credit financing. The ghetto market is simply not profitable enough to induce credit institutions to commit a significant amount of capital. One mechanism he proposes is the automatic loan guarantee to eliminate the risk factor in making minority loans. Another mechanism he proposes is tax incentives to encourage the flow of credit into the ghetto.

Community Development Corporation:[22] Recognizing the community development corporation structure as a possible way to deal with poverty, the Community Self-Determination Bill of 1968 was introduced in Congress. The general purpose of the bill was to give ghetto residents control over their own destinies by creating a community-owned structure which would expand employment and self-determination opportunities. The specific goals of the bill were (1) to give the residents an organizational structure with the power to develop the economic opportunities of the ghetto through the development of local businesses and (2) to improve and expand the range of public services in the community. Several community development proposals have been made; we are considering the particular proposal implicit in the Community Self-Determination Bill of 1968.

Public Works Programs for Area Redevelopment:[23] Public Works Programs create jobs and at the same time are directed at improving the quantity and quality of public facilities in poverty areas. These programs are mainly construction projects and include building highways, dams, schools and other public facilities. The two major tools today for area redevelopment are the Economic Development Act of 1965 and the Appalachian Regional Development Act. These acts authorize loans to private businesses and public works loans and grants to low income, high unemployment areas.

Assumptions Implicit In The Economic Development Approach The major assumption implicit in all economic development strategies is that unemployment is a major cause of poverty. Since employment is the major source of income in our society, any major reduction in the extent of poverty is likely to require an increase in employment opportunities for the poor. Aggregate strategies such as economic growth assume that a substantial proportion of the poor are sensitive to the progress of the general economy. The selective categorical development strategies such as Economic Opportunity Loans assume that many of the poor are participating in sub-economies which have become stagnant and isolated from the general economy. These programs aim at stimulating the sub-economies of the urban and rural depressed areas.

Another assumption is that strategies which benefit the poor through employment are preferable to strategies which give money to the poor without the employment requirement. In this respect the approach is consistent with the work ethic. There is less stigma associated with a program which enables the poor to earn an income. Such programs improve the self-image of the poor and aid in developing stability within the poor family and community.

It is implicitly assumed that the majority of the poor who are able to work are also willing to work. Development strategies imply that somehow the economic system is responsible for leaving many people without a decent job and income. This assumption is opposed to the view that the poor are so because they are lazy and indolent.

Implicit in aggregate strategies is the assumption that the general economy has the ability to reach many of the poor without any major changes in the economic structure. Such strategies rely exclusively on the "trickling down" of benefits through the existing economic system.

The categorical strategies assume the opposite, that changes in some of the relationships within the economic structure are necessary before the general economy can meet the needs of the poor. In line with this assumption, black capitalism programs and the CDC proposal seek to alter the structure of ownership of economic resources, putting more in the hands of the poor. Incentives to private industries for relocation and public works programs for area redevelopment seek to change the distribution of economic resources by developing specific areas.

Most of the categorical strategies assume that it is better to improve living conditions in the ghettos than to encourage ghetto dispersal. This should not be viewed as a segregationist position. It is based on the assumption that the ghetto residents stand to gain more through ghetto development than through ghetto dispersal. The assumption is generally made that the improved economic and social status of the ghetto residents made possible through ghetto development will in the long run facilitate racial integration.

Another assumption of the approach is that economic development strategies need to be supplemented by other strategies. All development strategies contain the implicit concession that a portion of the poor will not be reached. There is the realization that other approaches are necessary to reach these hard-core poor. In many cases other strategies are also needed even for those who benefit from economic development. For example, any black capitalism program must rely on education strategies to prepare the entrepreneurial talent for its program. An incentives program would need a manpower training program to develop a work force to meet the demands of a newly relocated industry. Put another way, the assumption is that the development approach may be the answer to the long-range goal of eliminating poverty; but until that goal is reached, several approaches working in conjunction are necessary.

Implicit in the black capitalism programs is the assumption that the small business is a viable economic unit upon which the development of the ghetto economy can be based. These programs seek to establish the individual entrepreneur within the economy of the ghetto. Certainly in the past, the individually owned business provided the vehicle by which many members of immigrant minority groups pulled themselves out of poverty. Since these earlier successes, however, basic changes in the economic structure have taken place which give the competitive advantage to corporate conglomerates and retail business chains. The individual businessman within the ghetto must often compete with the local representative of a national concern to realize his meager profit. For these reasons, many feel that black capitalism programs are not the ultimate answer to the developement of the ghetto economy.

Black capitalism programs are based on the belief that the development of a business middle class is important for the future of the black minority. Such a middle class would perform a dual function. On the one hand, it would provide a group from which to draw leaders for the black community and leadership models for young blacks in search of a future. On the other hand, this business class would maintain the social, economic, and political contacts outside the black community which are necessary for the development and eventual integration of the racial ghetto.

A further assumption implicit in the CDC proposal is that community ownership and control of indigenous resources is vital to the development of poverty stricken communities. A related assumption is that the residents of these communities are in the best position to make judgements as to what changes are needed. The CDC structure would provide the vehicle for such broad based community control.

It is also an assumption of the public works programs for area redevelopment that depressed areas are the result of physical and economic isolation from the mainstream of American life. This assumption is the basis for the emphasis of such programs on the improvement of public facilities, particularly the expansion and modernization of the highway systems in these areas. An example of a program with such emphasis is the Appalachian Regional Development Administration, which spends about three-fifths of its funds on highway construction. The underlying assumption here is that such improvements will increase the accessibility of these poverty areas, making them more attractive to private industry.

The proposal to provide incentives to private industry to relocate in the ghetto has the underlying assumption that the private sector may be more successful in developing these areas than the government. It is assumed that such a program would facilitate the utilization of private business expertise in the development of the sub-economy of the ghetto.

Evaluation Of Economic Development Strategies In this section, arguments are presented which apply to all, or most, of the economic development strategies. The purpose is to summarize the arguments for and against the approach as a means of combating poverty. The arguments in favor of economic development are considered first:

Economic development strategies encourage self-sufficiency. The primary mechanism of economic development strategies is employment. Each program seeks to create new and better employment opportunities for the poor which will enable them to become self-sufficient. But this same argument can also be viewed as a limitation, since economic development benefits can only reach those who are employable. The poor who, for any reason, are not employable cannot receive the primary benefits of the strategy. This latter category includes many of the poor.

Income is put into the hands of many of the poor. By increasing the number of jobs open to and filled by the poor, these strategies increase the money available to the poor. This provides a freedom of choice that is lacking in many strategies, particularly income-in-kind strategies.

They are conducive to a positive self-image among the poor. Unlike some strategies, such as AFDC, which involve substantial social stigma, economic development strategies do not. By creating employment opportunities, these strategies enhance the self-image of the unemployed and underemployed who obtain jobs. Benefits which are acquired as earned income have a more positive effect on self-image than do those which are not employment related.

They attempt to attack the causes of poverty. Instead of simply seeking to support those in poverty, economic development strategies attempt to solve the basic economic problems of the poor. This is especially true of the categorical strategies which view poverty as the result of economic isolation and stagnation which deprive the poor of a proportionate share of the general economic expansion. These strategies seek to remedy this by generating employment opportunities within a specific area or among a specific group. Such strategies, however, do not deal directly with another root cause of poverty, the lack of marketable skills. Economic development programs make little direct provision for training the unemployed poor.

The following are the major criticisms of the economic development strategies:

Economic development strategies do not meet the immediate needs of the poor. In general, economic development strategies aim at the long-range solutions to the economic difficulties of the poor. The immediate needs of providing food, clothing, and medical care are often not met directly by these strategies. The emphasis is more on effecting economic change than on meeting immediate needs. However, such strategies create new or better employment opportunities for the poor. In doing so, they provide income for those who receive these new jobs. This income is used, in turn, to meet immediate needs. The problem arises because there is often a time lag between the initiation of a program and the creation of new job opportunities.

There is uncertainty as to who receives the benefits of economic development strategies. All economic development strategies depend ultimately on the employment market to dispense benefits. There are very few direct controls over who gets hired as a result of a particular program. Therefore, there are no guarantees that the most needy will receive the benefits. On the contrary, the labor market works to benefit the most able, not the most needy. Black capitalism programs and the CDC proposal are exceptions to this general rule. However, even with these strategies there is relatively little control over who ultimately gets hired.

Administrative costs tend to be high. Most economic development programs have led to the establishment of elaborate bureaucracies to implement their goals. While there is considerable variation among programs, as compared to the other approaches, economic development programs rank poorly. The CDC proposal is an important exception to this generalization. While this proposal would establish a new bureaucratic structure, most of the positions would be filled by residents of the poor community, thus providing employment benefits for them.

Benefits from the various programs are generally inaccessible. Programs for economic development often vary in their accessibility from state to state and region to region. There has been a bias in favor of the development of urban centers with little attention and funding going to rural areas. This may stem, in part, from the tendency for many national programs to locate their regional offices in urban centers. Furthermore, aggregate strategies affect regions differently, depending upon the degree of isolation. Often, the benefits of such strategies will be felt least by those regions most in need of development.

A second cause of inaccessibility stems from the bureaucratic structures which surround development programs. With the Economic Opportunity Loan (EOL) program, for example, the application procedures called for are so complex and lengthy as to discourage application by the most needy.

Little of the actual spending for economic development programs reaches the poor. There is considerable leakage of funds. Since these programs rely mainly on the creation of jobs in the private sector to benefit the poor, a considerable portion of the funding goes to these private industries in the form of profits. Outstanding examples of this type of leakage are the public works programs for area redevelopment. The construction under these programs is done by private construction companies and the bulk of any jobs created for the poor are in the industries which are attracted. In each case there is leakage to the nonpoor.

Comparing Economic Development Strategies In this section, the various economic development strategies are compared on the basis of the standard set of 26 dimensions defined in the Appendix.

In Table 5.3 the following strategies are compared: (8) economic growth, (9) Economic Opportunity Loan program (EOL), (10) Cross' black capitalism proposal, (11) CDC proposal (as presented in the Community Self-Determination Bill), and (12) public works programs for area redevelopment.

By way of summary a comparison will be made among the ratings of the five economic development strategies considered above. For the purposes of this comparison, a subset of eighteen out of the original twenty-six dimensions has been selected. In Table 5.4 the total number of high and low ratings as well as a difference score is presented for each of the five economic development strategies.

The most noteworthy observation to be made on the basis of the information in Table 5.4 is that economic growth, an aggregate strategy, is rated higher than any of the categorical strategies. The economic growth strategy has a more substantial impact on the distribution of income than any of the other strategies. Its reliance on a trickling down of benefits is administratively simpler than a categorical strategy such as the Economic Opportunity Loan program. The strategy receives strong policical support because it benefits both the rich and the poor.

The lowest rated of the strategies considered is the Economic Opportunity Loan program. One factor contributing to this low rating is that it tends to encourage blacks to remain in the ghetto which in turn tends to slow the rate of racial integration. The program is also highly dependent on the state of the economy; when there is an economic recession, the strategy is less effective. The program does not include mechanisms to assure accountability to the poor and the benefits of the program are not easily accessible. As far as the poor are concerned, the major benefits come in the form of jobs; but to the job applicant these jobs are not distinguished from others.

ORGANIZATION

The strategies considered in this section are consistent with the organization approach. Several of the strategies considered could appropriately have been considered in a previous chapter or an earlier section of this chapter. The rent strike strategy is considered here and not included in the discussion of other housing strategies in Chapter 4. The unionization of farmworkers could have been considered in the section of this chapter on Manpower. However, not all organization strategies fit into any of the anti-poverty approaches as yet considered. For example, neither neighborhood organization nor the mobilization of low income voters fit into any of the major categories considered earlier.

Community Action Program:[24] Three goals that are often cited in regard to CAP are the expansion of political influence of the poor, democratization of social welfare and improvement of delivery of social welfare services. The expansion of political influence involves giving the poor more say in all the institutions that affect them. The democratization of social welfare means that the welfare clients have a greater voice in the type of welfare services they receive. Improved delivery of services means that the social welfare agency makes its services more accessible to clients and potential clients. Although welfare is a major target, the Community Action Program aims at making all the institutions of the community more responsive to the poor. This includes schools, legal services, and so forth.

Neighborhood Organization:[25] The focus here is on Saul Alinsky's approach to neighborhood organizing. He began organizing neighborhoods in the 1930s. His strategy was to go into a neighborhood and find a common problem around which residents could unite. He developed an enemy or target to organize against (for example, a local merchant who was overcharging or a slumlord). He created an umbrella organization from existing community organizations, such as churches, clubs, and unions. Alinsky's method is oriented toward conflict, not consensus. Rather than allying with liberals, he organized ghetto residents into a power block.

Mobilization of Low Income Voters:[26] The goal of mobilizing the poor to register and vote is to gain power through the election of candidates with policies favorable toward the poor. It assumes the poor represent a large enough block that, if united, could bring about changes.

Riots:[27] There has been an outbreak of rioting in black communities in recent years. Riots are an indication that a community is highly frustrated with its situation and sees no channels for action other than destruction. Riots have served as a warning to the nation that there is something seriously wrong in the cities. Riots are not understood by the public in America as a form of political protest. Historically in Europe, for instance, riots were understood to be an expression of dissatisfaction on the part of the lower classes who had no other means to express their grievances. Since representative institutions developed early in America, riots are not accepted in this light.

Rent Strikes:[28] Rent strikes are organized to alleviate housing problems. In general, rent strikes have two main goals. The first is to obtain greater legal rights for tenants. The existing legal relationship between landlords and tenants predominately favors the former. The second goal is to obtain repairs in run-down, neglected dwelling units.

National Welfare Rights Organization (NWRO):[29] NWRO was formed with the broader goal of bringing fiscal disruption to local and state budgets by dramatically increasing the cost of welfare. This was to be brought about by expanding the enrollment of those eligible for welfare and increasing the benefits paid to recipients. It was hoped that as a result of this pressure, national reforms would be instituted paving the way for a guaranteed annual income. Now based in Washington, D.C., NWRO has formed a national committee with members elected by and accountable directly to the membership. Biennial conventions are held to effect a periodical evaluation of the organization's goals.

Community Control of Education:[30] Disenchantment with the existing school structure and its seeming unresponsiveness to local needs has led to demands for decentralization. The failure of compensatory education and desegregation has added to the controversy and heightened the debate surrounding school accountability and control. Our focus is on the Oceanhill-Brownsville experiment in New York

City. This experiment was initiated in response to the suggestions of the Bundy Commision. The suggestions for community control involved a redistribution of power over school affairs, giving local communities significant control over their schools.

Unionization of Farm Workers:[31] Farmworkers were not covered by the National Labor Relations Act and as a result, have no legal rights of collective bargaining and do not fall under the minimum wage rule. In 1962, Cesar Chavez, a Mexican community organizer, formed the National Farmworkers Alliance (NFWA) in the San Joaquin Valley, in the heart of the California wine industry. He began with approximately 3,000 families and by 1968 his organization had grown to 17,000 families. Chavez has organized the workers to a point where they have won the right of collective bargaining and has signed agreements with the ten largest grape growers in California. These contracts provide substantial pay increases, fringe benefits, and increased power for the workers in their relations with the growers. He has since expanded his unionization efforts to other states with substantial minority group farmworker populations.

Action Against Discrimination in the Construction Industry:[32] In a number of cities, coalitions of black organizations have staged demonstrations and closed construction sites in order to emphasize their demand for more jobs. The most notable of these incidents have occurred in Pittsburgh, Seattle, and Chicago, but they have been attempted in almost every major American city. The demands include a quota of jobs for blacks, black control of recruiting and training, sweeping changes in the apprenticeship system and the provision that federal, state and local officials deny funding to any construction firm not meeting these demands.

Operation Breadbasket:[33] This program is a strategy designed to keep money within the community where the poor live and to increase its circulation. Breadbasket was originally conceived by Martin Luther King, Jr., as an organization to recruit, train and place blacks in meaningful, rewarding jobs. After King's death, Jesse Jackson, a black minister, stepped in to fill the power vacuum created in the black community of Chicago. He expanded the program into an economic development organization that provides jobs for ghetto residents and stimulates black owned and operated businesses within the ghetto in Chicago. Recently, Jackson has left the organization to start another more broadly based national organization.

Assumptions Implicit In The Organization Approach One of the most fundamental assumptions of the organization strategies is that the poor have been fragmented, disorganized, and unable to effectively articulate and document their needs. Organization strategies assume that the poor must develop power of their own in order to place themselves in a more effective bargaining position.

Another assumption is that the problems of poverty are rooted in the unequal distribution of resources within our society. Unlike many other strategies, which view the poor as responsible for their own poverty, organization strategies assume that changes must be made throughout society, not just in the life-style of the poor. This outlook can be most clearly seen in the National Welfare Rights Organization's view that the welfare bureaucracy, not the recipient, is the major cause of welfare ineffectiveness.

It is also implicitly assumed by most organization strategies that the poor are capable of and willing to make important decisions on the factors influencing their lives. In the past the assumption was that the poor were apathetic and unwilling to take on leadership roles or even unwilling to join in organizational activity. Those who advocate the organizational approach point out that the activities in which the poor do take a leadership role are often classified as deviant or immoral. They also say that many of the more legitimate organizational activities have systematically excluded the poor and have generally not been responsive to their needs. Organization strategies assume that more responsive organizations with realistic goals for the poor will effectively counteract the supposed apathy of the poor. The poor are assumed to be active participants, able to make significant contributions to organizational activity. Community control of education is a prime example of this assumption.

Certain programs have in addition, specific assumptions which need to be discussed. For instance, NWRO assumes that welfare is a right and should not be considered as a handout. NWRO assumes that by organizing, welfare recipients can significantly reduce their perceived stigma. Secondly it is held that constant pressure on the welfare bureacuracy will cause it to collapse from within, forcing changes in welfare policy.

An underlying assumption of the unionization of farmworkers, action against discrimination in the construction industry, and Operation Breadbasket is that the poor must organize to effectively compete in the economy of our society. They all assume that the poor, through organized activity, can significantly alter their employment and business opportunities.

Supporters of community control of education believe that present centralized bureaucracies are unable to provide meaningful education to the poor. It is assumed that community control of the decision making processes will provide more relevant, responsive educational structures.

A fundamental assumption of mobilization of low income voters is that the poor can effect meaningful changes in their living conditions through the electoral process. It is assumed that the system is open and flexible enough so that the poor can work within rather than outside it. This approach is in opposition to those who believe that our present system does not work and must be replaced.

Rent strikes are based on the assumption that organized tenants can put enough pressure on public and political opinion to change inadequate housing conditions. It is felt that changes in housing codes and in contractual agreements and the enforcement of these would place the tenant in a more favorable bargaining position vis-a-vis the landlord.

Neighborhood organization, as advocated by Saul Alinsky, assumes that those in power (businessmen, local politicians and so on) are most susceptible to confrontation tactics by an organized body of the poor at the local level. It assumes each neighborhood must determine its own needs and targets for protest. Until recently Alinsky and his advocates have assumed that a nationally oriented program was unwise and unworkable.

The Community Action Program was organized around two assumptions. Poverty was thought to be due, in part, to a limited opportunity structure rather than to individual pathology. This led to programs geared to increase opportunities for the poor and away from programs oriented toward the provision of services. Secondly, it was assumed that the poor, especially poor blacks, needed to be brought inside the political process. It was assumed that organized communities would be able to pressure their local power structures into being responsive to their needs.

Evaluation Of The Organization Strategy In this section both the advantages and disadvantages of the organization approach as a general strategy against poverty are briefly summarized. The advantages of the organization strategy are considered first:

The organization strategy can inform the larger society of the problems of the poor. Through effective use of the media, as in the case of NWRO and the unionization of farmworkers, the organized poor can dramatize their plight and bring the resources of the larger society to bear upon their problems.

It gives the poor a sense of dignity and hope. By organizing into groups around relevant social issues, the poor can improve their image of themselves in several ways. By meeting others in similar situations, an individual comes to understand that his problems are neither unique nor unsolvable. His self-image is improved because he knows he is not alone. The poor often see their lives as controlled by arbitrary factors beyond their control. Organizing breaks this sense of dependency and gives them a sense of control over their lives. The apathy often attributed to the poor may be due in large part to the unresponsiveness of institutions to the needs of the poor. Once the poor have the power to affect these institutions, their apathy may well diminish.

NWRO, for example, has evolved into an effective organizational weapon. As a result it has both reduced the stigma felt by welfare recipients and has shown that welfare recipients are not all apathetic.

Organization increases the political power of the poor. After organizing, the poor are better able to compete for existing resources and services than prior to becoming organized. As organized groups, their demands become more concrete and their ability to see that they are met increases substantially. The new power goes not only to those participating in the organization, but to all the poor.

Organization strategies are generally quite accountable to their recipients. Some programs, such as Operation Breadbasket and to some extent the unionization of farmworkers, are controlled by a select few with little or no accountability to the recipients. Most others, however, have built-in mechanisms to insure a high degree of accountability. Unlike massive federal manpower or housing programs, organization strategies allow the poor to set their own priorities and give them an active voice in the decision making process.

Benefits go to a significant proportion of the poor beyond those actually participating in the organization. Since organization strategies operate to improve the living conditions of a group, rather than an individual, the gains the organization can obtain help many of the poor.

The organization strategy can play an iconoclastic role by breaking down the myths about the poor. Earlier analyses of the poor which portrayed them as deviants who needed a strong dose of middle-class values have to some extent been changed by organizational activity. Because of their active participation in a variety of organizational settings, the poor are less frequently viewed as lazy.

The following are some of the limitations of the organizational strategy:

Effective organization requires resources which the poor, by themselves, lack. The poor often do not have the time, money and expertise for successful organizing. It is frequently necessary for those who are not themselves poor to begin the task of organizing. The danger is that middle-class, professional values may be forced upon or substituted for the indigenous values of the poor. Goals may be imposed upon the organization that the poor would not choose for themselves. As long as the poor need to rely on outside sources for money or technical aide, limitations on the nature of the organization will be present.

Concrete benefits from organized activity differ markedly from community to community. The organization strategy against poverty relies heavily on local participation and involvement. Levels of participation are dependent on a multitude of factors that may be present in one community and totally lacking in another. Attempts at greater centralization of organizations to make benefits more equal run the risk of destroying a basic premise of the organization strategy —grass roots participation and decision making.

For the poor, life is a struggle; there is little extra time or energy for organizing. The organization strategy generally does not meet the immediate, acute needs of the poor. Unlike income or manpower strategies which provide cash and jobs, the organization strategy deals with less tangible, longer range goals such as decision making power, community pride and development, and the like. It is probably true that the immediate problems of adequate food, clothing and shelter must be met before the poor can effectively organize for broader goals.

Organization strategies often bog down in administrative failures. The problems of organizational development are well documented. The larger and more successful an organization, the greater the complexity of administrative problems. Leadership becomes entrenched, membership participation is less meaningful and goals are side stepped. The poor are further hampered by their inexperience in organizational interaction. CAP is a classic example of the administrative problems that can beset the organization strategy. In response to pressure on the federal government from local goverments, CAP has shifted its role from initiator of community action to provider of services.

Comparing Organization Strategies In this section, ten of the organization strategies are compared on the basis of ratings along 28 dimensions. Some of the programs considered in the preceding two chapters are not included in these ratings. In some cases the information needed to make the ratings was not available, while in others the rating would have made little sense.

In Table 5.5 the following ten strategies are compared: (1) Community Action Program (CAP), (2) mobilization of low income voters, (3) neighborhood organizing, (4) riots, (5) rent strikes, (6) National Welfare Rights Organization (NWRO), (7) community control of education, (8) unionization of farmworkers, (9) action against discrimination in the construction industry, and (10) Operation Breadbasket.

A total of 28 dimensions are used to compare these strategies. Dimensions 1 through 26 correspond to the standard dimensions defined in the Appendix. Two new dimensions have been added: dimension 27, impact on public awareness of poverty, and dimension 28, utilization of the poor as leaders and decision makers. These two dimensions are defined below.

Dimension 27, impact on public awareness of poverty, is a measure of the degree to which alternative strategies raise the level of the

TABLE 5.5

RATINGS FOR COMPARING ALTERNATIVE ORGANIZATION STRATEGIES

DIMENSION FOR THE RATING*	ORGANIZATION STRATEGY BEING RATED**									
	1	2	3	4	5	6	7	8	9	10
1	2	1	1	2	1	2	1	2	2	2
2	3	2	2	3	2	2	2	2	2	2
3	3	3	5	3	3	5	5	5	3	3
4	5	5	5	4	4	5	5	5	5	5
5	4	3	3	4	3	3	3	5	5	5
6	3	3	3	3	3	1	3	5	5	5
7	5	3	3	3	3	1	3	5	5	5
8	3	1	3	1	3	3	1	3	5	1
9	5	1	3	1	3	3	1	3	5	5
10	5	5	5	5	5	5	5	5	1	5
11	3	3	3	3	3	3	3	3	1	1
12	1	1	1	1	1	5	1	5	1	1
13	1	1	1	1	1	2	1	1	1	1
14	1	5	5	1	5	5	5	5	1	1
15	1	1	1	1	1	1	1	5	5	5
16	3	1	1	1	1	1	1	1	1	1
17	3	5	5	x	5	5	5	3	3	3
18	3	1	1	x	1	3	1	3	1	3
19	3	1	5	1	1	1	3	5	3	5
20	1	3	3	1	1	5	1	3	1	3
21	3	1	2	3	1	2	1	1	1	1
22	3	1	1	3	1	5	1	1	1	1
23	3	3	1	3	1	5	1	5	1	1
24	2	1	3	2	1	2	1	1	1	1
25	3	5	5	3	3	5	5	5	5	5
26	3	1	1	1	1	1	1	1	1	1
27	1	1	1	5	1	5	1	5	3	3
28	1	5	5	5	5	5	5	5	3	3

x Strategy not rated on specified dimension.

* Dimensions 1-26 correspond to the 26 standard dimensions presented in the Appendix; 27 is public awareness of poverty; 28 is the poor as leaders and decision-makers.

** The numbers used to identify the 10 organization strategies are to be interpreted as follows:

(1) CAP
(2) Neighborhood Organization
(3) Mobilization of Low Income Voters
(4) Riots
(5) Rent Strikes
(6) NWRO
(7) Community Control of Education
(8) Unionization of Farmworkers
(9) Action Against Discrimination in the Construction Industry
(10) Operation Breadbasket

general public's consciousness of the poverty problem. For our purposes, awareness may or may not include a propensity to act. In addition, whether the impact produces positive or negative attitudes toward the problems is not an issue. Thus, riots and unionization of farmworkers receive the same rating. A rating of 5 indicates that the strategy has a widespread impact on the awareness of the public; a rating of 3 indicates that the strategy has a modest impact on public awareness; and a rating of 1 indicates that the strategy has little or no impact on public awareness of poverty.

Dimension 28, utilization of the poor as leaders and decision makers, is a measure of the degree to which the poor actually hold leadership and decision making positions. The relative success of the strategy is not taken into account. Thus, rent strikes and NWRO receive the same rating. A rating of 5 indicates that many actual decision making and leadership positions are held by the poor, and a rating of 1 indicates that relatively few of the important decision making positions are filled by the poor.

TABLE 5.6

SUMMARY OF RATINGS FOR ALTERNATIVE ORGANIZATION STRATEGIES ON SELECTED EVALUATIVE DIMENSIONS

SUMMARY OF THE RATINGS*	ORGANIZATION STRATEGY BEING RATED**									
	1	2	3	4	5	6	7	8	9	10
HIGH	4	3	5	0	2	6	4	9	7	7
LOW	4	8	4	8	7	5	9	2	8	6
DIFFERENCE SCORE (HIGH-LOW)	0	-5	1	-8	-5	1	-5	7	-1	1

* The summary is based on dimensions 2-9, 11-12, 14-21 of Table 5.5; the row marked HIGH is a summary of the total number of times the specified strategy received a rating of 5 in Table 5.5; the row marked LOW is a summary of the total number of times the specified strategy received a rating of 1; the DIFFERENCE SCORE is obtained by subtraction.

** The numbers used to identify the 10 organization strategies are to be interpreted as follows:

(1) CAP
(2) Neighborhood Organization
(3) Mobilization of Low Income Voters
(4) Riots
(5) Rent Strikes
(6) NWRO
(7) Community Control of Education
(8) Unionization of Farmworkers
(9) Action Against Discrimination in the Construction Industry
(10) Operation Breadbasket

By way of summary a comparison will be made among the ratings of the ten organization strategies considered above. In Table 5.6 the total number of high and low ratings as well as a difference score is presented for each strategy.

One observation that can be made on the basis of the information included in Table 5.6 is that the unionization of farmworkers receives the highest rating of the organization strategies. A major limitation of this strategy is that farmworkers make up only a small fraction of the poor. For farmworkers, however, it is a very effective strategy. Those farmworkers who have been organized have substantially increased their political influence at the local level, have increased their wages, and both of these factors have undoubtedly led to a more positive self-image. These same factors also contribute to family stability. The strategy is accountable to the recipients and to the extent that it has been successful in increasing wages it has met the acute needs of the poor. However, for many farmworkers these needs have been met only after long strikes and concomitant deprivation.

It can be observed in addition, on the basis of the information in Table 5.6, that riots receive an exceedingly low overall rating. One factor contributing to the low rating of this strategy is that it contributes to fear of integration on the part of whites. This in turn increases the resistance of middle-class residential areas to any influx of lower-class blacks. Needless to say this is one of the least popular of those we have considered.

Notes

1. E. Wright Bakke, *The Mission of Manpower Policy* (Kalamazoo, Michigan: The W.E. Upjohn Institute for Employment Research, 1969), p. 9; Sar A. Levitan, *Programs in Aid of the Poor for the 1970s* (Baltimore: Johns Hopkins Press, 1969), p. 60; U.S. Department of Labor, *Manpower Report of The President 1969* (Washington, D.C.: U.S. Government Printing Office, 1969), p. 129.
2. William Goldstein, "Opportunities Industrialization Centers," (Unpublished background paper of the Social Welfare Regional Research Institute, Boston College, 1970); U.S. Department of Labor, *Manpower Report of the President 1968* (Washington, D.C.: U.S. Government Printing Office, 1968), pp. 207-208.
3. Sar A. Levitan, Garth L. Mangum and Robert Taggart III, *Economic Opportunity in the Ghetto: the Partnership of Government and Business* (Baltimore: Johns Hopkins Press, 1970), pp. 21-22; U.S. Department of Labor, *Manpower Report of the President 1970* (Washington, D.C.: U.S. Government Printing Office, 1970), p. 22.
4. Robert A. Levine, *The Poor Ye Need Not Have With You* (Cambridge, Mass.: M.I.T. Press, 1970), p. 131; U.S. Department of Labor, *Manpower Report of the President 1971* (Washington, D.C.: U.S. Government Printing Office, 1971), p. 42; *Everyman's Guide to Federal Programs* (Washington, D.C.: New Community Press, 1968); *Manpower Report of the President 1970,* pp. 304-313.
5. Executive Office of the President, *Catalogue of Federal Domestic Assistance* (Washington, D.C.: U.S. Government Printing Office, 1970); *Manpower Report of the President 1971,* pp. 308-309; U.S. Department of Labor, *Making the Scene in Jobs, School, Training Through the Neighborhood Youth Corps.* (Washington, D.C.: U.S. Government Printing Office, 1968), p. 7. President's Commission on Income Maintenance Programs, *Background Papers* (Washington, D.C.: U.S. Government Printing Office, 1969), p. 389.
6. *Manpower Report of the President 1971,* pp. 125-126; *Manpower Report of the President 1970;* Levitan et al., *Economic Opportunity in the Ghetto,* pp. 62-67.
7. Levine, *The Poor Ye Need Not Have With You,* p.116; *Manpower Report of the President 1970,* pp. 59, 81; Martin Lowenthal, *Work and Welfare an Overview,* (Chestnut Hill, Mass: Boston College, Social Welfare Regional Research Institute, 1971), pp. 78–80.
8. Levitan et al., *Economic Opportunity in the Ghetto,* pp. 56, 281; *Everyman's Guide to Federal Programs,* pp. 395-397; Levine, *The Poor Ye Need Not Have With You,* pp. 123-127; *Manpower Report of the President 1970,* pp. 74-75; Lowenthal, *Work and Welfare,* pp. 81-87.

9. *Manpower Report of the President 1971,* p. 53; *Manpower Report of the President 1970,* pp. 74-75; Lowenthal, *Work and Welfare,* pp. 81-87.
10. *Background Papers,* p. 391; *Manpower Report of the President 1970,* p. 60; Sar A. Levitan and Garth L. Mangum, *Federal Training and Work Programs in the Sixties* (Ann Arbor, Michigan: Institute of Labor and Industrial Relations, 1967), p. 28.
11. Garth L. Mangum, "Guaranteeing Employment Opportunities." In *Social Policies for America in the Seventies,* edited by Robert Theobald (Garden City, New York: Doubleday, 1968). Michael Harrington, "Government Should Be the Employer of First Resort," *New York Times Magazine,* (March 26, 1972).
12. Levine, *The Poor Ye Need Not Have With You,* pp. 132-143; "Project Head Start: A Research Summary," *Integrated Education* 6, 5(1968): 45-54; U.S. Department of Health, Education, and Welfare, Office of Child Development, *Project Head Start 1968: The Development of a Program,* October, 1970, pp. 24-37.
13. Armando Rodreguez, "The Necessity for Bilingual Education," *Wilson Library Bulletin* 44, 7(1970): 724-730.
14. *Catalogue of Federal Domestic Assistance,* pp. 244-246.
15. *Catalogue of Federal Domestic Assistance,* p. 300.
16. Solomon Resnik and Barbara Kaplan, "Report Card on Open Admissions: Remedial Work Recommended," *New York Times Magazine,* (May 9, 1971). See also, Christopher Jencks et al., *Inequality* (New York: Basic Books, 1972).
17. James S. Coleman, *Equality of Educational Opportunity* (Washington, D.C.: U.S. Government Printing Office, 1966); John A. Morsell "Racial Desegregation and Integration in Public Education," *Journal of Negro Education* 38, 3(1969): 276-284; Gary Orfield, "The Debate Over School Desegregation," *New Republic* 162, 10(1970): 33-35; Jon P. Alston and Melvin P. Knapp, "Acceptance of School Integration 1965-1969," *Integrated Education* 9, 2(1971): 11-15. Also see Jencks et al., *Inequality.*
18. Center for the Study of Public Policy, *Education Vouchers: A Preliminary Report on Financing Education by Payments to Parents* (Cambridge, Mass.: Center for the Study of Public Policy, 1970). Also see Jencks et al., *Inequality.*
19. Lowell Galloway, "Foundations of the War on Poverty," *American Economic Review* 55, 15(1967): 122-131; Leon H. Keyserling, "The Problem of Problems: Economic Growth." In *Social Policies for America in the Seventies,* edited by Theobald.
20. Sar Levitan, Garth Mangum, and Robert Taggart III, *Economic Opportunity in the Ghetto,* p. 75.
21. Theodore Cross, *Black Capitalism* (New York, Atheneum, 1969).
22. The bill referred to as the Community Self-Determination Act of 1968 was introduced into the Senate by Senator Gaylord Nelson, 90th Congress, 2nd Session, 1968. Sar Levitan, "Community Self-Determination and Entrepreneurship: The Promise and Limitations," *Poverty and Human Resources Abstracts* 4, 1(1969): 16-24; Michael Brower, "The Criteria for Measuring the Success of a Community Development Corporation in a Ghetto,"

(Working paper for the Center for Community Economic Development, Cambridge, Mass.,) p. 21. See also Severyn T. Bruyn, "Notes on the Contradictions of Modern Business," *Sociological Inquiry* 42, 2(1972): 123-143.

23. Joseph Becker, *In Aid of the Unemployed* (Baltimore: Johns Hopkins Press, 1965), p. 167; Levitan, *Programs in Aid of the Poor for the 1970's* pp. 68-69; U.S. Department of Commerce, "Economic Growth in American Communities," in *Annual Report of the Redevelopment Administration* (Washington, D.C.: U.S. Government Printing Office, 1963), p. 6.

24. Peter Marris and Martin Rein, *Dilemmas of Social Reform* (New York: Atherton Press, 1967); Ralph Kramer, *Participation of the Poor* (Englewood Cliffs, New Jersey: Prentice-Hall, 1969); Neil Gilbert, *Clients or Constituents* (San Francisco: Jossey-Bass, 1970); The Poor Ye Need Not Have With You; Kenneth Clark and Jeannette Hopkins, *A Relevant War Against Poverty* (New York: Harper and Row, 1968); Severyn T. Bruyn, *Communities in Action: Pattern and Process* (New Haven: College and University Press, 1963).

25. Frank Riessman, *Strategies Against Poverty* (New York: Random House, 1969), pp. 4-7; Marion Sanders, *The Professional Radical: Conversations with Saul Alinsky* (Evanston, Ill.: Harper and Row, 1965); Saul Alinsky, *Reveille for Radicals* (Chicago: University of Chicago Press, 1946), p. 201.

26. Richard Cloward, "A Strategy of Disruption," *Center Diary* (January/February, 1967): 32-36.

27. Ralph W. Conant, "Rioting, Insurrection and Civil Disobedience," *American Scholar* 37, 3(1968): 420-433; Hazel Erskine, "The Polls: Demonstrations and Race Riots," *Public Opinion Quarterly* 31, 4(1967-1968): 655-677.

28. Michael Lipsky, "Rent Strikes: Poor Man's Weapon," *Trans-action* 6, 2(1969): 10-15; Richard Cloward and Frances Piven, "Finessing the Poor," *The Nation* 207, 11(1968): 332-334; "Rent Strikes in Public Housing," *Journal of Housing* 26, 8(1969): 351-352; Edward White, "Tenant Participation in Public Housing Management," *Journal of Housing* 26, 8(1969): 416-419.

29. Richard Cloward and Frances Piven, "A Strategy to End Poverty by Guaranteed Income," *The Nation* 202, 18(1966): 510-517; Richard Rog, "Now It's Welfare Lib," *New York Times Magazine* (September 27, 1970); "NWRO-Organizational Weapon," an interview with George Wiley in *Social Policy* 1, 2(1970).

30. Mario Fantini, "Participation, Decentralization, and Community Control and Quality Education," *The Record* 71, 1(1969): 93-107; Maurice Berube, "Community Control: Key to Educational Achievement," *Social Policy* 1, 2(1970): 42-46.

31. Irving Cohen, "LaHuelga, Delano and After," *Monthly Labor Review* 91, 6(1968): 13-16; Karen Kaziara, "Collective Bargaining on the Farm," *Monthly Labor Review* 91, 6(1968): 3-9.

32. Raymond Marshall, "The Impact of Civil Rights Legislation on Collective Bargaining in the Construction Industry," *Poverty and Human Resources Abstracts* 5, 1(1970): 4-17; Pacific Studies Center, "Black Monday's Sunday Allies," *Ramparts* 8, 7(1970): 34-38.

33. Richard Levine, "Jesse Jackson: Heir to Dr. King," *Harpers Magazine* 238, 1426(1969): 58-70.

6

Comparing Strategies Against Poverty

In the Introduction we outlined the three objectives of the present study. Firstly, to describe and evaluate the major anti-poverty programs and proposals consistent with each of six general approaches. Secondly, to compare programs and proposals within each of these six approaches. The preceding chapters have dealt with these objectives. The third objective was to compare programs and proposals across the six general anti-poverty strategies. While the use of the same dimensions for rating programs across general strategies makes such comparisons possible, such inter-category comparisons have not as yet received much attention. In this chapter comparisons will be made between the six general approaches. In addition the five highest rated strategies will be compared.

Since the National Welfare Rights Organization's negative income tax proposal receives the highest overall rating, the reader might conclude that this is the strategy we endorse most enthusiastically. Actually, despite its many merits, the strategy does have a major flaw: the high guaranteed minimum income called for ($6,500 per year) is not politically feasible at present nor is it likely to be at any time in the near future. In the last section of this chapter, an alternative to the NWRO negative income tax is presented. This strategy, referred to as a national income insurance plan, is a negative income tax plan which includes a guaranteed minimum income that would be politically feasible in the not too distant future. Within ten years it would provide a guaranteed minimum income rivalling that called for in the NWRO proposal. The national income insurance plan is the one anti-poverty strategy which we feel in the long run would do the most to reduce the extent of poverty in the United States. However, neither this plan, nor any other single anti-poverty strategy can reasonably be expected to do the job alone.

Comparing Anti-Poverty Approaches In this section comparisons are made among the six anti-poverty approaches considered in the preceding chapters. We will be particularly interested in whether or not there is a tendency for strategies within one approach to be consistently rated higher than strategies within other approaches. Data relevant to this question are presented in Table 6.1. The six vertical bars correspond to the six alternative anti-poverty approaches. In previous chapters, the ratings of the various strategies were summarized on the basis of a subset of 18 of the 26 standard dimensions selected as most appropriate for evaluative comparisons. The overall difference score was obtained by subtracting the number of dimensions on which the strategy has the lowest possible rating, 1, from the number of dimensions on which it had the highest possible rating, 5. In Table 6.1 there are horizontal marks along each of the bars; these correspond to the difference score ratings for various strategies consistent with the specified approach. The top horizontal mark corresponds to the highest rated strategy and the lowest horizontal mark corresponds to the lowest rated strategy. There are fewer horizontal marks than strategies rated because generally there are a few strategies within an approach with the same difference score.

The single most important conclusion to be drawn from the data presented in Table 6.1 is that there is considerable overlap in the ranges of the ratings among approaches. Any tendency for strategies consistent with a specified approach to be rated higher than those consistent with another is, at best, weak. There is evidence of a tendency for income strategies to be rated higher than income-in-kind strategies, but more dramatic than this tendency is the extent of the overlap between the two approaches.

The highest income strategy (the NWRO negative income tax proposal) is rated substantially higher than the highest rated education strategy (school vouchers) and the highest rated economic development strategy (economic growth), but it is not rated much above the highest rated manpower strategy (the government as employer of last resort), the highest rated organization strategy (unionization of farm-

TABLE 6.1

RANGES BETWEEN HIGHEST AND LOWEST RATED STRATEGY WITHIN EACH OF THE SIX MAJOR APPROACHES

DIFFERENCE SCORE* ANTI-POVERTY APPROACH BEING RATED**

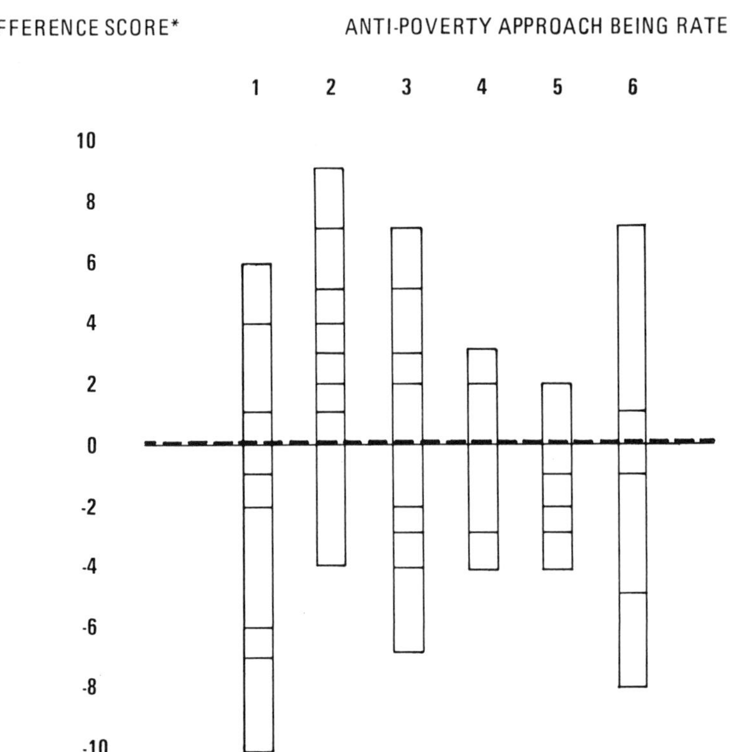

* The DIFFERENCE SCORE rating is the difference between the number of times a strategy receives the highest possible rating (5) and the number of times it receives the lowest possible rating (1).

** The numbers used to identify the 6 anti-poverty approaches are to be interpreted as follows:

(1) Income-in-kind
(2) Income
(3) Manpower
(4) Education
(5) Economic Development
(6) Organization

workers), and the highest rated income-in-kind strategy (national housing allowance). The lowest rated income-in-kind strategies (conventional public housing, leased housing, and rent supplement) are all rated substantially lower than the lowest rated income strategy (AFDC), the lowest rated education strategy (bilingual education), and the lowest rated economic development strategy (Economic Opportunity Loans). But the lowest rated income-in-kind strategies are not rated much below the lowest rated organization strategy (riots) and the lowest rated manpower strategy (Concentrated Employment Program).

The width of the range between the lowest and highest rated strategies varies among approaches. The range is large for income-in-kind (16 points), organization (15 points), manpower (14 points), and income (13 points); it is much smaller for education (7 points) and economic development (6 points). This data could be used to argue that there is generally less variability between strategies consistent with the education and economic development approaches, than is the case for strategies consistent with the other four approaches. But it is noteworthy that fewer strategies were rated within the education and economic development approaches; the difference in range may be due in large part to the number of strategies rated.

When the 63 strategies rated are divided into 47 programs and 16 proposals, it is evident that the proposals are disproportionately represented among the highest rated strategies. This is in part due to our failure to anticipate the problems which would arise were the proposals actually introduced as programs.

Within the income-in-kind, income, manpower, and education approaches there is evidence that the proposals tend to be rated higher than the programs. Given this tendency, it is reasonable to raise the question as to whether the conclusions drawn on the basis of the data in Table 6.1 would hold if only existing programs were considered. When the data for the 47 out of the 63 strategies which correspond to existing programs are presented in a format similar to that in Table 6.1, the conclusions drawn are quite similar. The most important difference is that there is no tendency for the highest rated income program (Social Security) to be rated higher than the highest rated organization program (unionization of farmworkers); they both receive the same rating. If the proposals are excluded, then the range between the highest and the lowest rated strategies within a specified approach tend to be reduced. For example, the range for strategies consistent with the income approach falls from 16 points to 12 points. With these few qualifications, the conclusions based on data for the 47 existing programs are the same as those based on all 63 strategies.

Comparisons Among The Five Highest Rated Strategies In

the preceding section our focus was on comparisons among general anti-poverty approaches. Here, the focus is on comparisons among the five strategies with the highest difference scores. The median difference score for all sixty-three strategies is 0. The NWRO negative income tax proposal with a difference score of 9 is the highest rated strategy. The unionization of farmworkers, Social Security, and the government as employer of last resort proposal all have difference scores of 7. The national housing allowance proposal has a difference score of 6. These five include all strategies with difference scores greater than 5.

The ratings for each of these strategies along the standard dimensions are summarized in Table 6.2 below. In earlier chapters each of these strategies has been rated and compared with other strategies within the same approach. The income-in-kind, income, manpower, and organization approaches are represented by these strategies; education and economic development are not represented.

Among the strategies being considered, three of the five are proposals. Since only 25 percent of the original 63 strategies were proposals, this indicates that proposals are disproportionately represented among the most highly rated strategies. One interpretation of this is that it is easier to propose a good strategy than it is to get it accepted. As was mentioned earlier, an alternative view is that a proposed program is likely to run into unanticipated snags when it is introduced as an operational program.

Both the NWRO negative income tax proposal and the government as employer of last resort proposal would be exceedingly expensive. The NWRO NIT proposal would cost approximately $52 billion per year; the government as employer of last resort proposal would cost approximately $25 billion per year. While this contributes to relatively low ratings with respect to popularity in the general population there are many more dimensions, including impact on the distribution of income, for which the cost contributes to high ratings. Thus our rating scheme leads to high ratings even though neither of these proposals is in a cost range which will be politically feasible in the foreseeable future. This illustrates a limitation of the procedure we have used which calls for giving equal weight to each dimension considered.

Social Security and the unionization of farmworkers both receive the same overall rating. Yet there is a substantial gap in scope between these strategies. The Social Security program distributes in excess of $16 billion per year to approximately 33 percent of the poor. In contrast, the efforts to unionize farmworkers have provided less than $1 billion annually to less than 1 percent of the poor. A more important consideration than the presently limited scope of the movement to unionize farmworkers, is the fact that this strategy does not have the

TABLE 6.2

RATINGS FOR COMPARING THE FIVE HIGHEST RATED STRATEGIES

DIMENSION FOR THE RATING*	STRATEGY BEING RATED**				
	1	2	3	4	5
1	1	5	5	2	5
2	4	5	5	2	5
3	3	5	3	5	5
4	3	5	4	5	5
5	5	5	4	5	5
6	1	5	5	5	1
7	1	5	3	5	1
8	1	3	3	3	3
9	5	3	3	3	5
10	3	3	3	5	3
11	5	5	5	3	5
12	5	5	5	5	5
13	5	1	3	1	5
14	5	5	1	5	5
15	5	5	5	5	5
16	5	5	5	1	5
17	1	1	1	3	1
18	5	1	5	3	5
19	3	3	5	5	1
20	5	1	5	3	5
21	5	4	3	1	5
22	5	5	3	1	5
23	3	3	3	5	1
24	3	3	3	1	4
25	5	5	5	5	5
26	4	5	5	1	5

* Dimensions 1-26 correspond to the 26 standard dimensions presented in Appendix A.

** The numbers used to identify the 5 strategies are to be interpreted as follows:

(1) National Housing Allowance
(2) Government As Employer of Last Resort
(3) Social Security
(4) Unionization of Farmworkers
(5) NWRO NIT Proposal

potential to become a major program for dealing with poverty nationally; farmworkers make up too small a fraction of the poor.

The high rating of the unionization of farmworkers strategy is in part due to characteristics of the unionization strategy more generally. There is no question as to the economic benefits that the American labor movement has brought to those unionized. But due to efforts by unions to protect the interests of those who are already members, often at the expense of those who are not, the approach is of limited value to people close to the bottom of the income distribution. Many of the poor are employed in secondary or low-wage sectors of the economy which are difficult to organize. In the past farmworkers were considered one such group. Chavez's success suggests that there may be more potential for organization in the low-wage sector than is generally thought.

The discussion that follows is based on the ratings of the five strategies along the 26 standard dimensions. Each dimension is considered separately.

1. Impact On Distribution Of Income: The national housing allowance proposal receives a low rating because its benefits are classified as income-in-kind. The unionization of farmworkers receives a low rating because the number of recipients involved is so small. Social Security distributes approximately $16 billion per year to the poor; the NWRO NIT proposal would distribute $25 billion per year to the poor; the government as employer of last resort proposal would distribute approximately $16 billion per year to the poor; and the unionization of farmworkers has increased the incomes of farmworkers by less than $1 billion per year.

2. Impact On Distribution Of Basic Goods And Services: Four of the five strategies are rated the same here as on the preceding dimension. The rating of the national housing allowance proposal is higher due to the impact it would have on the value of the housing available to the poor; we have estimated this at $6 billion per year.

3. Impact On Distribution Of Political Influence: The national housing allowance proposal would contribute little if anything to the political influence of the poor. The same is true of the Social Security program. The government as employer of last resort and the NWRO NIT would contribute to the political influence of the poor in that these proposals would substantially reduce the economic dependence of the poor on the local employers, bureaucrats, and politicians. Political disagreement could be expressed with less fear of economic sanctions. Unionization of farmworkers not only makes those involved less economically dependent, but also gives them a focus for organized political activity.

4. Impact On Self-Concept: Most of the strategies considered would have a positive impact on self-concept. The national housing allowance proposal might also have some positive impact in that recipients would be able to live in higher quality housing, but this impact would be minimal.

5. Impact On Family Stability: All five of these strategies would tend to contribute to family stability. There is no evidence to date indicating that a negative income tax program would contribute to family instability. However, some argue that a high guaranteed minimum income would make a family less dependent on the head for support; this in turn might lead to lower family stability.

6. Encouragement Of Economic Self-Sufficiency: The national housing allowance and the NWRO NIT both receive low ratings because they do not encourage employment in any way. In contrast, the government as employer of last resort and the unionization of farmworkers are both strategies which provide benefits to those who work. Social Security is a special case. It is work related in that a person must have been in the labor force for a specified length of time to be eligible, but once a person reaches age 65, the program makes it economically more feasible to stop working.

7. Impact On Work Incentives: The national housing allowance and the NWRO NIT are rated low due to high tax on earned income. The government as employer of last resort and unionization of farmworkers both contribute to increasing wages and consequently to increasing the work incentive. The Social Security program is not rated as high as the other work related strategies because of the high tax rate on earned income for those who qualify for benefits.

8. Impact On Racial Integration: The national housing allowance proposal receives a low rating because it would make it possible for low income whites in many urban areas to escape to the suburbs; fewer blacks would be able to locate in the predominantly white suburbs. The net result would be a trend toward increased racial separation. The other four strategies would not substantially change the extent of racial integration.

9. Impact On Separation Between Social Classes: The national housing allowance proposal receives a high rating because it would increase the proportion of persons from lower and working class backgrounds living in middle class areas. This shift would predominantly involve whites. The NWRO NIT is rated high because the added income would have much the same effect as a national housing allowance in residential separation between social classes

10. Marginal Impact: The unionization of farmworkers is the only strategy in which the impact would increase with increased participation. This is a characteristic the strategy shares with most organizational strategies.

11. Dependence On The State Of The Economy: Unionization of farmworkers has little dependence on the state of the economy. But for the other four strategies benefits in the form of payments or number of jobs created would increase during periods of recession.

12. Equity In Benefit Levels: All five strategies have high ratings on this dimension.

13. Consideration Of Individual Need: The national housing allowance and the NWRO NIT would both take into consideration family size, family assets, and all sources of income in the determination of benefits. The government as employer of last resort and unionization of farmworkers, however, would not take into consideration variation between families in the determination of benefit levels. Social Security does take into consideration earned income, but not unearned income. Thus there are many wealthy persons who receive Social Security in spite of substantial income from investments.

14. Creaming: Social Security provides higher benefits to those who have had higher incomes prior to retirement. Thus it generally turns out that the poorest recipients tend to receive lower benefits. All other strategies receive high ratings indicating that there would be relatively little creaming.

15. Adequacy For Meeting Acute Needs Of The Poor: All five strategies are rated high on this dimension.

16. Accessibility Of Program Benefits: Unionization of farmworkers receives a low rating because the benefits are available only in those few areas which have so far been organized. Most farmworkers live in areas in which these benefits are unavailable. All of the other strategies are rated high in accessibility of program benefits.

17. Accountability To Recipients: Unionization of farmworkers is rated higher than the other strategies because it is a grass roots organization. Chavez has to date remained in close touch with those he has organized. The other four strategies would be or are large scale federal programs directed from Washington with little effort to be accountable to special local interests. In the case of income strategies, accountability is less relevant than in the case of manpower strategies such as the government as employer of last resort.

18. Administrative Success: The government as employer of last resort is given a low rating on this dimension because we anticipate that there would be administrative problems. Even the much smaller existing manpower programs have difficulty placing trainees. With a program assuring jobs to all, the problems would be multiplied. The other strategies would be less likely to have administrative problems.

19. Popularity: The NWRO NIT proposal receives the lowest rating because it would provide a guaranteed minimum income of $6,500 to everyone without any work requirement. The opposition to so generous a program would be sufficiently strong to make the strategy politically unfeasible. It is also not likely to be politically feasible at any point in the near future. Social Security is popular because the recipient is viewed as having paid for his benefits over the years in payroll taxes. Unionization of farmworkers is rated high because it would cost the public very little and is considered a legitimate way to press for higher wages.

20. Political Vulnerability: Government as employer of last resort receives a low rating because there is a past record of cutbacks in federal employment projects with improved economic conditions. The NWRO NIT would include a very substantial recipient population. This would make it difficult to terminate the program once it was introduced, unless there were serious complications for the overall economy which could be attributed to the program. But political opposition from those who are not poor would in all likelihood keep it from being introduced in the first place.

21. Percentage Of The Poor Who Benefit In One Year: Unionization of farmworkers receives a low rating because the farmworkers, whom Chavez has organized, make up such a small segment of the poor. The other four strategies would all provide benefits to a wide range of the poor. The NWRO NIT would provide to all the poor and many of the near poor.

22. Percentage Of Target Population Reached: Unionization of farmworkers receives a low rating because, as mentioned above, Chavez has so far organized only a small fraction of all farmworkers. Social Security misses many of those in the low wage sector of the economy. Those who have worked in this sector are often forced to retire without the benefits of Social Security.

23. Percentage Of Benefits Going To The Nonpoor: The NWRO NIT receives a low rating because a substantial fraction of the benefits would go to those with incomes above the poverty line, but the largest benefits would go to those with the least income. Unionization of farmworkers is rated high because virtually all those who have been organized to date have had poverty wages prior to organization.

24. Percentage Of Total Population Who Benefit During One Year: Unionization of farmworkers is rated lowest for reasons which have been mentioned above. The NWRO NIT proposal would benefit nearly 50 percent of the total population.

25. Duration Of Recipient Status: The typical recipient is likely to remain a recipient for well over five years for all of these strategies.

26. Current Spending Level: Unionization of farmworkers is lowest because it costs less to organize than to provide benefits directly. The spending level for the national housing allowance would be in the range of $8 billion per year. The government as employer of last resort would cost approximately $25 billion per year. Social Security currently costs $26 billion per year. The NWRO NIT would cost approximately $52 billion per year.

National Income Insurance Plan The national income insurance plan considered in this section is a variation on the negative income tax. The plan would within ten years eliminate poverty as it exists today; by then, no families would have incomes below what today is considered the poverty line. In addition, the income gap between the poorest segment of society and the median American family would be substantially reduced. In an effort to facilitate movement from a program which would be politically feasible today to a program which would achieve these objectives, the proposal calls for starting with a modest program which includes provisions for subsequent evolution into a much more ambitious program.

The concept of income insurance is not new. Both Etzioni and Jencks have previously discussed the possibility. Our national income insurance plan differs from the anti-poverty insurance proposed by Etzioni in many specifics.[1] One important difference is that Etzioni's plan would be financed by a consortium of private insurance companies; our plan would be federally financed. His plan would have a work component. Employable recipients would be required to accept work offered by local employment agencies to remain eligible. Our proposal has no such work component.

Jencks has proposed an income insurance plan in which the government would guarantee a worker an income equal to half the income she or he could be expected to earn as determined by careful actuarial projections.[2] These projections would take into consideration family background, level of education, occupation, and other such characteristics. When the worker earned less than his predicted income, the government would make up half the difference; when he earned more than his predicted income, he would have to pay the government half the difference. As Jencks points out, there are some problems that would have to be worked out; not the least of which is that black and female workers would be guaranteed less than equally qualified white, male workers.

Our income insurance plan is so named because it would provide social insurance benefits whenever the family income fell below a specified level. The plan would be financed in large part by a payroll tax similar to that presently used in connection with the Social Security program.

A basic component of any negative tax proposal is the level of the guaranteed minimum income. This is a major determinant of the impact of the program on the distribution of income. For the income insurance plan, the guaranteed minimum income would initially be set at a low level. The plan calls for a guaranteed minimum income initially equal to 25 percent of the median American family income. In 1972, the median income was approximately $10,000 so the guaranteed minimum income would have been $2,500 for a family of four. This guaranteed minimum income would be made available to all families and single individuals; the level would be adjusted for family size in the same way that the Social Security Administration's poverty index is adjusted. The proposed guarantee level is substantially below the poverty line which was approximately $4,000 per year for a family of four in 1972.

The major reason for suggesting such a low level guaranteed minimum income to begin with is to increase the political feasibility of the overall proposal. The higher the level of the guaranteed minimum income, the greater the number of recipients and the higher the cost of the program. The estimated net increase in federal expenditures would initially be only $6.7 billion per year.

Another reason for suggesting a low guaranteed minimum income initially is to minimize the impact of the program on labor force participation. Were a program introduced with a relatively high guaranteed minimum income, it is possible that there would be a substantial increase in voluntary unemployment. Those who lost their jobs would be under less pressure to find jobs. Undoubtedly, some workers would leave jobs which offered low wages and poor working conditions. A sharp impact on labor force participation would lead to strong pressures on Congress to rescind the program. By starting with a modest program with increments, it would be easier to deal with any disruptions of the overall economy.

The suggestion that the guaranteed minimum income originally should be low is also related to the proposed mechanism for increasing the level of the guaranteed minimum income. We are assuming that it is preferable to start with a low guaranteed minimum income to increase the overall political feasibility of the provision for automatic increments in the level of the guaranteed minimum income. While the initial cost of the proposal would be only $6.7 billion annually, through automatic increments it would cost in the range of $50 billion per year ten years later.

Central to the national income insurance plan would be the provision for increasing the magnitude of the guaranteed munimum income. If there were no provision for automatically incrementing the level of the guaranteed minimum income over time, the potential impact of the plan would be substantially reduced. The national income insurance plan would include the provision that the level of the guaranteed minimum income be uniformly incremented from the original 25 percent of the median income to 50 percent of the median income ten years later.[3] This provision would lead to a substantial reduction in the gap between the poor family and the median American family.

The incremental procedure which has been suggested is only one of several possible alternatives. It establishes two basic precedents. One is that the magnitude of the guaranteed minimum income be increased in some way each year so as to take into consideration the rise in incomes generally. The other is that the gap between those at the bottom of the income distribution and the median income will be gradually reduced.

A less ambitious alternative would be to increment the guaranteed minimum income so as to keep it at 25 percent of the median income. This would lead to a gradual improvement in the standard of living provided, but it would not reduce the gap between the guaranteed minimum income and the median income. On the contrary, the dollar gap would gradually increase over time.

A still less ambitious alternative would be to include a provision for incrementing the level of the guaranteed minimum income so as to take into consideration increases in the cost of living. This would protect recipients against a decrease in standard of living due to inflation, but it would not lead to any improvement in living standards. Since the guaranteed minimum income in the initial proposal is substantially below the poverty line, this alternative would not achieve the objective of assuring at least a minimally adequate standard of living for all Americans within ten years.

The national income insurance plan calls for a 50 percent marginal tax rate on all sources of income up to the breakeven point (recall that the breakeven point is the income at which the tax on other sources of income just equals the guaranteed minimum). If the guaranteed minimum income were $2,500, the breakeven point would be $5,000. This tax rate is high relative to what those in the lowest income brackets presently pay. A lower tax rate has been avoided so as to keep down the total cost of the program.

The national income insurance plan would be financed by a federal surtax on all sources of income above the breakeven point. This surtax would be progressive with the minimum and maximum tax rates adjusted to take into consideration the tax revenues needed to pay for the program. Initially the surtax would be designed to raise $6.7 billion annually; within ten years the tax would have to produce in excess of $50 billion annually. As the level of the guaranteed minimum income increased, so would the surtax. For wage earners the surtax would take the form of a payroll tax. As is presently the case with the Social Security tax, the employee would pay half and the employer would pay half. The individual would be responsible for paying the full surtax himself on all other sources of income. The tax revenues so generated would be paid into a national income insurance trust fund comparable to the Social Security trust fund. The program would be financed out of this trust fund, not from general federal revenues.

As outlined above, the national income insurance plan does not attempt to take into consideration inequality in family assets. A possible modification would be to include as imputed income, 10 percent of the value of all assets in excess of some specified level such as the median American income for the preceding year; this would work out to approximately $10,000 in 1972. Any consideration of assets substantially increases the administrative cost of the program. The provision to discount assets up to a specified level is designed to reduce administrative costs. Such a modification would be desirable only if the gains in equity would more than offset increases in administrative cost; such increases would eventually be reflected in higher tax rates and lower benefit levels.

As with the other strategies we have considered, there are arguments both for and against the national income insurance plan. We will first answer some of the most likely criticisms and then consider some of the arguments in support of the plan:

Initially the plan would not provide even a minimally adequate standard of living. If we use the poverty line as a measure of adequacy, this criticism is quite valid. It can be countered by the assertion that the plan would increase the standard of living for many, while decreasing it for relatively few. If this plan were introduced, it would replace several existing welfare programs including AFDC. In some states families would suffer a reduction in living standard unless a state program were introduced to supplement the federal program, but most of those who would be forced to live on $2,500 per year are living on less than that today. Another argument is that while several negative income tax plans have been proposed which would assure a more adequate standard of living, their cost generally makes them politically unfeasible. The national income insurance plan would not provide an adequate living standard initially, but within ten years it would provide a standard of living which would be substantially more adequate than that which would be provided by any proposal politically feasible today.

The provision for automatic yearly increments in the level of the guaranteed minimum income makes the plan politically unfeasible. It is no accident that the Social Security program does not even have an automatic cost of living increase, to say nothing of an increment based on increases in the median income. Congress wants to maintain control of increments for, among other reasons, the credit in election years for having recently voted for increases in Social

Security benefits. Were a negative income tax program introduced, it is likely that Congress would want to maintain similar control over any increments in benefits. The provision in the national income insurance plan for automatic increases in the guaranteed minimum income might well make it politically unfeasible. If this provision were eliminated in the effort to increase political support for the plan, its potential impact would be drastically curtailed. The likely strength of the opposition to the provision for automatic yearly increments in the level of the guaranteed minimum income is probably the greatest weakness of the plan.

The plan has no provision for making recipients self-sufficient. The national income insurance plan cannot be viewed as a replacement for existing educational and training programs. Such programs would be needed even if the income insurance plan were introduced. The plan could eventually replace existing social insurance and Public Assistance programs, but it would not meet the need for medical care, housing, education, jobs and job training, or economic growth and development.

The plan might lead to a substantial increase in unemployment. To date there is no evidence of such an impact in the experimental studies of the negative income tax approach. But these short term experiments may not prove to be an accurate guide to the impact of a long-term program. Assuming that there were an increase in unemployment, it is important to note that it would be voluntary. Many of those involved would be leaving jobs in the secondary sector which offer low wages, poor working conditions, or both. The procedure of starting with a modest program and gradually incrementing it would allow time to make the adjustments that might be needed to deal with any increase in unemployment which might occur.

The plan could prove to be exceedingly inflationary. Any program with a built in cost of living increase tends to exert some inflationary pressure; the procedure called for in this plan which bases increases on changes in the median income would exert even greater inflationary pressure. While the plan would exert even greater inflationary pressure, the actual extent of the resulting inflation would be considerably mitigated by other factors. Appropriate fiscal or monetary countermeasures by the federal government could keep the level of inflation at an acceptable level even with such a program in effect. It is also noteworthy that the existence of a program which would provide a guaranteed minimum income adjusted yearly for increases in the national median income would in some respects reduce the need for keeping inflation to a minimum. A major reason often mentioned for keeping inflation low is to protect those living off a low fixed income. Many of these people would do better under this program with a moderate level of inflation than they would without it even if inflation were kept substantially lower.

The plan would do very little to alter the inequality in the distribution of wealth in America. Most of those who would favor a more equitable distribution of income feel that the extent of the inequality in the distribution of wealth is an equally, if not more, important issue. The income insurance plan would have a substantial impact on the distribution of income, but very little impact on the distribution of wealth. Other strategies, including higher inheritance taxes and the elimination of various loopholes in the present inheritance tax system, would be more effective for reducing the extent of the inequality in the distribution of wealth. Another measure, briefly mentioned earlier, would be to include as taxable income an imputed income equal to 10 percent of all assets above a specified level.

The following are some of the major arguments in favor of the national income insurance plan:

The national income insurance plan would be universalistic; that is, it would provide benefits to all poor persons. At present all anti-poverty and welfare programs in the United States are categorical; they provide benefits to certain categories of the poor while excluding others. One justification offered for this approach is that it encourages tailoring programs to the specific needs of various categories of the poor. This would in itself be a desirable characteristic, but when put into practice the approach serves to exclude certain categories of the poor. The major rationale for breaking with the categorical approach is that efforts to restrict benefits to those who are clearly deserving inevitably leads to the exclusion of many who under careful scrutiny also turn out to be deserving. An obvious case in point is the exclusion of children living in families headed by able-bodied males. In contrast, a universalistic program such as the national income insurance plan would assure that at least some benefits reach all of the poor.

The plan would eventually provide sufficient economic security to encourage long-term efforts to become self-sufficient. When first introduced the program would not provide sufficient economic security so as to encourage such efforts. But as the level of the guaranteed minimum income increased, long-range efforts would become increasingly common. Undoubtedly, many would decide to live on the guaranteed minimum income without making an effort to become self-sufficient, but many more would take advantage of the opportunity to improve their economic position. When a family has to worry about where the money is going to come from for next week's grocery bills, little attention can be given to such luxuries as obtaining more education or skill training; but an assured steady income would in many cases free the family of such immediate economic worries. It would also make the poor credit worthy in the eyes of many commercial and financial institutions.

The plan would lead to gradual inprovement in working con-

ditions and higher wages in many industries. It would free many of the poor of their present dependence on the low-wage labor market. This would lead to an increase in the cost of many of the services presently supplied by the low-wage labor market. It would also lead to the collapse of those industries which are dependent on the present pool of low wage labor for their existence. Those who view virtually any kind of employment as preferable to unemployment would see this result as a limitation of the strategy.

The plan would provide a focus around which the poor and near-poor could organize nationally. The success of the National Welfare Rights Organization illustrates the potential impact of the poor when they have a focus and common interest for organization. One objective around which the poor could organize would be efforts to get the level of the guaranteed minimum income increased. This would be particularly crucial if the automatic mechanism for incrementation were not included in the original program. But even if the procedure were included, the guaranteed minimum income would remain at 50 percent of the median income after that level had been reached. At that point the poor and near-poor could push for still further increase in the level of the guaranteed minimum income. The precedent of the previous increments could be used to argue for still further increments. It would be reasonable to continue pushing for increments until the inflation generated and the disruption to the economy outweighed the increases in benefit levels. The poor could also push for a reduction in the 50 percent marginal tax rate on income below the breakeven point. The eventual goal could be to transform the curvilinear schedule of marginal tax rates into a progressive schedule starting at 20 percent and increasing.

Such a plan would lead to a more equitable distribution of income in the United States. The low initial level of the guaranteed minimum income would have relatively little impact; but if appropriate mechanisms for incrementing the guaranteed minimum income were included, the eventual impact on the distribution of income would be substantial. To some a more equitable distribution of income would be valued for its impact on the distribution of scarce goods, services, opportunities, political influence, and the like. Others would value a more equitable distribution because it would contribute to reducing the extent of various forms of social pathology presently associated with poverty.

The national income insurance plan would reduce the extent of both the absolute and the relative deprivation of the poor. However, even with improvement in the relative economic position of the poor, the psychological feeling of deprivation may remain high. Improvements in objective conditions do not necessarily lead to reduced feelings of deprivation because expectations can and often do increase at a more rapid pace than these improvements.

A more equitable distribution of income would clearly benefit those at the lower end of the income distribution. There would also be some benefits to those at the upper end. For example, spending presently associated with various poverty related social problems could be reduced. But is is unlikely that such savings would be considered worth the added tax burden to those in the upper income brackets. As much as the social reformer wants to argue that redistribution of income is in everyone's best interest, most of those who would as a result carry a heavier tax burden are not going to view redistribution in these terms. Since those with high incomes have a disproportionate amount of political influence, any efforts to markedly change the income distribution are going to face stiff opposition.

Two important questions remain to be considered. (1) Is it likely that a national income insurance plan or some other such negative income tax plan will be introduced as a federal program at any time in the near future? (2) If such a program is introduced, will it be just another liberal reform or will it lead to fundamental changes in the social structure and dominant value orientation of our society?

The negative income tax was originally proposed by Milton Friedman, one of the foremost conservative economists in the country. The approach was subsequently backed by the Nixon Administration in the form of the FAP proposal. The major reason that the approach appeals to conservatives is that it would be considerably more efficient than the complex maze of programs for the poor that exists today. Many take the view that such a program would replace not only existing federal and state welfare programs, but in addition, a number of others in such areas as housing, education, and manpower. In short, the approach is viewed as a way to cut welfare spending.

The approach has also received support from liberals; Senator McGovern called for a form of the negative income tax in his bid for the Democratic Presidential nomination in 1972.[4] To liberals, the approach is seen to be less stigmatizing, more efficient, and more equitable than the present welfare system. It is viewed as a way to deliver more in the way of welfare benefit per dollar of federal welfare spending. Liberals are less likely to view the approach as a replacement for other social welfare programs and generally do not argue that the approach can or should be used to reduce the overall extent of social welfare spending.

The present welfare system is under attack from all sides; there is general agreement that the existing structure is not adequate for dealing with today's welfare needs. The negative income tax approach is the only approach that has been seriously suggested as a replacement for the existing welfare system. As we have seen, there are strong arguments for the negative income tax approach from both liberal and conservative perspectives. In view of these considerations, it is not unreasonable to argue that it is only a matter of time before a negative income tax of some sort is introduced. Nixon's FAP proposal was rejected by the Senate, but it did pass the more conservative House by an almost two-to-one vote.[5]

We now turn to the second question. If such a program is introduced, will it lead to fundamental changes in the social structure and dominant value orientation? Once a national income insurance plan or some other such negative income tax plan is introduced, a situation will exist in which national mass political organization of the poor will be feasible on a scale never before possible. There have been several national organizations of blacks, a national organization of welfare recipients, and there is emerging an effort to create a national organization of the elderly but there has never been a national organization of all the poor.

The existing maze of separate welfare programs has made it all but impossible for the various segments of the poor to unify. But the introduction of a negative income tax will provide a clear source of common economic interest for all segments of the poor including poor whites, poor blacks, the aged, the working poor, female headed families, the disabled, and other presently disparate segments of the poor.

Any such program will include as one component a guaranteed minimum income. It will be in the interest of all categories of the poor to push for increases in the guaranteed minimum income. Any such program will also include a relatively high marginal tax rate on earned income and many of the poor can be expected to support efforts to get this rate reduced. These two objectives will provide a focus for efforts to organize the poor. The goals will be clear and the potential benefits obvious; there will be no need to appeal to distant and abstract objectives.

For any politically feasible negative income tax plan the initial guaranteed minimum income will be low and the marginal tax rate on earned income will be high. In view of this, it is likely that there will be considerable support in the general population for a gradual increase in the size of the guaranteed minimum income and a gradual decrease in the marginal tax rate. Legislators will undoubtedly use such benefits to seek votes in much the same way they presently use increments in Social Security benefits.

However, such concessions no matter how small will increase the number of people below the breakeven point. This will increase the number with an objective economic interest in supporting the program. These concessions will reward the efforts of those working to organize the poor and encourage further organizational efforts. Since increments in the guaranteed minimum income can come in a wide assortment of sizes, it will be difficult to resist at least modest increases.

As the years pass and the level of the guaranteed minimum income increases, more and more of those at the lower end of the income distribution will become recipients, and, what is equally important, they will become politically united. First, the poor will be united with the near-poor and, subsequently, many of those presently in the working and lower middle classes will be united with them. The recipient population may eventually constitute a voting majority. Even before this point is reached, the recipients will become a major voting block. They can be expected to back reform legislation designed to undercut the control the rich and corporate interests have over government decision making. One form this may take would be restrictions on the size and source of campaign contributions. This segment of the population can also be expected to back legislation designed to reform the tax structure. Among such reforms might well be higher inheritance taxes and the elimination of various inheritance tax loopholes. These and other such measures will undoubtedly have a marked impact on the distribution of wealth and political power.

Suppose a negative income tax is introduced and it starts to have some of the effects outlined above; wouldn't the rich be quick to note the threat to their power and to take the necessary steps to emasculate the program if not to eliminate it all together? There is a good chance they would. But there is also a possibility that such efforts would fail. Once the program was introduced it would begin to gain momentum. The larger the recipient population became, the stronger the resistance would be to efforts to cut it back. The rich might have to settle for short term efforts to stem the expansion of the program, and the forces contributing to expansion might well prove too strong to be permanently halted. Were the program financed through a payroll tax in the way Social Security is presently financed, the benefits would be viewed as having been earned. This would considerably increase the permanence and legitimacy of the program. It would make it a program with potential benefits to a wide range of the income distribution, not just to those receiving benefits at any one time.

How about the middle income segment of the population, those who would not receive benefits from the program, but who would be paying higher taxes to finance it? Again this segment of the population, which at the outset would constitute a clear majority, might decide to push for elimination of the program and could succeed in this effort. However, it is possible that this would not occur. When the program was first introduced, the cost would be low and the majority of those in the middle income range might well support it. But as the level of the guaranteed income increased, so would the cost. This would undoubtedly reduce the extent of support among nonrecipients. But this does not mean that opposition among nonrecipients would be universal. Many in the middle and upper income ranges are willing to support social welfare efforts which do not have any direct economic benefit to themselves. There is considerable variation in ideological orientation among those in this segment of the population, and at least a substantial minority could be expected to support even a rather generous guaranteed minimum income level. The program would be safe as long as the number of recipients together with the minority of nonrecipients who support it remained a clear voting majority. Eventually the program would provide direct benefits to more than half of the voting population and would be freed of dependence on support from nonrecipients. When this point was reached the program would be quite secure.

A national income insurance plan would eventually have a major impact on norms and values. In particular, the work ethic and related aspects of the individualistic value orientation which so pervades our society today would be undercut. The key to this impact would be the objective situation where it will be no longer necessary to work. Those who will be willing to live at an unusually low standard of living will be able to do so without working. While this option would be all but impossible at first, it would become a very real option as the level of the guaranteed minimum income increased.

This would lead to many other changes. Many workers would leave the most unattractive jobs. Some of these jobs would disappear altogether; others would be automated or come to pay considerably higher wages. Employers would be forced to pay much more attention to working conditions, the structure of work, and employee morale.

It is impossible to fully anticipate the forces that would be set in motion by the introduction of a national income insurance program or other such negative income tax program. But it is clear that such a program would eventually lead to major shifts in the distribution of income, wealth, and political power. These changes would undoubtedly have a major impact on the dominant value orientation as well as on the social and economic structure of our society. Such a program would most definitely not be just another liberal reform.[6]

We have discussed both the successes and the failures of many of the liberal reform anti-poverty strategies of the 1960s. It is our hope that the observations we have made, and those of other studies that our efforts may stimulate, will be put to use in the formulation of public policy when it again becomes fashionable for the federal government to seriously deal with the problems of poverty and economic inequality. With more funding and more time, many of the strategies we have considered would undoubtedly have had much more impact than they did. But it is our contention that some of the strategies with the greatest potential were never introduced as actual programs. Among such strategies we would include many of the negative income tax proposals. While there have been a few experiments, there are many important questions that cannot be answered by small scale, short term experiments. But based on what we know, it is evident that unlike most liberal reform strategies to date, the negative income tax has the potential for a major impact on the extent of poverty and economic inequality in America.

Notes

1. See Amitai Etzioni, "Antipoverty Insurance: A Mode of Private Sector Participation," *Public Administration Review* (November/December, 1969): 614-622; Amitai Etzioni, "A New Kind of Insurance," *Columbia Forum* (Spring, 1970): 18-23.
2. See Christopher Jenks et al., *Inequality* (New York: Basic Books, 1972), pp. 228-229.
3. More ambitious goals have been suggested. For example, Rainwater has proposed that the goal be to bring the lowest income category (Guaranteed minimum income) up to a level at which it would include the median income. See Lee Rainwater, "The Problem of Lower-Class Culture and Poverty-War Strategy," in *On Understanding Poverty,* ed. by Daniel P. Moynihan (New York: Basic Books, 1969).
4. In the 1968 Democratic Presidential primaries, Eugene McCarthy spoke out in favor of a guaranteed minimum income; Robert Kennedy spoke out in opposition to the idea. See Daniel P. Moynihan, *The Politics of a Guaranteed Income* (New York: Random House, 1973), pp. 61-62.
5. The FAP bill was defeated in the Senate Finance Committee by liberal votes. Many of those who most strongly opposed the FAP bill were in favor of greater benefits. Moynihan, *The Politics of a Guaranteed Income,* p. 15. Most of the liberal criticism centered on the work provision and the level of the guaranteed minimum income. We feel that a much more serious limitation was that it was to be restricted to families with dependent children; this provision would have considerably reduced its impact on the political unification of those at the lower end of the income distribution.
6. The result would be a radical reform or, in the words of Gorz, a non-reformist reform. For a discussion of the distinction between reformist and non-reformist reforms see Andre Gorz, *Strategy for Labor* (Boston: Beacon Press, 1967).

APPENDIX

DEFINITIONS OF THE 26 STANDARD DIMENSIONS FOR COMPARING ANTI-POVERTY STRATEGIES

1. Impact On Distribution Of Income: This is a measure of the short term impact of the program on the share of all income that goes to those who are poor. This includes money distributed by income maintenance, work experience, job training, and scholarship programs. It also includes income from employment for those who would otherwise have been unemployed. Some programs provide income-in-kind. Such contributions are not considered here; but they are considered in the next dimension. Some programs provide education and job training. The contributions of such programs are not considered here because they tend to be long-term. A rating of 5 indicates that the program distributes over $15 billion per year to the poor; a rating of 4 indicates that the program distributes between $5 billion and $15 billion; a rating of 3 indicates that the program distributes between $1 and $5 billion; a rating of 2 indicates that the program distributes income to the poor, but the amount is less than $1 billion per year; and a rating of 1 indicates that the program does not in the short run increase the income of the poor.

2. Impact On Distribution Of Basic Goods And Services: This is a measure of the short term impact of the program on the share of all goods and services that go to the poor. It includes the value of housing, food, medical care, education, job training, and other such goods and services. It also includes the value of any income that is distributed because such income is used in large part to purchase these goods and services. A rating of 5 indicates that the value of the goods and services delivered to the poor is over $15 billion per year; a rating of 4 indicates that the value is between $5 and $15 billion; a rating of 3 indicates the value is between $1 and $5 billion; a rating of 2 indicates that the program distributes goods, services, or income to the poor, but the value is less than $1 billion per year; and a rating of 1 indicates that the program does not in the short run increase the share of goods and services available to the poor.

3. Impact On Distribution Of Political Influence: This is a measure of the extent to which the program increases the political influence of the poor. This includes influence at both local and national levels, but the emphasis is on local control. A strategy which makes the poor less dependent on local authorities increases their political influence at the local level. A strategy which increases the control of the poor over education, local business, or the delivery of social services contributes in an important sense to their political influence; for this reason there is some overlap between this dimension and dimension 17. A rating of 5 indicates that the program substantially increases the relative political influence of the poor; a rating of 3 indicates there is a small increase; and a rating of 1 indicates that the strategy does not change the relative influence of the poor.

4. Impact On Self-Concept: This is a measure of the impact of the program on the recipient's (or participant's) self-concept. It is a measure of the extent to which the poor feel stigmatized by the program. At issue is the extent to which the program fosters a positive self-concept by encouraging the recipient to think of himself or herself as capable, successful, and trustworthy as opposed to a negative self-concept by encouraging the recipient to think of himself as incompetent, dependent, and untrustworthy. A rating of 5 indicates that the program supports a positive self-concept; a 3 indicates that the program has a very little impact either way on self-concept; a 1 indicates that the program fosters a negative self-concept.

5. Impact On Family Stability: This is a measure of the extent to which the program encourages or discourages family stability. A rating of 5 indicates that the program encourages stability; a rating of 3 indicates that the program has little if any impact on stability; and a rating of 1 indicates that the program discourages family stability.

6. Encouragement Of Economic Self-Sufficiency: This is a measure of the extent to which the program encourages economic self-sufficiency as opposed to economic dependency. A program which provides jobs, job training, or education aimed at increasing employability encourages economic self-sufficiency. A program which provides money, goods, or services without requiring work encourages economic dependency; this is particularly so if there is no limit on the length of time for which such benefits can be received. A rating of 5 indicates that the program encourages self-sufficiency; a rating of 3 indicates that the program has little impact on economic self-sufficiency; and a rating of 1 indicates that the program encourages economic dependency.

7. Impact On Work Incentives: This is a measure of the extent to which the program provides work incentives or work disincentives. A program which excludes those who are employed or calls for a high tax rate on any earned income decreases the incentive to work. A program which pays a person to participate in job training increases the incentive to work as does a program which increases the number of jobs offering attractive wages and opportunities for advancement. A rating of 5 indicates that the program increases the incentive to work; a rating of 3 indicates that the program has little impact on work incentives; and a rating of 1 indicates that the program tends to decrease the incentive to work.

8. Impact On Racial Integration: This is a measure of the extent to which the program tends to increase racial integration in residential, school, and work situations. A rating of 5 indicates that the program contributes to greater racial integration; a rating of 3 indicates that the program does not have much impact one way or another on the extent of racial integration; and a rating of

1 indicates that the program slows the rate of integration or contributes to further segregation.

9. Impact On Separation Between Social Classes: This is a measure of the extent to which the program contributes to increasing or decreasing the separation of social classes in residential, school, and work situations. A rating of 5 indicates that the program contributes to reducing the extent of separation; a rating of 3 indicates that the program does not have much impact one way or another on the extent of separation; and a rating of 1 indicates that the program encourages separation between social classes.

10. Marginal Impact: This is a measure of the extent to which the impact of the program is likely to increase or decrease as the number of people participating increases. The potential effectiveness of the U.S. Employment Service decreases as the number of people seeking to utilize its services increases; that is, as the number of people looking for jobs increases, the success of the program in finding them decreases. In contrast, as the number of the poor who register and vote increases, the potential effectiveness of the approach also increases. With respect to publicly funded programs the assumption is made that the per recipient expenditure would remain constant; that is, the situation of dividing a fixed allotment more and more ways is not at issue. A rating of 5 indicates that as the number of recipients (or participants) increases, the potential benefit to each increases; a rating of 3 indicates that there is little change in the potential impact as the number of recipients increases; a rating of 1 indicates that as the number of recipients increases there is likely to be a substantial reduction in the potential benefits to each from the program.

11. Dependence On The State Of The Economy: This is a measure of the extent to which the value of the program as a strategy against poverty is influenced by the state of the economy. Some programs such as U.S. Employment Service are likely to offer less during a recession; others such as Head Start are not directly influenced by the state of the economy; and still others such as a negative income tax provide greater benefits when incomes decline in periods of economic recession. A rating of 5 indicates that the program is likely to deliver more during a period of economic recession; a rating of 3 indicates that there is little relationship between the economy and what the program delivers; a rating of 1 indicates that the program is likely to deliver less during a period of economic recession.

12. Equity In Benefit Levels: This is a measure of the extent to which benefits are the same for eligible persons in similar circumstances. It takes into consideration variation in benefit levels between regions of the country or between categories of the poor when the variation cannot be justified on the basis of objective differences in need. It also takes into consideration the extent to which the discretion allowed local program administrators allows arbitrary variation in benefits. A rating of 5 indicates that there is considerable equity in benefit levels; a rating of 1 indicates that there is considerable inequity in benefit levels.

13. Consideration Of Individual Need: This is a measure of the extent to which economic need is taken into consideration in the determination of who is eligible for benefits and the size of benefits. The rating of a program corresponds to the highest rating for which it meets all the criteria. A rating of 5 indicates that family size, family assets, earned income, and unearned income are taken into consideration in the determination of benefit size. The criteria for a rating of 4 are the same as for a rating of 5 with the one exception that family assets are not taken into consideration. The criteria for a rating of 3 are the same as those for a rating of 4 except that unearned income is not taken into consideration. A rating of 2 indicates that some economic criteria are used to determine who is eligible to receive benefits from the program. A rating of 1 indicates that economic need is not a determinant of who is eligible to receive benefits from the program. Note that it is quite possible for a strategy which takes into consideration both family assets and family income to curtail benefits more gradually than a strategy which takes into consideration family income alone. This dimension does not differentiate between two programs both of which take into consideration family income, but to different degrees. One might curtail benefits much more sharply than the other as family income increases.

14. Creaming: This is a measure of the extent to which the program fails to reach a representative cross-section of the poor and instead reaches the most qualified of the poor. Often in the effort to assure a good record the most qualified of those eligible are selected; the result is that many of those with the greatest need for benefits are overlooked. A rating of 5 indicates that relatively little creaming goes on; a rating of 1 indicates that a substantial amount goes on.

15. Adequacy For Meeting Acute Needs Of The Poor: This is a measure of the extent to which the program provides the money, goods, or services needed to meet acute present needs of the poor. Hunger is an acute present need; in contrast, the need for job training is not an acute present need. A rating of 5 indicates that the program is useful for meeting acute present needs of the poor; a rating of 1 indicates that the program is not useful for meeting such needs.

16. Accessibility Of Program Benefits: This is a measure of how accessible the benefits of the program are to those who are eligible for them. A program which cannot be easily reached by potential recipients because offices are located only in major cities is low in accessibility. A program with complex and poorly publicized eligibility procedures is also low in accessibility. A distinction is made between programs which have national coverage and those which are more experimental in nature existing in only a few areas. For a national program the rating takes into consideration accessibility to all persons who are potentially eligible. For a local program, such as open enrollment in New York City, the rating is based on those eligible persons in the local area. A rating of 5 indicates that the program benefits are relatively high in accessibility; a rating of 1 indicates that the program benefits are relatively low in accessibility.

17. Accountability To Recipients: This is a measure of the extent to which those who administer the program are responsive to the desires of recipients about how the program is run and about making modifications as the need arises. A rating of 5 indicates that the program is relatively high in the extent of accountability to recipients; a rating of 1 indicates that there is little accountability to recipients.

18. Administrative Success: This is a measure of the extent to which the program suffers from administrative problems. The form that administrative problems takes varies considerably from one program to another. One sign of poor administration is inadequate articulation with other administrative units which are necessary for the success of the program; for example, a job training program that does a poor job of placing its trainees would get a lower rating than a program with a good record on this account. Another measure is the man-hours of administration that are required relative to other similar types of programs for the delivery of an equivalent amount of goods and services. Another measure is the extent to which the success of the program is hampered by conflicting local interests. A rating of 5 indicates that the program has a relatively successful administrative record; a rating of 1 indicates a relatively poor record.

19. Popularity: This is a measure of the popularity of the program within society. A program that is consistent with the "work ethic" is likely to be more popular than a program that provides benefits without requiring work. A program which keeps the poor separated from the nonpoor is likely to be more popular than one involving integration. A program which provides benefits for many of the nonpoor is likely to be more popular than one that restricts its benefits to the poor. A rating of 5 indicates that the program is relatively popular among the nonpoor; a rating of 1 indicates that the program is relatively unpopular among the nonpoor.

20. Political Vulnerability: This is a measure of the extent to which the support for the program is (or would be in the case of a proposal) vulnerable to cutbacks in funding due to fluctuations in the political climate (e.g., during a change between Democratic and Republican administrations). Older larger programs such as Social Security are quite invulnerable. Another component of political vulnerability is the extent to which lack of cooperation from local authorities can reduce the effectiveness of the program; opposition to school integration is an example of this. A rating of 5 indicates that the program is relatively invulnerable to shifts in the political climate; a rating of 1 indicates that the program is relatively vulnerable to such shifts in political climate.

21. Percentage Of The Poor Who Benefit In One Year: This is a measure of the percentage of all poor persons who benefit from the program in the course of a year. A program which tends to increase the earning potential for heads of household is counted as contributing to all members of the household. A program which contributes goods or services to a family member which would otherwise be paid for out of family income is counted as contributing to the entire family. A rating of 5 indicates that more than 90 percent of the poor benefit during the course of a year; a rating of 4 indicates a figure between 50 and 90 percent; a rating of 3 indicates that between 10 and 50 percent benefit; a rating of 2 indicates that between 1 and 10 percent benefit; and a rating of 1 indicates that less than 1 percent benefit.

22. Percentage Of Target Population Reached: This is a measure of the percentage of all persons (poor and nonpoor) in the category of persons potentially eligible for the program who actually benefit from it. A distinction is made between programs which have national coverage and those which are more experimental in nature existing in only a few areas. For a national program the rating takes into consideration all persons in the country in the relevant categories. For a local program, such as Operation Breadbasket in Chicago, the rating takes into consideration all persons in the relevant categories living in the local area. A rating of 5 indicates that more than 90 percent of the target population is reached; a rating of 3 indicates that between 10 and 90 percent are reached; and a rating of 1 indicates that less than 10 percent of the target population is reached.

23. Percentage Of The Benefits Going To The Nonpoor: This is a measure of the percentage of income, goods, and services delivered by the program that end up going to the nonpoor. In some cases this represents unintended leakage as in the case of Public Assistance benefits that get to the nonpoor. In other cases such as with Social Security it is the intent of the program to provide benefits to the nonpoor as well as the poor. A rating of 5 indicates that less than 10 percent of the cash value of the benefits are delivered to the nonpoor; a rating of 3 indicates that between 10 and 50 percent of the benefits reach the nonpoor; a rating of 1 indicates that more than 50 percent of the benefits go to the nonpoor.

24. Percentage Of Total Population Who Benefit During One Year: This is a measure of the percentage of the total U.S. population directly benefitting from the program in the course of a year. A rating of 5 indicates that more than 50 percent of the population benefit in the course of a year; a rating of 4 indicates that between 25 and 50 percent benefit; a rating of 3 indicates between 5 and 25 percent; a rating of 2 indicates between 1 and 5 percent; and a rating of 1 indicates that less than 1 percent of the U.S. population benefit from the program in the course of a year.

25. Duration Of Recipient Status: This is a measure of the length of time a recipient of a program is likely to be in the recipient status over his or her lifetime. Many of those who use the services of the U.S. Employment Service only remain in a recipient status for a matter of weeks over their entire lifetime. In contrast, many people remain recipients of Social Security for ten years or more. A rating of 5 indicates that the median cumulative duration of time spent in a recipient status is more than 5 years; a rating of 3 indicates that the duration is 1 to 5 years; and a rating of 1 indicates a duration of under a year. There are a number of programs such as health insurance in which a person is covered over an extended period of time, but actually takes advantage of the potential benefits only periodically. Our ratings are based on the cumulative number of days that the recipient takes advantage of potential benefits.

26. Current Spending Level: This is a measure of the amount spent on the program each year. A rating of 5 indicates a spending level of over $20 billion each year. A rating of 4 indicates a spending level of $1 - $20 billion per year. A rating of 3 indicates a spending level of $100 million to $1 billion per year. A rating of 2 indicates a spending level of $20 - $100 million per year. A rating of 1 indicates a spending level of under $20 million per year. The spending level includes all sources including federal, state, local, and private.

REFERENCES

Abrams, Charles. "Some Blessings of Urban Renewal." *Urban Renewal: The Record and the Controversy.* Edited by James Q. Wilson. Cambridge, Mass.: M.I.T. Press, 1966.

Abu-Lughod, Janet, and Foley, Mary Mix. "The Consumer Votes by Moving." *Urban Housing.* Edited by Margy Ellin Meyerson, Grace Milgram, and William L.C. Wheaton. New York: Free Press, 1966.

Ackerson, Nels, and Sharf, Lawrence. "Community Development Corporations: Financing and Operation." *Harvard Law Review* 83, 7(1970): 1558-1671.

Alinsky, Saul. *Reveille for Radicals.* Chicago: University of Chicago Press, 1946.

Alston, John P., and Knapp, Melvin P. "Acceptance of School Integration 1965-1969." *Integrated Education* 9, 2(1971): 11-15.

Anderson, Martin. *The Federal Bulldozer: A Critical Analysis of Urban Renewal, 1949-1962.* Cambridge, Mass.: M.I.T. Press, 1964.

Anderson, Odin W. "Infant Mortality and Social and Cultural Factors." *Patients, Physicians, and Illness.* Edited by E. Gartly Jaco. Glencoe, Ill.: Free Press, 1958.

Arnold, Mark. "Whither Legal Services." *Juris Doctor* (February, 1971): 3-8.

Atkinson, Carolyn. "Coalition Building and Mobilization Against Poverty." *American Behavioral Scientist* 12, 2(1968): 48-52.

Bakke, E. Wright. *The Mission of Manpower Policy,* Kalamazoo, Michigan: The W.E. Upjohn Institute for Employment Research, 1969.

Banfield, Edward. "An Act of Corporate Citizenship." *Programs in Aid of the Disadvantaged.* Edited by Peter Doeringer. Englewood Cliffs, N.J.: Prentice-Hall, 1969.

———. *The Unheavenly City.* Boston: Little, Brown and Company, 1970.

Bazell, R. J. "Health Insurance." *Science* 171, 3973(1971): 783-785.

Becker, Joseph. *In Aid of the Unemployed.* Baltimore: Johns Hopkins Press, 1965.

Bell, Carolyn Shaw. *The Economics of The Ghetto.* New York: Western Publishing Company, Inc., 1970.

Bell, Winifred. "Services for People: An Appraisal." *Social Work* 15, 3(1970): 5-12.

Bellin, Lowell E., and Kavaler, Florence. "Policing Publicly Funded Health Care for Poor Quality, Overutilization, and Fraud—The New York City Medicaid Experience." *American Journal of Public Health* 60, 5(1970): 811-820.

Bendix, Reinhardt, and Lipset, Seymour M., eds. *Class, Status, and Power.* New York: Free Press, 1966.

Bergman, Barbara R. "Investment in the Human Resources of Negroes." *Race and Poverty: The Economics of Discrimination.* Edited by John F. Kain. Englewood Cliffs, N.J.: Prentice-Hall, 1969.

Bernard, S.E. *Fatherless Families: Their Economic and Social Adjustment.* Waltham, Mass.: Brandeis University, 1965.

———. "The Nixon Family Assistance Plan: How It Will Fail and Why I Support It." *Poverty and Human Resources Abstracts* 5, 5(1970): 5-13.

Berube, Maurice. "Community Control: Key to Educational Achievement." *Social Policy* 1, 2(1970): 42-46.

Birnbaum, Norman. "Is There a Post-industrial Revolution?" *Social Policy* 1, 2(1970): 3-13.

Bickel, Alexander M. "Desegregation Where Do We Go From Here?" *New Republic* 162, 6(1970): 20-22.

Bluestone, Barry. "The Poor Who Do Have Jobs." *Dissent* 15, 1(1968): 410-419.

Blum, Zahava D., and Rossi, Peter H. "Social Class Research and Images of the Poor: A Bibliographic Review." *On Understanding Poverty.* Edited by Daniel P. Moynihan. New York: Basic Books 1969.

Bozell,R. J. "Health Insurance." *Science* 171, 3973(1971): 783-785.

Brazer, Harvey E. "The Federal Income Tax and the Poor: Where Do We Go From Here?" *California Law Review* 57, 2(1969): 422-449.

Brazer, Harvey E.; Cohen, Wilbur J.; David, Martin H.; and Morgan, James N. *Income and Welfare in the United States.* New York: McGraw-Hill, 1962.

Break, George F. "The Effects of Taxation on Work Incentives." *Private Wants and Public Needs.* Edited by Edmund S. Phelps. New York: Norton, 1962.

Brightman, Jay, and Allaway, Norman "Evaluation of Medical and Dental Care Under the Medical Assistance Programs." *American Journal of Public Health* 59, 12(1969): 2215-2220.

Brower, Michael. "The Criteria for Measuring the Success of a Community Development Corporation in the Ghetto." *Working Paper for the Center for Community Economic Development.* Cambridge, Mass.: n.d.

Bruyn, Severyn T. *Communities in Action: Pattern and Process.* New Haven: College and University Press, 1963.

———. "Notes on the Contradictions of Modern Business." *Sociological Inquiry* 42, 2(1972): 123-143.

Bullock, Paul. "On Organizing the Poor." *Trans-action* 15, 1(1967): 65-70.

Buxbaum, Robert C.; Goldberg, George A.; and Trowbridge, Frederick L. "Issues in the Development of Neighborhood Health Centers." *Inquiry* 6, 1(1969): 37-48.

Campbell, Angus; Converse, Phillip E.; Miller, Warren E.; and Stokes, Donald E. *The American Voter.* New York: John Wiley and Sons, 1960.

Center for the Study of Public Policy. *Educational Vouchers: A Preliminary Report on Financing Education by Payments to Parents.* Cambridge, Mass.: Center for the Study of Public Policy, 1970.

Chilman, Catherine S. "Fertility and Poverty in the U.S.: Some Implications for Family Planning Programs, Evaluation and Research." *Journal of Marriage and the Family* 30, 2(1968): 207-227.

Citizens' Board of Inquiry. *Hunger USA.* Boston: Beacon Press, 1968.

Clark, Kenneth. *Dark Ghetto.* New York: Harper Torch Books, 1965.

———. "Efficiency as a Prod to Social Action." *Monthly Labor Review* 92, 8(1969): 54-56.

Clark, Kenneth, and Hopkins, Jeannette. *A Relevant War Against Poverty.* New York and Evanston: Harper and Row, 1968.

Clift, Virgil A. "Curriculum Strategy Based on the Personality Characteristics of Disadvantaged Youth." *Journal of Negro Education* 38, 2(1969): 94-104.

Cloward, Richard. "A Strategy of Disruption." *The Center Diary* (January/February, 1967): 32-36.

Cloward, Richard, and Piven, Frances. "Finessing the Poor." *Nation* 207, 11(1968): 332-334.

———. "A Strategy to End Poverty by Guaranteed Income." *Nation* 202, 18(1966): 510-517.

———. "The Urban Crisis and the Consolidation of National Power." *Urban Riots: Violence and Social Change.* Edited by Robert Connery. New York: Columbia University, The Academy of Political Science, 1968.

Cohen, Irving. "La Huelga, Delano and After." *Monthly Labor Review* 91, 6(1968): 13-16.

Cohen, Wilbur J. "The Developmental Approach to Social Challenges." *Children,* 15, 6(1968): 210-213.

Coleman, James S. *Equality of Educational Opportunity.* Washington, D.C.: U.S. Government Printing Office, 1966.

Coll, Blanch D. *Perspectives in Public Welfare.* Washington, D.C.: U.S. Government Printing Office, 1969.

Colorado, State of. *The Incentive Budgeting Demonstration Project, Final Report.* Colorado State Department of Welfare, December, 1961.

Conant, Ralph W. "Rioting, Insurrection and Civil Disobedience." *American Scholar* 37, 3(1968): 420-433.

Connery, Robert, ed. *Urban Riots: Violence and Social Change.* New York: Columbia University, The Academy of Political Science, 1968.

Cornsweet, Donna M., and Rappaport, Lydia, "Preventive Intervention Potentials in Public Child Care Center." *Child Welfare* 48, 1(1969): 6-13.

Cowen, David L. "Denver's Neighborhood Health Program." *Public Health Reports* 84, 9(1969): 761-766.

Cross, Theodore. *Black Capitalism* New York: Atheneum, 1969.

Cuyahoga County Welfare Department and Community Action for Youth, Cleveland. *Employment Incentives and Social Services: A Demonstration Program in Public Welfare,* 1965.

David, Stephen. "Leadership of the Poor in Poverty Program." *Urban Riots: Violence and Social Change.* Edited by Robert Connery. New York: Columbia University, The Academy of Political Science, 1968.

Delorean, John Z. "The Problem." *Black Economic Development.* Edited by William Haddad and Douglas Pugh. Engelwood Cliffs, New Jersey: Prentice-Hall, 1969.

Dohrenwend, Bruce P., and Dohrenwend, Barbara S. *Social Status and Psychological Disorder.* New York: Wiley and Sons, 1969

Downs, Anthony. *Who Are The Urban Poor?* New York: Committee for Economic Development, 1970.

Dumois, Ana. "Organizing A Community Around Health." *Social Policy* 1, 5(1971): 10-14.

Ehrenreich, J., and Fein, O. "National Health Insurance." *Current* 129 (May, 1971): 24-31.

Ellis, John M. "Socio-economic Differentials in Mortality from Chronic Diseases." *Patients, Physicians, and Illness.* Edited by E. Gartly Jaco. Glencoe, Ill.: Free Press, 1958.

Emerson, Lola. "The League's Day Care Project: Findings to Guide the Community in Providing Day Care Services." *Child Welfare* 48, 7(1969): 402-406.

Ennis, Philip H. *Criminal Victimization in the United States: A Report of a National Survey.* Washington, D.C.: U.S. Government Printing Office, 1967

Eppley, David B. "The AFDC Family in the 1960's." *Welfare in Review* 8, 5(1970): 8-16.

Erskine, Hazel. "The Polls: Demonstrations and Race Riots." *Public Opinion Quarterly* 31, 4(1967-1968): 665-677.

Etzioni, Amitai. "A New Kind of Insurance." *Columbia Forum* (Spring,1970): 18-23.———. "Antipoverty Insurance: A Mode of Private Sector Participation." *Public Administration Review* 29, 6(1969): 614-622.

Etzioni, Amitai, and Atkinson, Carolyn O. *Social Implications of Alternative Income Transfer Systems.* Washington, D.C.: Bureau of Social Science Research, 1969.

Everyman's Guide to Federal Programs. Washington, D.C.: New Community Press, 1968.

Executive Office of the President. *Catalogue of Federal Domestic Assistance.* Washington, D.C.: U.S. Government Printing Office, April, 1970.

Falk, Isadore S. "Beyond Medicare." *American Journal of Public Health* 59, 4(1969): 608-623.

Fantini, Mario. "Participation, Decentralization, and Community Control and Quality Education." *The Record* 71, 1(1969): 93-107.

Ferman, Louis A.; Kornbluh, Joyce; and Haber, Alan, eds. *Poverty in America.* Ann Arbor: University of Michigan Press, 1965.

Finch, R. and Egeberge, R. "The Role of Prepaid Group Practice in Relieving the Medical Care Crisis." *Harvard Law Review* 84, 4(1971): 889-1001.

Fried, Marc. "Grieving for a Lost Home." *The Urban Condition: People and Property in the Metropolis.* Edited by Leonard J. Duhl. New York: Basic Books, 1963.

———. *The World of the Urban Working Class.* Cambridge: Harvard University Press, 1973.

Fried, Marc, and Gleicher, Peggy. "Some Sources of Residential Satisfaction in an Urban Slum." *Urban Renewal: People, Politics and Planning.* Edited by J. Bellush and M. Hausknecht. Garden City, N.Y.: Doubleday, 1967.

Fried, Marc. *The World of the Urban Working Class.* Cambridge: Harvard University Press, 1973.

Friedman, Rose. *Poverty Definition and Perspective.* Washington, D.C.: American Enterprise Institute, 1965.

Friedman, Milton. *Capitalism and Freedom.* Chicago: University of Chicago Press, 1962.

Frisch, Rose E. "Present Status of the Supposition that Malnutrition Causes Permanent Mental Retardation." *The American Journal of Clinical Nutrition,* 23, 2(1970): 189-195.

Fucher, John H. "School Parks for Equal Opportunities." *Journal of Negro Education* 37, 3(1968): 301-309.

Fuchs, Victor R. "Redefining Poverty and Redistributing Income." *The Public Interest* 8, (Summer, 1967): 89-94.

Galloway, Lowell. "Foundations of the War on Poverty." *American Economic Review* 55, 15(1967): 122-131.

Gans, Herbert J. "Income Grants and 'Dirty Work'." *Public Interest* 6(Winter 1967): 110-113.

———. "The Negro Family: Reflections on the Moynihan Report." *The Moynihan Report and the Politics of Controversy.* Edited by Lee Rainwater and William L. Yancey. Cambridge, Mass.: M.I.T.Press, 1967

———. "Culture and Class in the Study of Poverty: An Approach to Anti-Poverty Research." *On Understanding Poverty.* Edited by Daniel P. Moynihan. New York: Basic Books, 1969.

———. "The Uses of Poverty: The Poor Pay All." *Social Policy* 2, 2(1971): 20-24.

———. "The Positive Functions of Poverty." *American Journal of Sociology* 78, 2(1972): 275-289.

———. *More Equality.* New York: Pantheon, 1973.

Gilbert, Neil. *Clients or Constituents.* San Francisco: Jossey-Bass, 1970.

Gittell, Marilyn. "Community Control in Education." *Urban Riots: Violence and Social Change.* Edited by Robert Connery. New York: Columbia University, The Academy of Policital Science, 1968.

Glazer, Nathan. "The Missing Bootstrap." *Saturday Review* 52, 3(1969).

Glickstein, Howard. "Federal Educational Programs and Minority Groups." *Journal of Negro Education* 38, 3(1969): 303-304.

Gold, Martin. "Undetected Delinquent Behavior." *Journal of Research in Crime and Delinquency* 3, 1(1966): 27-46.

Goldstein, William. "Opportunities Industrialization Centers." Unpublished background paper of the Social Welfare Regional Research Institute, Boston College, 1970.

Goode, William J. "Economic Factors and Marital Stability." *American Sociological Review* 16, 1(1951): 802-812.

Gordon, David. "Income and Welfare in New York City." *Public Interest* 16, (Summer, 1969): 64-88.

Gorz, Andre. *Strategy for Labor.* Boston: Beacon Press, 1967.

Green, Christopher. *Negative Taxes and Poverty Problem.* Washington, D.C.: Brookings Institution, 1967.

Grisby, William C. "A General Strategy for Urban Renewal." *Urban Renewal: The Record and the Controversy.* Edited by James Q. Wilson. Cambridge, Mass.: M.I.T. Press, 1966.

Haddad, William. and Pugh, Douglas. eds. *Black Economic Development.* Englewood Cliffs, N.J.: Prentice-Hall, 1969.

Handler, Jane. *Neighborhood Legal Services: New Dimensions in the Law.* Report prepared for the Office of Juvenile Delinquency and Youth Development, Department of Health, Education and Welfare. Washington, D.C.: U.S. Government Printing Office, 1966.

Handler, Joel F., and Hollingsworth, Ellen Jane. "The Administration of Social Services and the Structure of Dependency: The Views of AFDC Recipients." *Social Service Review* 43, 4(1969): 406-420.

———. "How Obnoxious is the 'Obnoxious Means Test'?" *Wisconsin Law Review* 1, (1970): 114-135.

Hardt, Robert H., and Hunt, Donald E. "The Effects of Upward Bound Programs." *Journal of Social Issues* 25, 3(1969): 117-129.

Harrington, Michael. "Government Should Be The Employer of First Resort." *New York Times Magazine* (March 26, 1972).

Hartman, Chester W., and Carr, Greg. "Housing Authorities Reconsidered." *Journal of the American Institute of Planners* 35, 1(1969): 10-21.

Harvard Educational Review. *Equal Educational Opportunities.* Cambridge, Mass.: Harvard University Press, 1969.

———. *Perspectives on Inequality.* Cambridge, Mass.: Harvard University Press, 1973.

Hausman, Leonard J. "Potential for Financial Self-Support among AFDC and AFDC-UP Recipients." *Southern Economic Journal* 36, 1(1969): 60-66.

"Health and Community Control." *Social Policy* 1, 1(1970): 41-46.

Heffernan, Joseph, Jr. "Negative Income Tax Studies: Some Preliminary Results of the Graduated-Work-Incentive Experiment." *Social Service Review* 46, 1(1972).

———. "Research Notes on the Conventional Political Behavior of the Poor." *The Journal of Human Resources* 4, 2(1969): 253-259.

Heilburn, James. "An Economic Development Program for the Ghetto." *Urban Riots: Violence and Social Change.* Edited by Robert Connery. New York: Columbia University, The Academy of Political Science, 1968.

Hildebrand, George H. *Poverty Income Maintenance and the Negative Income Tax.* Ithaca, N.Y.: New York State School of Industrial and Labor Relations, 1967.

———. "Second Thoughts on the Negative Income Tax." *Industrial Relations* 6, 2(1967): 138-154.

Hill, Herbert. "Racial Inequality in Employment: The Patterns of Discrimination." *The Annals of the American Academy of Political and Social Science* 357(1965): 30-47.

Hunter, Robert. *Poverty.* New York: Macmillan, 1904.

Hurley, Rodger. *Poverty and Mental Retardation.* New York: Vintage Books, 1969.

Hyman, Herbert H. "The Value Systems of Different Classes: A Social Psychological Contribution to the Analysis of Stratification." *Class, Status, and Power.* Edited by Reinhardt Bendix and Seymour M. Lipset. New York: Free Press, 1966.

Jaco, E. Gartly. ed. *Patients, Physicians, and Illness.* Glencoe, Ill.: Free Press, 1958.

Jaffe, Frederick S. "Family Planning and Poverty." *Journal of Marriage and the Family* 26, 4(1964): 467-470.

Jaffe, Frederick S., and Polygar, Steven. "Family Planning and Public Policy:

Is the 'Culture of Poverty' the New Cop Out?" *Journal of Marriage and the Family* 30, 2(1968): 228-235.

Jencks, Christopher. "The Moynihan Report." *The Moynihan Report and The Politics of Controversy.* Edited by Lee Rainwater and William L. Yancey. Cambridge, Mass.: M.I.T. Press, 1967.

Jencks, Christopher; Smith, Marshall; Acland, Henry; Bane, Mary Jo; Cohen, David; Gintis, Herbert; Heyns, Barbara; and Michelson, Stephan. *Inequality.* New York: Basic Books, 1972.

Jensen, Arthur R. "How Much Can We Boost IQ and Scholastic Achievement?" *Harvard Educational Review* 39, 1(1969): 1-123.

Jordan, Joan. "Working Women and The Equal Rights Amendment." *Transaction* 8, 1 and 2(1970): 16-22.

Kain, John F. "The Distribution and Movement of Jobs and Industry." *The Metropolitan Enigma.* Edited by James Q. Wilson. Cambridge, Mass.: Harvard University Press, 1968.

———, ed. *Race and Poverty: The Economics of Discrimination.* Englewood Cliffs, N.J.: Prentice-Hall, 1969.

Kaplan, Barbara, and Resnik, Solomon. "Report Card on Open Admissions: Remedial Work Recommended." *New York Times Magazine* (May 9, 1971).

Kaziara, Karen. "Collective Bargaining on the Farm." *Monthly Labor Review* 91, 6(1968): 3-9.

Kershaw, David M. "The Negative Income Tax Experiment in New Jersey." Paper presented at the Conference on Public Welfare Issues, New Brunswick, N.J.: April 26, 1969.

Keyserling, Leon H. "The Problem of Problems: Economic Growth." *Social Policies for America in the Seventies: Nine Divergent Views.* Edited by Robert Theobald. Garden City, New York: Doubleday, 1969.

Kramer, Ralph. *Participation of the Poor.* Englewood Cliffs, New Jersey: Prentice-Hall, 1969.

Kriesberg, Louis, and Treiman, Beatrice R. "Socio-economic Status and the Utilization of Dentists' Services." *Journal of the American College of Dentists* 27, 3(1960): 147-165.

Lampman, Robert J. "Expanding the American System of Transfers to Do More for the Poor." *Wisconsin Law Review* 2, (1969): 541-549.

———. "Negative Rates Income Taxation." Unpublished paper prepared for Office Of Economic Opportunity, August, 1965.

———. "Transfer Approaches to Distribution Policy." *The American Economic Review* 60, 2(1970): 270-279.

Landman, Lynn. "U.S., Underdeveloped Land in Family Planning." *Journal of Marriage and the Family* 30, 2(1968): 191-201.

Lane, Robert E. *Political Ideology: Why The American Common Man Believes What He Does.* Glencoe, Ill.: Free Press, 1962.

Larson, Richard G. "School Curriculum and the Urban Disadvantaged: A Historical Review and Some Thoughts About Tomorrow." *Journal of Negro Education* 38, 4(1969): 351-360.

Lenzer, Terry. "Legal Services Fight for the Poor but Who Fights for Legal Services," *Juris Doctor* (February, 1971): 9-10.

Levine, Richard. "Jesse Jackson: Heir to Dr. King." *Harpers Magazine* 238, 1426(1969): 58-70.

Levine, Robert A. *The Poor Ye Need Not Have With You.* Cambridge, Mass.: M.I.T. Press, 1970.

Levitan, Sar A. *The Great Society's Poor Law: A New Approach to Poverty.* Baltimore: The Johns Hopkins Press, 1969.

———. *Programs in Aid of the Poor for the 1970s.* Baltimore: The Johns Hopkins Press, 1969.

Levitan, Sar A., and Mangum, Garth L. *Federal Training and Work Programs in the Sixties.* Ann Arbor, Michigan: Institute of Labor and Industrial Relations, 1967.

Levitan, Sar A.; Mangum, Garth L.; and Taggart, Robert III. *Economic Opportunity in the Ghetto: The Partnership of Government and Business.* Baltimore: The Johns Hopkins Press, 1970.

Lewis, Oscar. *La Vida.* New York: Random House, 1966.

Lidman, Russell. "Costs and Distributional Implications of McGovern's Minimum Income Grant Proposal." Discussion Paper 131-72, Madison, Wisconsin: University of Wisconsin, Institute for Research on Poverty, 1972.

Lipsky, Michael. "Rent Strikes: Poor Man's Weapon." *Trans-action* 6, 2(1969): 10-15.

Lipsky, Michael, and Neumann, Carl A. "Landlord-Tenant Relations in the U.S. and West Germany: Comparison of Legal Approaches." *Tulane Law Review* 44, 1(1969): 36-66.

Locke-Anderson, W., and Ledebur, L.C. "Programs for the Economic Development of the American Negro Community." *American Journal of Economics and Sociology* 30, 1(1971): 27-46.

Loring, William C., Jr. "Housing Characteristics and Social Disorganization." *Social Problems* 3, 3(1956): 160-168.

Lowenthal, Martin. *Work and Welfare: An Overview.* Chestnut Hill, Mass.: Social Welfare Regional Research Institute, Boston College, 1971.

Lumer, Hyman. *Poverty: Its Roots and Its Future.* New York: International Publishers, 1965.

———. "Why People are Poor." *American Society, Inc.* Edited by Maurice Zeitlin. Chicago: Markham, 1970.

Magid, Alvin. and Weaver, Thomas. eds. *Poverty.* San Francisco, California: Chandler Publishing Co., 1969.

Mangum, Garth L. "Guaranteeing Employment Opportunities," *Social Policies for America in the Seventies.* Edited by Robert Theobald. New York: Anchor Books, 1969.

March, Michael S. "The Neighborhood Center Concept." *Public Welfare* 26, 2(1968): 97-112.

Marmor, Theodore, "On Comparing Income Maintenance Alternatives." *American Political Scene Review* 65, 1(1971): 83–96.

Marris, Peter, and Rein, Martin. *Dilemmas of Social Reform.* New York: Atherton Press, 1967.

Marshall, Raymond. "The Impact of Civil Rights Legislation on Collective Bargaining in the Construction Industry." *Poverty and Human Resources Abstracts* 5, 1(1970): 4-17.

McGovern, George. "A Human Security Plan." An Address before the Citizen's Committee for Children, New York, N.Y., January 20, 1970.

———. "George McGovern: On Taxing and Redistributing Income." *The New York Review of Books* (May 4, 1972).

Means, Gardiner. "Job Opportunities and Poverty." *Poverty As A Public Issue.* Edited by Ben Seligman. New York: Free Press, 1965.

Meier, Gitta. "Implementing the Objectives of Family Planning Programs." *Social Casework* 50, 4(1969): 195-203.

Meyers, Robert J. "Administrative Expenses of the Social Security Program." *Social Security Bulletin* 32, 9(1969): 20-27.

Meyerson, Ellin; Milgram, Grace; and Wheaton, William L.C., eds. *Urban Housing.* New York: Free Press, 1966.

Michael, John A. "High School Climates and Plans for Entering College." *Public Opinion Quarterly* 25, 1(1961): 585-595.

Miller, Herman P., ed. *Poverty American Style.* Belmont, Calif.: Wadsworth, 1968.

Miller, S.M., and Roby, Pamela A. *The Future of Inequality.* New York: Basic Books, 1970.

Miller, S. M.; Rein, Martin; Roby, Pamela; and Gross, Bertram M. "Poverty, Inequality and Conflict." *The Annals of the American Academy of Political and Social Science* 373(1967): 18–52.

Miller, S.M.; Riessman, Frank; and Seagull, Arthur A. "Poverty and Self-Indulgence: A Critique of the Non-deferred Gratification Pattern." *Poverty in America.* Edited by Louis A. Ferman, Alan Haber, and Joyce L. Kornbluh. Ann Arbor: University of Michigan Press, 1965.

Miller, Walter B. "Focal Concerns of Lower Class Culture." *Poverty in America.* Edited by Louis A. Ferman, Alan Haber, and Joyce L. Kornbluh. Ann Arbor: University of Michigan Press, 1965.

Minsky, Hyman P. "Tight Full Employment: Let's Heat Up the Economy." *Poverty American Style.* Edited by Herman P. Miller. Belmont, Calif.: Wadsworth, 1968.

Mitchell, Robert E. "Some Social Implications of High Density Housing." *American Sociological Review* 36, 1(1971): 18-29.

Moody, Kimberly. "Poverty and Politics." *New Politics* 6, 2(1967): 37-42.

More Than Shelter: Social Needs in Low and Moderate-Income Housing. A report prepared for the consideration of the National Commision on Urban Problems. Washington, D.C.: U.S. Government Printing Office, 1968.

Morgan, James N.; David, Martin H.;Cohen, Wilbur J.; and Brazer, Harvey E. *Income and Welfare in the United States.* New York: McGraw-Hill, 1962.

Morsell, John A. "Racial Desegregation and Integration in Public Education." *Journal of Negro Education* 38, 3(1969): 276-284.

Moynihan, Daniel P. *Maximum Feasible Misunderstanding.* New York: Free Press, 1969.

———, ed. *On Understanding Poverty.* New York: Basic Books, 1969.

———. *The Politics of a Guaranteed Income.* New York: Random House, 1973.

Muth, Richard F. "Urban Residential Land and Housing Markets." *Issues in Urban Economics,* Edited by Harvey Perloff, and Lowdon Wingo, Jr. Baltimore: The Johns Hopkins Press, 1968.

National Welfare Rights Organization. "Guaranteed Adequate Income: A Social Program for the 1970's." n.d.

———. "NWRO Proposals for a Guaranteed Adequate Income." n.d.

Netzer, Dick. *Economics and Urban Problems.* New York: Basic Books, 1970.

Neugeboren, Bernard. "Opportunity-Centered Social Services." *Social Work* 15, 2(1970): 47–52.

"NWRO—Organizational Weapon." Interview with George Wiley. *Social Policy* 1, 2(1970).

O'Donnell, Edward J. and Sullivan, Marilyn M. "Service Delivery and Social Action Through the Neighborhood Center: A Review of Research." *Welfare in Review* 7, 6(1969): 1-12.

Office of Senator George McGovern. "Background Material on Senator McGovern's Human Security Program." n.d.

Office of the President. *The Budget of the United States Government, Appendix and District of Columbia.* Washington, D.C.: U.S. Government Printing Office, 1970.

Orfield, Gary. "The Debate Over School Desegregation." *New Republic* 162, 10(1970): 33-35.

Orshansky, Mollie. "Counting the Poor: Another Look at the Poverty Profile." *Social Security Bulletin* 28, 1(1965): 3-29.

———. "The Shape of Poverty." *Social Security Bulletin* 31, 3(1968): 3-32.

———. "Who Was Poor in 1966?" Research and Statistics Note No. 23, Office of Research and Statistics, Social Security Administration, U.S. Department of Health, Education and Welfare, 1967.

Pearl, Arthur. "New Careers: One Solution to Poverty." *Social Policies for America in the Seventies.* Edited by Robert Theobald. New York: Anchor Books, 1969.

Pechman, Joseph A.; Aaron, Henry J.; and Taussig, Michael K. *Social Security.* Washington, D.C.: Brookings Institution, 1968.

Perloff, Harvey, and Wingo, Lowdon, Jr., eds. *Issues in Urban Economics.* Baltimore: The Johns Hopkins Press, 1968.

Perry, George. "Inflation vs. Unemployment, Worsening Trade-Off." *Monthly Labor Review* 94, 2(1971): 68-70.

Pettigrew, Thomas F. "The Metropolitan Educational Park." *The Science Teacher* 36, 9(1969): 23-26.

Phelps, Edmund S., ed. *Private Wants and Public Needs.* New York: Norton, 1962.

Phipps, Anthony. "Locational Choices of Direct Housing Allowance Recipients." Paper prepared for Midwest Council for Model Cities, December 1972.

Piven, Frances Fox, and Cloward, Richard A. *Regulating the Poor.* New York: Random House, 1971.

"The Poor People and the White Press." *Columbia Journalism Review* 7, 3(1968): 61-65.

Presidents Commission on Income Maintenance Programs. *Background Papers.* Washington, D.C.: U.S. Government Printing Office, 1969.

"Project Head Start: A Research Summary." *Integrated Education* 6, 5(1968): 45-54.

Rainwater, Lee. *And the Poor Get Children.* Chicago: Quadrangle, 1960.

———. "The Problem of Lower-Class Culture and Poverty-War Strategy." *On Understanding Poverty,* Edited by Daniel P. Moynihan. New York: Basic Books, 1969.

———. *Behind Ghetto Walls,* Chicago: Aldine, 1970.

———. "Economic Inequality and the Credit Income Tax." *Working Papers for a New Society* 1, 1(1973): 50-61.

———. *What Money Buys: Inequality and the Social Meaning of Income.* New York: Basic Books, 1974.

Rainwater, Lee, and Yancey, William L. eds. *The Moynihan Report and the Politics of Controversy.* Cambridge, Mass.: M.I.T. Press, 1967.

Report of the President's Commission on Income Maintenance Programs, Poverty Amid Plenty. Ben W. Heineman, Chairman. Washington, D.C.: U.S. Government Printing Office, 1969.

Report of the President's Committee on Urban Housing, A Decent Home. Washington, D.C.: U.S. Government Printing Office, 1968.

Rhys–Williams, Lady Juliette. *Something to Look Forward To.* London: MacDonald, 1943.

Riessman, Frank. *Strategies Against Poverty.* New York: Random House, 1969.

Riessman, Leonard. "Readiness to Succeed: Mobility Aspirations and Modernism Among the Poor." *Urban Affairs Quarterly* 4, 1(1969): 379-395.

"Rent Strikes in Public Housing." *Journal of Housing* 26, 7(1969): 351-352.

Rodreguez, Armando. "The Necessity for Bilingual Education." *Wilson Library Bulletin* 44, 7(1970): 724-730.

Rog, Richard. "Now It's Welfare Lib." *New York Times Magazine* (September 27, 1970).

Rolph, Earl R. "The Case for a Negative Income Tax Device." *Industrial Relations* 6, 2(1967): 155-165.

Rosenberg, Morris. *Society and the Adolescent Self-Image,* Princeton, N.J.: Princeton University Press, 1965.

Ross, John A. "Social Class and Medical Care." *Journal of Health and Human Behavior* 3, 1(1962): 35-40.

Ryan, William. *Blaming the Victim.* New York: Pantheon Books, 1971.

———. "Savage Discovery: The Moynihan Report." *The Moynihan Report and the Politics of Controversy.* Edited by Lee Rainwater, and William L. Yancey. Cambridge, Mass.: M.I.T. Press, 1967.

Salaman, Lester. "Family Assistance: The Stakes in the Rural South." *New Republic* 164, 8(1970): 17-18.

Samuels, Howard. "Compensatory Capitalism." *Black Economic Development.* Edited by William Haddad and Douglas Pugh. Englewood Cliffs, N.J.: Prentice-Hall, 1969.

Samuelson, Paul, and Rosow, Robert. "Problems of Achieving and Maintaining a Stable Price Level." *American Economic Review* 50, 2(1960): 177-194.

Sanders, Marion. *The Professional Radical: Conversations with Saul Alinsky.* Evanston, Illinois: Harper and Row, 1965.

Schmitt, Robert C. "Density, Health, and Social Disorganization." *Journal of the American Institute of Planners* 32, 1(1969): 38-40.

Schneider, Louis, and Lysgaard, Sverre. "The Deferred Gratification Pattern: A Preliminary Study." *American Sociological Review 18,* 1(1953): 142–149.

Schorr, Alvin L. *Poor Kids.* New York: Basic Books, 1966.

Schwartz, Edward E. "A Way to End the Means Test." *Social Work* 9, 3(1964): 3-12.

"Services for People: Preliminary Recommendations, Task Force on Organization of Social Services." *Welfare In Review* 7, 1(1969): 9-13.

Sexton, Brendan. " 'Middle-Class' Workers and the New Politics." *Dissent* 16, 3(1969): 231-238.

Shapiro, Sam. "Ill Serving Medicaid Eligibles." *American Journal of Public Health* 59, 4(1969): 635-641.

Shostak, Arthur B.; Van Til, Jon; and Van Til, Sally Bould. *Privilege in America: An End to Inequality?* Englewood Cliffs, N.J.: Prentice–Hall, 1973.

Siegel, Paul M. "On the Cost of Being a Negro." *Sociological Inquiry* 35(1965): 41-58.

Silver, Arthur. "Official Interpretation of Racial Riots." *Urban Riots: Violence and Social Change.* Edited by Robert Connery. New York: Columbia University, The Academy of Political Science, 1968.

Silverstein, Lee. úPoor. Chicago: The Foundation, 1967.

Siporin, Max. "Social Treatment: A New-Old Helping Method." *Social Work* 15, 3(1970): 13-25.

Spencer, Esther. Medicaid: Lessons and Warnings." *Social Policy* 1, 5(1971): 47-51.

Spiegel, Hans. *Citizen Participation in Urban Development. Vol. 2.* Washington, D.C.: Center for Community Affairs, 1968.

Spraggins, Rinsley L. "New Educational Goals and Direction: A Perspective of Title I, ESEA." *Journal of Negro Education* 37, 1(1968): 45-54.

Steiner, Gilbert Y. "Day Care Centers: Hype or Hope?" *Trans-action 8,* 9–10(1971): 50–57.

Sternlieb, George. *The Tenement Landlord.* New Brunswick, N.J.: Rutgers University Press, 1966.

Stigler, George. Poor. Chicago: The Foundation, 1967.

Siporin, Max. "Social Treatment: A New-Old Helping Method." *Social Work* 15, 3(1970): 13-25.

Spencer, Esther. Medicaid: Lessons and Warnings." *Social Policy* 1, 5(1971): 47-51.

Spiegel, Hans. *Citizen Participation in Urban Development. Vol. 2.* Washington, D.C.: Center for Community Affairs, 1968.

Spraggins, Rinsley L. "New Educational Goals and Direction: A Perspective of Title I, ESEA." *Journal of Negro Education* 37, 1(1968): 45-54.

Steiner, Gilbert Y. "Day Care Centers: Hype or Hope?" *Trans-action 8,* 9–10(1971): 50–57.

Sternlieb, George. *The Tenement Landlord.* New Brunswick, N.J.: Rutgers University Press, 1966.

Stigler, George. "The Economics of Minimum Wage Legislation." *American Economic Review* 36, 3(1946): 358-365.

Stoeckle, John D. "The Future of Health Care." *Poverty and Health.* Edited by John Kosa, Aaron Antonovsky, and Irving Kenneth Zola. Cambridge, Mass.: Harvard University Press, 1969.

Suelzle, Marijean. "Women in Labor." *Trans-action* 8, 1(1970): 50-58.

Taeuber, Karl E. "The Effect of Income Redistribution on Racial Residential Segregation." *Urban Affairs Quarterly* 4, 1(1968): 5-14.

Taggart, Robert III. *Low-Income Housing: A Critique of Federal Aid.* Baltimore: The John Hopkins Press, 1970.

TenHouten, Warren D. "The Black Family: Myth and Reality." *Psychiatry* 33, 2(1970): 145-155.

Terrell, Robert. "Poor People Goodbye." *Commonwealth* 88, 16(1968): 453-454.

Theobald, Robert. *Free Men and Free Markets.* Garden City, N.Y.: Doubleday, 1963.

———. ed. *The Guaranteed Income.* Garden City, N.Y.: Doubleday, 1965.

———. ed. *Social Policies for America in the Seventies.* New York: Anchor Books, 1969.

Thurow, Lester C. *Poverty and Discrimination.* Washington, D.C.: The Brookings Institution, 1969.

Tobier, Arthur. "Cooperative Communities, North and South." *U.S. Congressional Record,* 90th Congress, 2nd Session, 114, 129(1968): S9269-9285.

Tobin, James. "Improving the Economic Status of the Negro." *Daedalus* 94, 4(1965): 878-898.

———. "Raising the Incomes of the Poor." *Agenda for the Nation* Edited by Kermit Gordon. Washington, D.C.: Brookings Institution, 1968.

Tobin, James; Pechman, Joseph A.; and Miezhowski, Peter. "Is a Negative Income Tax Practical?" *Yale Law Journal 77,* 1(1967): 1–27.

Ulmer, Melville J. "The Family Assistance Plan: Work and Welfare." *New Republic* 165, 1(1971): 12-14.

U.S. Bureau of the Census. *Current Population Reports.* Series P–60, No. 76, "24 Million Americans—Poverty in the United States: 1969." Washington, D.C.: U.S. Government Printing Office. 1970.

U.S. Bureau of the Census. *Current Population Reports.* Series P-60, No. 77, "Poverty Increases by 1.2 Million in 1970." Washington, D.C.: U.S. Government Printing Office, 1970.

U.S. Bureau of the Census. *Statistical Abstract of the United States: 1970.* 91st. ed. Washington, D.C.: U.S. Government Printing Office, 1970.

U.S. Department of Agriculture. "Food and Nutrition Service News." Information Division, New York, July 22, 1971.

U.S. Department of Commerce. *"Economic Growth in American Communities."* Annual Report of the Area Redevelopment Administration. Washington, D.C.: U.S. Government Printing Office, 1963.

U.S. Department of Health, Education and Welfare. *1970 Annual Report.* Washington, D.C.: U.S. Government Printing Office, 1970.

U.S. Department of Health, Education and Welfare. *Toward a Social Report.* Ann Arbor: University of Michigan Press, 1970.

U.S. Department of Health, Education and Welfare, Office of the Assistant Secretary (Program Coordination). *Income and Benefit Programs,* 1966.

U.S. Department of Health, Education and Welfare, Office of Child Development. *Project Head Start 1968: The Development of a Program.* October, 1970.

U.S. Department of Health, Education and Welfare, Social Security Administration, Children's Bureau. *Working Mothers and Day Care Services in the U.S., Facts About Children,* 1962.

U.S. Department of Health, Education and Welfare, Social and Rehabilitation Service, National Center for Social Statistics. *Preliminary Report of Findings —1969 AFDC Study,* March, 1970.

U.S. Department of Housing and Urban Development. *1969 HUD Statistical Yearbook.* Washington, D.C.: U.S. Government Printing Office, 1969.

U.S. Department of Labor. *An Assessment of Technical Assistance and Training Needs in New Carrers Project.* Washington, D.C.: U.S. Government Printing Office, July, 1969.

U.S. Department of Labor. *Making the Scene in Jobs, School Training through the Neighborhood Youth Corps.* Washington, D.C.: U.S. Government Printing Office, 1968.

U.S. Department of Labor. *Manpower Report of the President 1968.* Washington, D.C.: U.S. Government Printing Office, 1968.

U.S. Department of Labor. *Manpower Report of the President 1969.* Washington, D.C.: U.S. Government Printing Office, 1969.

U.S. Department of Labor. *Manpower Report of the President 1970.* Washington, D.C.: U.S. Government Printing Office, 1970.

U.S. Department of Labor. *Manpower Report of the President.* Washington, D.C.: U.S. Government Printing Office, 1971.

U.S. Department of Labor, Manpower Administration. *Handbook for the JOBS Program,* 1969.

U.S. Department of Labor. *Unemployment Insurance: State Laws and Experience.* BES No. U-198-R. Revised May, 1968.

U.S. Department of Labor, Bureau of Labor Statistics. *Bulletin,* No. 1570-5, 1969.

U.S. Senate. *The JOBS Program, Background Information Prepared for the Subcommittee on Employment, Manpower and Poverty of the Committee on Labor and Public Welfare,* 1970.

U.S. Senate, Select Committee on Nutrition and Human Needs. *Hearings, Nutrition and Human Needs.* Parts 1-12, 90th Congress, 2nd sess., and 91st Congress, 1st sess., 1969; and 91st Congress, 2nd sess., 1970.

Upton, Marcella E. "The Impact of Day Care in a Poverty Area." *Child Welfare* 48, 4(1969): 231-234.

Vadakin, James C. "A Critique of the Guaranteed Annual Income." *Public Interest* 11 (Spring, 1968): 53-66.

———. *Children, Poverty and Family Allowances.* New York: Basic Books, 1968.

Wald, Patricia M. *Law and Poverty 1965.* A Report to the National Conference on Law and Poverty. Washington, D.C.: The Conference, 1965.

Watson, T. J., Jr. "Health Service: Is the Next Step Socialism?" *Vital Speeches of the Day* 37, 8(1971): 249-251.

Watts, Harold W. "Adjusted and Extended Preliminary Results from the Urban Graduated Work Incentive Experiment." Discussion Paper 69-70 revised, Institute for Research on Poverty, University of Wisconsin, 1970.

———. "Income Redistribution: How It Is and How It Can Be." Unpublished paper for the Democratic Platform Hearings, June 17, 1972.

Weaver, Robert C. "New Directions in Urban Renewal." *Urban Renewal: The Record and the Controversy.* Edited by James Q. Wilson. Cambridge, Mass.: M.I.T. Press, 1966.

White, Edward. "Tenant Participation in Public Housing Management." *Journal of Housing* 26, 8(1969): 416-419.

Williams, Kenton. "Some Implications for Services." *Public Welfare* 27, 4(1969): 327-332.

Williamson, John B. "Welfare Policy and Population Policy: A Conflict in Goals?" *Urban and Social Change Review* 4, 1(1970): 21-23.

———. "Beliefs About the Motivation of the Poor and Attitudes Toward Poverty Policy." *Social Problems,* in press.

———. "Beliefs about the Welfare Poor." *Sociology and Social Research 58,* 2(1974): 163–175.

———. "The Stigma of Alternative Forms of Public Aid to the Poor." *Annual Proceedings of the American Sociological Association.* 1974.

Williamson, John B.; Boren, Jerry; and Evans, Linda, eds. *Social Problems: The Contemporary Debates.* Boston: Little, Brown and Company, 1974.

Williamson, John B.; Boren, Jerry F.; Cooney, Nancy A.; Evans, Linda; Foley, Michael F.; Garber, Jody; Mifflen, Frank J.; Steiman, Richard; Theberge, Nancy; and Turek, Donna J. B. *Reducing Inequality: Comparisons Among Alternative Anti-Poverty Programs and Proposals.* Ann Arbor: University Microfilms, 1973.

Willner, Milton. "Unsupervised Family Day Care in New York City." *Child Welfare* 48, 6(1969): 342-347.

Wilson, James Q., ed. *The Metroplitan Enigma.* Cambridge, Mass.: Harvard University Press, 1968.

———. ed. *Urban Renewal: The Record and the Controversy.* Cambridge, Mass.: M.I.T. Press, 1966.

Yablonsky, Lewis. *The Hippie Trip.* New York: Western Publishing Co., 1968.

Yerby, Alonzo S. "The Disadvantaged and Health Care." *American Journal of Public Health* 56, 1(1966): 5-9.

Young, Whitney M. Jr. "Minorities and Community Control of the Schools." *Journal of Negro Education* 38, 3(1969): 285-290.

Zeitlin, Maurice, ed. *American Society, Inc.* Chicago: Markham, 1970.

Name Index

Subject Index

Community Control of Education, 177–179, 182. See Organization Strategies